PLACES IN TIME

Exploring
Ancient Egypt

PLACES IN TIME

Series editors Brian M. Fagan and Chris Scarre

PLACES IN TIME

Exploring Ancient Egypt

Ian Shaw

OXFORD
UNIVERSITY PRESS
2003

THIS BOOK IS DEDICATED TO

Joanna Defrates

OXFORD
UNIVERSITY PRESS

Oxford New York

Auckland Bangkok Buenos Aires Cape Town Chennai
Dar es Salaam Delhi Hong Kong Istanbul Karachi Kolkata
Kuala Lumpur Madrid Melbourne Mexico City Mumbai
Nairobi São Paulo Shanghai Taipei Tokyo Toronto

Copyright © 2003 by Ian Shaw

Published by Oxford University Press, Inc.
198 Madison Avenue, New York, New York 10016
http://www.oup-usa.org

Oxford is a registered trademark of Oxford University Press

Library of Congress Cataloging-in-Publication Data

Shaw, Ian, 1961–
    Exploring ancient Egypt / Ian Shaw.
        p. cm.—(Places in time)
Includes bibliographical references and index.
    ISBN 0-19-511678-X (alk. paper)
    1. Egypt—Antiquities. 2. Egypt—Civilization—To 332 B.C. 3.
Egypt—Civilization—332 B.C. -638 A.D. I. Title. II. Series.
    DT61 .S59 2002
    932—dc21
                                                    2002006004

1 3 5 7 9 8 6 4 2
Printed in Hong Kong
on acid-free paper

Designed by Joan Greenfield

Contents

vi

—

Preface

This book is intended to provide interested nonspecialists with a good overview of the nature and history of three and a half millennia of ancient Egyptian civilization, from around 3100 B.C. to the fourth century A.D. This aim is achieved not by a conventional historical narrative or thematic approach but through detailed studies of nineteen of the most important surviving ancient Egyptian sites. All the sites have long histories, based on many different types of archaeological and textual information, and all of them include certain monuments or sets of objects that have radically transformed Egyptologists' views of Egyptian history or culture. Each site has the potential to supply a wide range of evidence covering many different eras and aspects of life, but the degree to which these sources of data have been fully exploited has depended largely on the aims and techniques of individual archaeologists.

This book also aims to capture something of the diversity of ancient Egypt. The nineteen sites are simply different facets of a single, gradually changing cultural system, and each chapter describes a set of remains rooted in a specific geographical and historical context. Certain general themes emerge inevitably from the discussions of the sites: For instance, how early can Egypt be described as a fully "urbanized" and unified state? How did the Egyptians view their own past? Other, more specific questions are raised by the remains at particular places, such as the question of whether the earliest kings were buried at Abydos or Saqqara, or the debate concerning the degree to which the Deir el-Medina village can be interpreted as a microcosm of New Kingdom society.

The chapters of this book represent snapshots of Egyptian civilization, demonstrating to the reader that individual archaeological projects can present only part of the picture. Not even the chapters on different sites within ancient Thebes can fully encapsulate the various manifestations of the pharaonic period as a whole. Each chapter includes a description of the geographical context of the site in question, as well as information concerning the period during which it was occupied or used, a history of its discovery and excavation, a basic summary of its main monuments, and discussion of its significance with regard to Egyptian civilization as well as to the human past as a whole.

In the course of describing and interpreting a set of nineteen archaeological sites the book confronts the reader with some of the problems and dilemmas with which archaeologists are constantly obliged to deal. How old is this settlement, and why was it abandoned? Why is the decoration of this tomb so different from all the others? What kinds of rituals might have taken place within the walls of this shrine or temple? Very few of these questions have straightforward or easy answers, but the story of each of the nineteen sites is intended to show that meticulous and methodical surveys, excavations, and epigraphic projects have often provided clues and fresh theories that allow such questions to be addressed scientifically and logically, rather than through mere intuition or guesswork.

The Selection of Sites

The nineteen sites have been chosen to reflect a diverse range of chronological, geographical, and cultural viewpoints on ancient Egypt. Thus, the Middle Kingdom is represented by the pyramid and town at Lahun, the painted rock tombs of local governors at Beni Hasan, and the mines and religious monuments of the Sinai desert. In terms of chronological coverage, the emphasis is primarily on sites of the pharaonic, Ptolemaic, and Roman periods, which tend to be better preserved and open to visitors. Only the chapters on Hierakonpolis and Abydos include any substantial discussion of Egyptian prehistory, since few of the classic Predynastic sites (such as Naqada or el-Badari) have any prominent surviving remains that currently can be visited or examined.

One of the foremost problems of Egyptology is the recurrent bias toward data from Upper (southern) Egypt. Despite the work undertaken at Nile Delta sites, both in the late nineteenth century and in the late twentieth, the prevailing view of Egyptian society and history is heavily biased toward Upper Egypt and is dominated, in particular, by the rich remains of the Theban region. This situation stems partly from the survival of more impressive standing architectural remains in Upper Egypt, but also from the relatively poor conditions for preservation in the Delta, where high population, submergence of archaeological deposits below the groundwater level, and the agricultural use of tell sites for fertilizer have tended to reduce the attraction (and the visibility) of Lower Egyptian archaeological sites. Although the initiation of a number of new projects at Delta sites in the 1980s and 1990s has begun to redress this imbalance, it will be many years before the weight of evidence is spread equally across southern and northern Egypt.

Most of the sites in this book are at least partially accessible to visitors, but a few (such as Wadi Maghara and Serabit el-Khadim) are situated in more remote locations, and a few (such as the Early Dynastic royal tombs at Abydos) are not usually accessible to tourists. In a few cases, such as the Shunet el-Zebib at Abydos and the Qubbet el-Hawa necropolis at Aswan, the sites have long been open to visitors but tend to be less frequently visited simply because they are rarely included in standard tour-group itineraries.

Each chapter incorporates a map of the principal archaeological remains at the site, accompanied by drawings and photographs of certain monuments and artifacts. The text describes several different aspects of the site, including the history of its exploration and the surviving monuments, and discusses briefly the historical issues and controversies arising from the finds.

Names and Technical Terms

The spellings of ancient Egyptian kings' names vary tremendously from one book to another, which can be confusing to readers who are unfamiliar with them. For example, the king cited here as "Amenhotep III" may be found elsewhere as "Amenhotpe III," "Amunhotep III," or even (in the Greek form) "Amenophis III." I have chosen the spellings that are as consistent as possible with the transliteration of the original Egyptian; any confusion can be clarified by consulting the index with its cross-references.

A number of Egyptological or archaeological technical terms may be unfamiliar to the general reader (e.g., mastaba-tomb, nomarch, or serekh). These are usually defined briefly when first mentioned, and the glossary at the back of the book provides longer definitions.

A Note on Further Reading

Suggestions for further reading appear at the end of each chapter. These describe the literature that is available on that particular site, as well as works of broader coverage that may be helpful to the general reader. In most cases, some reference is made to the relevant specialist literature, for those who wish to delve deeper or to explore particular aspects of a site. The literature on these sites is in many languages, however, and often difficult to find. In a number of cases, the descriptions given in these chapters are the only ones yet available in English, except for short summary notices.

A site without its associated finds is a mere skeleton. It is the artifacts and food remains found at a site that enable the archaeologist to bring it to life.

Where relevant, therefore, a note has been included indicating where the objects from the individual sites may now be seen on display. In many cases, a great deal of the relevant material can be viewed at a major regional or national museum, but in other instances the finds have been split between two or more museums. I have tried to indicate this in each case, so that readers who want to use the book as a basis for archaeological itineraries can take in the relevant museums on their travels.

We should remember, however, that all major Egyptian sites yield thousands—if not hundreds of thousands—of objects. In nineteenth-century excavations, and even in some twentieth-century fieldwork, many of the finds were thrown away. Today, most are put in storage. Either way, what is displayed in a museum is likely to be only the edited highlights of what the archaeologists discovered.

Acknowledgments

I would like to express my gratitude to Dr. Chris Scarre and Professor Brian Fagan, the co-editors of the Places in Time series, for asking me to write this book, and to the staff at the New York offices of Oxford University Press (especially Catherine Carter and Mark Gallagher) for showing such enormous patience during the time that I have been writing it. Finally. I must also thank Ann, Nia, and Elin, as well as my parents, for being so long-suffering while I toiled away on the manuscript.

Introduction

Each of the sites featured in this volume was chosen to provide glimpses of different aspects of ancient Egyptian civilization in a particular place and at a specific point in time. If the sites are to be appreciated in their full historical and cultural contexts, however, they need to be viewed against three sets of background material: first, our current understanding of the geography, prehistory, and history of the people of the Nile Valley; second, the nature of ancient Egyptian religious and funerary beliefs; and third, the story of Egyptology since its beginnings as a scholarly discipline in the late eighteenth century. This introduction provides overviews of each of these aspects of the study of ancient Egypt.

The Land and the People

In the late fourth millennium B.C., a distinctive civilization emerged at the northern end of the Nile Valley. Its rich agricultural land was sustained not by rainfall (which is negligible throughout most of Egypt), but by the seemingly miraculous annual flooding of the river, which not only waters the fields but also deposits new layers of fertile silt along the banks. The Nile River, running north from its source in East Africa to the Mediterranean coast, is the single most important element in the geography of Egypt. It clearly divides the country into two sections: Upper Egypt, the southern part, consists

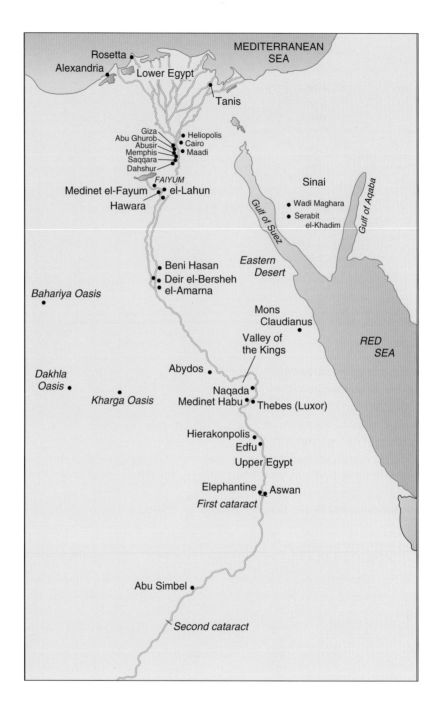

Map of Egypt, showing the sites and regions featured in this book.

of the thin strip of land on either side of the river from Aswan to Cairo; Lower Egypt essentially comprises the northern region, where the Nile fans out into several branches, forming a large and fertile delta before flowing into the sea. The ancient Egyptians called their country Kemet ("black land"),

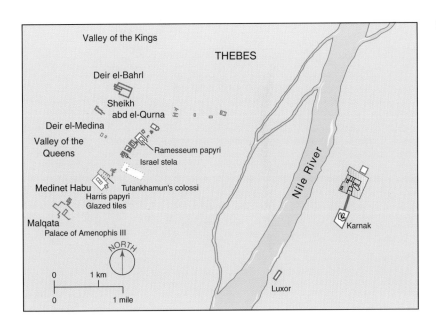

in contrast to the surrounding Deshret ("red land"), because, apart from the Mediterranean to the north, it was completely surrounded by vast areas of desert. Within this simple and curiously symmetrical geographical setting there developed a style of art and architecture that invariably shared these qualities of balance and harmony.

Egypt is in an unusual geographical position at the junction of three continents, with its northern border facing Europe across the Mediterranean, its southern and western borders in Africa, and its eastern border separated from western Asia only by the Red Sea and the Sinai Peninsula. In many respects, the physical geography of Egypt has remained constant for at least five thousand years, but a rich variety of human adaptive strategies developed within its constraints. The nature and scale of agricultural exploitation in the Nile Valley, Delta, and oases have undergone numerous changes, while dependence on the resources of the surrounding deserts has also varied enormously from one period to another, tending to reflect dramatic fluctuations in demand for various commodities and raw materials. Correspondingly, the different routes taken by hunting, trading, and mining expeditions over the centuries have imprinted on the landscape a record of the changing patterns of exploitation.

THE NILE

Egypt without the Nile River is inconceivable. Many other civilizations have grown up around rivers and floodplains, but it is clear that the northernmost stretch of the Nile has exerted an unusually overriding influence on Egyptian society and economy from the Paleolithic period to the present day.

The First Cataract at Aswan, with its distinctive granite boulders scattered across a typical Nile landscape, marked the border between Egypt and Nubia in the early pharaonic period. By the Middle Kingdom the frontier had been extended down to the second cataract, but Aswan retained its role as an important commercial city.

Unlike other rivers in the ancient Near Eastern world, the waters of the Nile rose every year between July and September, flooding the surrounding valley and depositing new layers of fertile silt. This apparently miraculous phenomenon, known as the annual inundation of the Nile, was the most crucial factor in the Egyptian economy until modern times because the success of the annual harvest was directly related to the extent of the flooding, ultimately dependent on the monsoon rains in the Ethiopian Highlands far to the south.

The gradual accumulation of fertile Nile alluvium, carried down every summer for twenty-five millennia since the time that the Nile Valley became a silt flood plain, has prevented the Mediterranean Sea from eroding Egypt's northern coastline and has transformed the fan-shaped Delta region from a succession of prehistoric swamps and "turtleback" islands into some of the richest farming land of modern Egypt. Rainfall in the Nile Valley is almost nonexistent (although there has been a slight increase since the creation of Lake Nasser), and even in the Delta annual precipitation is only about 4 to 8 inches (10–20 centimeters). Since prehistory, therefore, the rise and fall of the Nile has been the most significant variable in the environment of Egypt.

Many facets of the so-called hydraulic civilization of ancient Egypt, from religious myths to social and economic cycles, inevitably hinged on the annual inundation. Throughout the pharaonic, Greco-Roman, Coptic, and Islamic periods, there was an understandable preoccupation with measuring the fluctuating height of the Nile. The techniques of measurement ranged from simple rock carvings in the Early Dynastic Period (particularly in the region of Aswan) to specially constructed stone-lined pits, such as the ninth-century Nilometer on Roda Island, the oldest Islamic monument in Cairo.

CLIMATE, FLORA, AND FAUNA

Modern Egypt has only two seasons: a hot summer from May through October, and a cool winter from November through April. Temperatures range from about 6° C (42° F) at night in winter up to a maximum of around 46° C (116° F) at the height of summer. There is a growing body of archaeological evidence concerning the climate of Egypt in earlier times, based primarily on the results of paleobotany and radiocarbon dating. The first Egyptians of the Paleolithic period appeared in the grasslands of northeastern Africa around 400,000 B.C., but it was not until the onset of a drier climate around 25,000 B.C. that these populations were forced into the Nile Valley. This gradual process of desiccation eventually led to the formation of the Eastern and Western deserts. During the Mesolithic period (c. 10,000–5000 B.C.), a number of semi-nomadic cultures inhabited the immediate area of the Nile Valley, relying on hunting and fishing for their subsistence. Finally, a gradual moistening of the climate around 6000 B.C. encouraged the development of more settled Neolithic communities along the Nile, relying primarily on animal and plant domestication.

There was a surprising degree of innovation in animal husbandry during the pharaonic period. In addition to rearing cattle, sheep, goats, and pigs, the Egyptian farmers of the Old Kingdom experimented with the domestication of the gazelle, oryx, hyena, and ibex. In the Middle Kingdom, the indigenous fleeceless sheep began to be replaced by a wool-bearing species

Many New Kingdom tombs of high officials included agricultural scenes showing the production of the food essential for funerary offerings. In this instance, from the eighteenth-dynasty Theban tomb of Nakht (c. 1400 B.C.), grain is being winnowed (lifted up in wooden scoops so that the chaff blows away in the wind).

introduced from western Asia; by the New Kingdom, both the horse and the zebu (a hump-backed ox) had also been introduced. The principal domesticated animals in modern Egypt are sheep, goats, poultry, water buffalo, horses, donkeys, and camels.

The detailed pictograms of the hieroglyphic script and the scenes painted on the walls of ancient tombs and temples provide abundant evidence of the rich animal and plant life of the late Predynastic and pharaonic periods. With considerable accuracy and detail, they portray numerous species that have now become extinct in Egypt or that have retreated farther south into tropical Africa, such as the hippopotamus and the crocodile. As early as the middle of the Old Kingdom (c. 2600 B.C.), the elephant, rhinoceros, giraffe, and gerenuk gazelle were no longer to be found north of Aswan, and the number of lions and leopards was greatly reduced. It is not clear to what extent this change was caused by overhunting by humans or by the gradual desiccation that took place during the early pharaonic period. Certainly the complete absence of forests in Egypt means that many types of wildlife are correspondingly rare, with only a few ibex surviving in the Eastern Desert and the Sinai, and a scattering of wild boars, jungle cats, and lynx in the Delta.

The vegetation of ancient Egypt has changed as well. The once prolific papyrus plant has virtually disappeared, while recently introduced species of eucalyptus, cypress, and elm are thriving in the modern climate. The main crops grown in the pharaonic period were barley, wheat, and flax. The sheer fertility of the Egyptian soil seems to have discouraged innovation in this area, although a few new varieties of grain and vegetables were eventually introduced during the Ptolemaic and Roman periods.

THE PEOPLE OF THE NILE VALLEY

The human geography of the modern Arab Republic of Egypt is one of its most remarkable characteristics: the modern nation covers an area of about 400,000 square miles (one million square kilometers), but less than 5 percent of this territory is under cultivation. More than 96 percent of the country's population of more than 55 million is squeezed into an area of only about 15,000 square miles (40,000 square kilometers, roughly the size of Denmark).

A number of calculations have been made of the fluctuations in the size of the Egyptian population since prehistoric times, using evidence for the quantity and quality of agricultural exploitation as a rough guide. In the late Predynastic Period (c. 4000 B.C.), the area of cultivable land has been estimated at about 6,000 square miles (15,600 square kilometers), and the population is thought to have been no more than 350,000. But by the late second millennium B.C., after the development of various irrigation techniques (particularly the introduction of the shaduf, a counterweighted device for raising water), the available agricultural land had increased to about 9,000 square miles (23,000 square kilometers), and the population may have been as high as three million.

Ancient Egypt was divided into forty-two "nomes" (provinces, or sepat), twenty-two in Upper Egypt and twenty in Lower Egypt. Each nome had its own standard and symbol, often derived from the animal or fetish originally worshiped in that region, such as the "Hare Nome" or the "Ibis Nome." Each province had its own capital and governor, or nomarch. The title "nomarch" was often a hereditary one, passed down through powerful local families. In times of political stability, the nomarchs were subject to the overall control of the king, but in periods of weak central rule or civil war, there was a tendency for Egypt to split up into these smaller units, until one family of nomarchs became powerful enough to defeat the rest and gain control of the entire country. The geographical distribution of the population gradually shifted northward during pharaonic times, so that by the Ptolemaic Period, the Delta was both more populous and more powerful than Upper Egypt.

The Historical Framework

The earliest human artifacts in the Nile Valley are finds of large stone hand-axes currently dated at about 400,000–300,000 years B.P. (before present). The earliest known remains of a human being—the Paleolithic burial of a child discovered in 1994 at the Upper Egyptian site of Taramsa Hill (near Dendera)—date to about 55,000 B.P. The next major watershed in Egyptian culture was the Neolithic period, when agriculture began to replace hunting and gathering as the main subsistence strategy, from about 5500 B.C. on. The time between about 4500 and 3000 B.C. is known as the Predynastic Period because it was essentially the last prehistoric epoch before the Egyptian people became united into one nation under the rule of a succession of so-called dynasties (series of kings linked either by kinship or by the location of their main residence).

Ancient Egyptian political history from around 3000 B.C. to 395 A.D. is traditionally divided into three sections: the pharaonic, Ptolemaic, and Roman periods. By far the longest of the three was the pharaonic period (c. 3000–332 B.C.), which was made up of a sequence of thirty dynasties, conventionally grouped into the Early Dynastic Period, the Old Kingdom, the First Intermediate Period, the Middle Kingdom, the Second Intermediate Period, the New Kingdom, the Third Intermediate Period, and the Late Period. The three "intermediate" periods have proved to be particularly awkward phases for historians, partly because there were often multiple rulers or dynasties reigning simultaneously in different parts of the country.

The names and relative dates of the various rulers and dynasties in the pharaonic period are derived from a number of textual sources. These range from the Aegyptiaca, a history compiled by an Egyptian priest named Manetho in the early third century B.C., to the much earlier "king-lists," lists of the names of rulers recorded mainly on the walls of tombs and temples, but also occurring in the form of papyri (such as the nineteenth-dynasty document

Many of the pottery vessels produced by the Predynastic Naqada II culture were painted with scenes of boats and riverine landscapes. This example (h. 29 cm), now in the British Museum, dates to the mid-fourth millennium B.C. and comes from the cemetery at el-Amra; the principal motif is a boat in which one of the cabins is surmounted by a female figure with hands raised above her head.

known as the Royal Turin Canon) or remote desert rock inscriptions (such as the list in the Wadi Hammamat siltstone quarries). It is usually presumed that Manetho used king-lists of these types as his sources.

The "traditional" absolute chronology of Egypt tends to rely on complex webs of textual references, combining such elements as names, dates, and genealogical information into an overall historical framework that is more reliable for some periods than for others. The two most important documents for assigning absolute dates to the traditional Egyptian chronological framework are two records of the "heliacal rising" of the Dog Star, Sirius; one, dating to the twelfth dynasty, is a letter from Kahun, written on day 16, month 4 of the second season in year 7 of the reign of Senusret III; the other, dating to the eighteenth dynasty, is Papyrus Ebers, a Theban medical document from day 9, month 3 of the third season of year 9 in the reign of Amenhotep I. By assigning absolute dates to each of these documents, Egyptologists have been able to extrapolate a set of absolute dates for the whole of the pharaonic period, on the basis of records of the lengths of reign

of the other kings of the Middle and New Kingdoms. In addition, because of its well-respected traditional chronological framework, Egyptology was one of the first archaeological disciplines to benefit from radiocarbon dating. Since the late 1940s, when a series of Egyptian artifacts was used as a benchmark in order to assess the reliability of the newly invented radiocarbon dating technique, a consensus has emerged that the two chronologies agree broadly.

KINGS AND DYNASTIES

During the Early Dynastic Period (the first two dynasties), many of the major aspects of social and political structure in the pharaonic period emerged. Much of the archaeological and textual material pertaining to this period derives from the cemeteries of Abydos and Saqqara (see chapters 2 and 3). The tombs of kings and high officials have yielded some of the earliest Egyptian textual evidence, primarily in the form of stone stelae, wooden and ivory labels, inscribed pottery jars, and clay seal impressions. On the basis of these documents, together with the evidence of radiocarbon dating, archaeologists have been able to construct a rough chronology for the period. The sequence of first-dynasty kings is now widely accepted as Narmer, Aha, Djer, Djet, Den, Anedjib, Semerkhet, and Ka'a, with Queen Merneith serving as a regent, probably either before or after the reign of Den. The chronology of the early second-dynasty kings, who were probably buried at Saqqara, is more nebulous: perhaps Hetepsekhemwy, Raneb, Nynetjer, Weneg, and Sened. The last two rulers of the second dynasty were Peribsen and Khasekhemwy, both buried at Abydos.

The temple of King Sety I at Abydos contains a wall relief depicting the king with his son Ramesses II; the latter is writing down all the names of his royal ancestors, listed to the right of the figures. This inscription—the so-called Abydos King-list—appears to be in roughly the right chronological order, but we now know that some names, such as the eighteenth-dynasty "heretic" Akhenaten, have deliberately been omitted.

The early years of the Old Kingdom were dominated by two figures: the third-dynasty ruler Djoser and his chief architect, Imhotep. Djoser's Step Pyramid at Saqqara was the first stone-built Egyptian tomb, and the labyrinth of corridors carved out below the pyramid complex contain some of the earliest royal reliefs, showing the striding figure of Djoser engaged in the celebration of the sed-festival (royal jubilee), with the hawk god Horus hovering protectively above him. The majority of Old Kingdom paintings and reliefs derive from funerary monuments, including the pyramid complexes of the third- to sixth-dynasty pharaohs in the necropolis of the ancient capital, Memphis, just south of modern Cairo, extending from Abu Rawash in the north to Dahshur in the south (see chapters 3–5). From the fourth dynasty on, each royal funerary complex consisted of a pyramidal tomb (entered through corridors leading to one or more burial chambers) with a mortuary temple on its east face, and a stone causeway leading down to a valley temple, where the embalming and mummification of the pharaoh may have taken place. Starting in the reign of the fifth-dynasty ruler Unas, the internal corridors and chambers were decorated with the so-called Pyramid Texts, a set of ancient spells concerned with the fate of the king in the afterlife.

At the end of the sixth dynasty, the growing prosperity of some provincial governors, or nomarchs, was reflected in the rich decoration of their tombs, at a time when the pyramid complexes of the pharaohs were diminishing in size. It is not clear whether the Old Kingdom state went into decline because of environmental factors—such as an insufficiency or excess of annual floodwaters over the fields—or because of social, political, or economic mismanagement (or perhaps a combination of all these factors). In any case, there is a perceptible decline in the standards of art and architecture during the succeeding First Intermediate Period (c. 2181–2055 B.C.), no doubt primarily because there was no longer a single ruler strong enough to maintain a central workforce of skilled craftsmen producing funerary equipment of consistent quality. During this period, the political fragmentation of the country is mirrored in the emergence of a number of provincial artistic styles, the occasional technical deficiencies of which are sometimes balanced by a sense of individual experimentation that can be refreshing to the modern eye.

The Middle Kingdom began with the reunification of Upper and Lower Egypt into a single state by the Theban eleventh-dynasty ruler Mentuhotep II, whose family had claimed the kingship for several generations although they had, until his reign, controlled only a small area of Upper Egypt. In his later years, Mentuhotep II constructed a cult temple over the site of his tomb in a bay of the western Theban cliffs, known today as Deir el-Bahari. This complex was in one sense an architectural crystallization of his political successes, combining a revival of the Old Kingdom royal funerary monuments of the Memphite necropolis with a spectacular sequence of columned terraces reminiscent of the mortuary chapels of his Theban ancestors. His immediate successor, Mentuhotep III, had a comparatively short reign and perhaps left behind a smaller, unfinished funerary complex in the vicinity of Deir el-Bahari (although it has recently been persuasively argued that this monument might actually have been built for Amenemhat I, prior to the construction of his pyramid complex at Lisht). The last eleventh-dynasty ruler, Mentuhotep IV, is an even more ephemeral and shadowy figure, known primarily from the inscriptions recording his quarrying expeditions.

The first twelfth-dynasty ruler, Amenemhat I, established a new capital, Itj-tawy, at a still-undiscovered site somewhere to the north of the Faiyum region. The pyramid complexes of the twelfth-dynasty rulers at Lisht, Dahshur, Hawara, and Lahun (all situated in the region between the southern Faiyum and Memphis) were very much a return to the traditions of the Old Kingdom, although the pyramids themselves were somewhat smaller, the masonry was of poorer quality, and the interior corridors were no longer inscribed with the Pyramid Texts.

The twelfth dynasty was the most stable ruling family in the history of Egypt; the reigns of its eight kings covered a period of about two hundred years. The lengths of these reigns are listed in the Turin Royal Canon, and they have been broadly corroborated by many contemporary inscriptions and papyri. The funerary art of nonroyal individuals during the Middle Kingdom (2055–1650 B.C.) reached its peak in the large rock tombs of the governors buried at provincial sites such as Deir el-Bersha and Beni Hasan in Middle Egypt (the region roughly extending from the southern edge of the Faiyum down to Abydos) (see chapter 8), where the repertory of wall-paintings was enlarged to embrace large-scale depictions of wrestling and warfare (perhaps deriving from reliefs in Old Kingdom pyramid temples, only a few fragments of which have survived) alongside more traditional scenes such as the deceased receiving offerings or hunting and fishing in the marshes.

By the late seventeenth century B.C., the last Middle Kingdom rulers (the late thirteenth dynasty) had retreated south to the Theban region, and the eastern Delta region was taken over by Asiatic rulers, the so-called Hyksos. The excavations at Tell el-Dab'a, the site of Avaris, the Hyksos capital in the Delta, suggest that these Asiatic kings simply usurped and copied traditional Egyptian sculptures and reliefs. The material culture of many of the people inhabiting their Delta strongholds was more typical of Middle Bronze Age Palestine.

After the expulsion of the Hyksos rulers, Egypt embarked on more than four hundred years of economic and social stability: the New Kingdom. During this time, there was apparently constant growth in trade and diplomatic contacts with the Aegean and Near Eastern civilizations. On the west bank at Thebes are the remains of temples dedicated to the funerary cults of the New Kingdom pharaohs, the earliest being that of Queen Hatshepsut at Deir el-Bahari. In the Valley of the Kings and the Valley of the Queens are the last resting places of the New Kingdom pharaohs and their families,

The upper part of a colossal statue of Akhenaten from the temple built in the early part of his reign, in the eastern part of the Karnak temple complex (now in the Egyptian Museum, Cairo). The representations of most Egyptian kings show them as idealized, physically perfect individuals, but Akhenaten chose to be portrayed with grotesque facial features and an androgynous physique, perhaps for symbolic, religious reasons.

ranging from the gently curving passages of the tomb of Thutmose I (c. 1500 B.C.) to the single monumental descending corridor that leads to the burial chamber of Ramesses XI, the last ruler of the twentieth dynasty (c. 1070 B.C.). The mythological scenes in the pharaohs' tombs contrast to some extent with the more intimate details of family life and funerary arrangements in the tombs of high officials at Qurnet Murai, Sheikh Abd el-Qurna, and Asasif, and with those of the royal tomb-workers at Deir el-Medina.

Although Thebes appears to have been the spiritual focus of New Kingdom Egypt, the administrative center of the eighteenth dynasty—as in many earlier periods—was the northern city of Memphis, near modern Cairo, where the royal residence was situated. Recent investigations at the New Kingdom necropolis of Memphis have revealed the tombs of some eighteenth-dynasty high officials, including the military commander (and later king) Horemheb, the chancellor Maya, and the vizier Aper-el.

The most unusual phase of the New Kingdom was undoubtedly the time of Akhenaten in the mid-fourteenth century B.C., the so-called Amarna Period. After the first few years of his reign, when he was still known as Amenhotep, this pharaoh appears to have developed an obsession with the cult of the Aten (literally, the "sun-disk"), a considerably more abstract deity than those of the traditional Egyptian pantheon. He eventually changed his name to Akhenaten ("he who is effective on the Aten's behalf") and established the city of Akhetaten ("horizon of the Aten") as a new capital, built on virgin ground at the site now known as el-Amarna, in Middle Egypt. Although the precise motivations behind the "heresies" of the Amarna Period are uncertain, it is nevertheless apparent that the cult of the Aten was to some extent a logical outcome of the gradual growth of the solar cult in preceding reigns; it is equally apparent, however, that much of the cultural change that took place in the Amarna Period was a product of the mind of Akhenaten himself. His successors, Tutankhamun, Aye, and Horemheb, clearly wasted little time in restoring traditional forms of art and worship.

The Amarna Period and its immediate aftermath were followed by the nineteenth and twentieth dynasties, now known as the Ramessid Period because eleven of its pharaohs took the name Ramesses ("Ra has engendered him"). During the Ramessid Period, a new royal residence was established at Piramesse in the eastern Delta, immediately north of ancient Avaris; however, many of the reliefs and statues from this site were moved during the twenty-first to twenty-third dynasties to be reused in the temples of the nearby city of Tanis, where the rulers of the "Libyan Period" attempted to create a northern version of the precinct of Amun.

During the first millennium B.C., there were only a few periods of completely indigenous Egyptian rule. The country fell victim to a succession of foreign rulers, from the steady infiltration of Libyans during the Third Intermediate Period to the military conquests of the Nubians, Assyrians, and Persians. From the twenty-first dynasty on, kings were no longer buried in western Thebes; consequently, in most cases neither their tombs nor their mummies have survived. In the Third Intermediate Period, the isolated rock-cut tombs of the Valley of the Kings were replaced by small family vaults excavated within the precincts of temples, suggesting that a major change in royal funerary practices had taken place, probably as a result of the Libyan origins of the pharaohs concerned. A set of such vaults, some of which still contained royal mummies and substantial amounts of funerary equipment, was excavated in 1939 by Pierre Montet in the temple of Amun at the Delta site of Tanis (see chapter 16).

Some of the finest nonroyal art of the Late Period comes from the tomb of Mentuemhet, a remarkable individual who retained power over the Theban region throughout the tumultuous period in the seventh century B.C. when the Kushite kings of the twenty-fifth dynasty were first overthrown by an Assyrian invasion and then replaced by the twenty-sixth-dynasty rulers at Sais in the Delta. The "archaizing" tombs of Mentuemhet and other twenty-fifth and twenty-sixth-dynasty Theban officials, such as Pabasa and Iby, are all characterized by a sense of freshness and internal consistency that belies the variety of their sources. In one of the most extreme cases of archaism, the late twenty-sixth-dynasty vizier Nespakashuty took over and remodeled an eleventh-dynasty tomb, decorating its interior walls with scenes of offering bearers that harked back as far as fourth-dynasty funerary art.

In the spring of 525 B.C., the Achaemenid ruler Cambyses II (reigned 525–522 B.C.) defeated the armies of the Egyptian king Psamtek III (r. 526–525 B.C.) at Pelusium and went on to capture Memphis. The most interesting single document surviving from the ensuing First Persian Period (or twenty-seventh dynasty, 525–404 B.C.) is a long text inscribed on the statue of Udjahorresnet, an Egyptian priest and doctor who appears to have collaborated with the new regime, although there is some evidence that he looked after such local interests as the maintenance of the cult of the goddess Neith at his home city of Sais. After a brief period of renewed indigenous rule (the thirtieth dynasty), Egypt was subject to a second period of Persian domination, covering the decade between 343 B.C. and the arrival of Alexander the Great in 332 B.C.

The policy pursued by Alexander, in which he portrayed himself as an Egyptian ruler and effectively grafted the new administration onto the existing political and religious structure, appears to have been followed by his Ptolemaic successors with varying degrees of enthusiasm and success. The construction and decoration of temples continued unabated during the Greco-Roman Period, but there were many other traditional aspects of Egyptian culture that went into decline. None of the tombs of the Ptolemaic pharaohs has been discovered, although it is likely that their necropolis lay somewhere within the Ptolemaic capital at Alexandria, the very position of which indicated the Ptolemies' realignment of Egypt toward the Mediterranean region rather than Africa or western Asia.

Ptolemy I devised the new religious cult of Serapis from the existing worship of Osiris-Apis, perhaps hoping to use it as a unifying political force, but it was instead the cult of the goddess Isis that grew and spread from Egypt. The Macedonians and other Greeks had been familiar to the Egyptians long before the arrival of Alexander, since the Egyptian army in the Late Period (712–332 B.C.) had always included many Greek mercenaries. Ptolemaic rule, however, did not remain popular, and there were revolts in the Theban area in 208–186 B.C. and 88–86 B.C. As Ptolemaic rule weakened, the Ptolemies relied ever more heavily on Rome. Eventually the actions of Cleopatra VII (51–30 B.C.), the daughter of Ptolemy XII (55–51 B.C.) and sister-wife of Ptolemy XIII (51–47 B.C.), provided a pretext for the Roman conquest of Egypt under Augustus (r. 30 B.C.–14 A.D.). Augustus appointed himself pharaoh on 30 August in 30 B.C., thenceforth treating Egypt as an imperial estate rather than a Roman province. This special status was retained under subsequent emperors.

Superficially, Roman rule was a continuation of the Ptolemaic Period (Greek remained the official language, and Alexandria the dominant city), except that no ruling family was resident in Egypt. This had important consequences in that it may have removed any incentive for Egypt to create wealth, given that it was effectively being exploited at a distance as a source of food for Rome. Improvements in irrigation that had been introduced by the Ptolemies were exploited to the full by the Roman administration, and the produce was gathered up in tax by governors who could be held personally liable for any shortfalls.

During the reign of Marcus Aurelius (r. 161–180 A.D.), Egypt was seriously affected by a plague that seems to have resulted in a significant decrease in population. Conditions improved slightly under Septimius Severus (r. 193–211 A.D.), who reorganized the local administration and carried out various building projects, notably the repair of the Colossi of Memnon at Thebes. Although the Faiyum region, heavily settled by Greeks, continued to be favored by Roman visitors (who needed special permission to visit the country), it too gradually underwent depopulation, evident by the fourth century A.D. In 384 A.D., Emperor Theodosius (r. 379–395 A.D.) issued an edict commanding the closing of all pagan temples and ordering the adherence of the entire populace to Christianity. The end of Theodosius's reign, when the Roman empire finally split up into autonomous western and eastern regions, is traditionally regarded as the end of the history of "ancient" Egypt and the beginning of the Coptic (or Byzantine) Period.

CULTURAL CHANGE

After almost two centuries of excavation, it is now possible to outline the history of Egypt in terms of broad processes of change in material culture. Unlike the political history of the previous section, this kind of narrative is concerned not with the careers or achievements of specific individuals but with long sequences of technological developments and innovations.

Most of our knowledge of Egyptian technology during the earliest period of Egyptian prehistory—the Paleolithic period—centers on the production of stone tools and weapons and the earliest known chert quarries, such as those at Nazlet Khater and Saqqara (c. 40,000 B.P.). A much more varied range of crafts has survived from the Neolithic period. Apart from the domestication of plants and animals and the emergence of pottery (the two factors that tend to characterize this phase in most cultures), there also are surviving indications of basketry, rope-making, and bone-working.

By the Predynastic Period, the Egyptians' irrigation techniques had improved, expanding the agricultural capacity of the Nile Valley. By this time, they were also producing large numbers of stone vessels and making pottery on a previously unparalleled scale (between 3800 and 3500 B.C. at Hierakonpolis). From at least the Naqada Period on, they were brewing beer and cultivating grapes. They were also able to build wattle-and-daub buildings, smelt copper (by 4000 B.C.), mine gold, and work lead, gold, and silver into artifacts. Some of the weaving techniques developed in basketry and rope-making had begun to be applied to linen textile production. The earliest depiction of a ground (or "horizontal") loom dates from the Badarian Period (c. 4500–3800 B.C.); the painting, executed on a pottery vessel, shows four corner pegs holding two beams, one at either end, with the warp running between them; three bars depicted in the middle of the loom may perhaps be the laze rod, heddle rod, and some form of beater. It was also around this time that the first faience was manufactured, initially in the form of simple beads and later as small animal figurines.

The Predynastic development that most obviously foreshadowed the pharaonic period, however, was the increasing use of images and symbols that are assumed to be the forerunners of hieroglyphics. By the fourth millennium B.C., the Egyptians' use of pictorial symbols had evolved into the earliest stage of a sophisticated writing system. The oldest surviving sheet of papyrus (unfortunately uninscribed) was found in a first-dynasty tomb at Saqqara (c. 3000 B.C.). In the Early Dynastic Period, the first elite tombs incorporating stone masonry were built, the granite quarries at Aswan began to be exploited, and specialized copper tools began to be used for woodworking. Other Early Dynastic developments were the introduction of dyed threads and dyed cloth, and the earliest definite evidence of wine production. By the second dynasty (c. 2890–2686 B.C.), if not earlier, certain forms of artificial mummification had been introduced.

From the third dynasty (c. 2686–2613 B.C.) on, limestone quarries began to be exploited on a huge scale, primarily for the construction of pyramid complexes. From this date we also have the earliest evidence for the laminating of sheets of timber. By the fourth dynasty (c. 2613–2494 B.C.), "Egyptian blue" had begun to be used both as a sculpting material and as a pigment, and the earliest surviving faience workshop had come into existence at Abydos. Around this date, mummification techniques, at least for the elite, began to include evisceration and treatment with drying agents. By the fifth dynasty (c. 2494–2345 B.C.), the potter's wheel had been introduced, although it was not until the First Intermediate Period (c. 2160–2055 B.C.) that it was widely used.

From the eleventh dynasty (c. 2055–1985 B.C.) on, sandstone quarries were exploited for building and sculptural material. By the Middle Kingdom (c. 2055–1650 B.C.), excerebration (removal of the brain) had become part of the mummification process, which had by now spread to the "middle classes." Techniques of gold granulation were also introduced at this time. From the early New Kingdom we have the earliest examples of Egyptian wood-turning, and the introduction of topped-slag furnaces for copper processing. By at least the reign of Thutmose III (1479–1425 B.C.), glass was being processed and perhaps even manufactured by Egyptians, who probably adopted techniques developed at an earlier date in the Near Eastern polity of Mitanni. Around 1500 B.C., the first vertical loom is attested in Egypt. Unlike the horizontal loom, which was pegged out across the ground, the vertical (or "two-beamed") loom was usually placed against a wall, with weavers working upward from its base; the lower beam was either set into a shallow hollow in the ground or rested on grooved blocks, examples of which have survived in some New Kingdom houses.

By the Late Period (664–332 B.C.), specialized techniques of gold refinement had been developed, and from about 600 B.C., iron-working became fairly widespread. In a temple of the early Ptolemaic Period (fourth century B.C.) we have the first representation of a wooden object being turned on a lathe, although the lathe was used as early as the New Kingdom (see above). It was around this time that artificial mummification became more widespread throughout all levels of the population. During the Ptolemaic Period, stake-and-strand basketry was introduced, and lime mortar began to be used in mud-brick buildings. By the Roman Period, silver-working had become more common, and by the first century A.D., cotton was in general use for textiles, gradually replacing linen.

Although ancient Egypt is often regarded as a remarkably conservative and intractable civilization, even the briefest study of the material culture of the Nile Valley shows that the Egyptians had an enormous capacity to absorb new modes of production and innovative techniques and to exploit new materials when necessary. The nature of the Egyptian political and social systems—which were indeed remarkably rigid and enduring—should not blind us to the vitality and flexibility of much of their material culture.

Egyptian Religion

Ancient Egyptian official religion, which involved the worship of a large number of gods and goddesses, was concerned with the maintenance of the divine order. It was regarded as essential that life be lived in accordance with *maat* (personified as Maat, the goddess embodying universal truth and harmony), and that the encroachment of chaos be prevented. The temples and their associated priesthoods therefore served as a perpetual means of stabilizing the universe. Every day the priests attended to the needs of the deities, each of whom was thought to be manifested in a cult image housed in a temple shrine, making offerings to them and thus keeping the forces of chaos at bay.

TEMPLES

Apart from the cult temples associated with the royal pyramids, only a small number of early Egyptian temples dedicated to deities rather than to dead kings have survived. Most were dismantled by later pharaohs seeking convenient sources of building stone. By the fifth dynasty, the sun god Ra had become Egypt's closest equivalent to a state god. Many of the fifth and sixth-dynasty kings built sun temples; the similarity of these to pyramid complexes, together with their proximity to the royal necropolis, suggests that they were built for the afterlife rather than for the purposes of the living.

A sun temple, like a pyramid complex, consisted of a valley temple linked by a causeway to the upper temple. The main feature of the upper temple was a massive pedestal with an obelisk, a symbol of the sun god, which was approached via a large court open to the rays of the sun and centered on a large altar. The sun temple of Nyuserra at Abu Ghurob (see chapter 5) has yielded some of the finest religious art of its date, including a fascinating set of painted reliefs from the "Room of the Seasons" which depict the various plants, animals, and agricultural activities associated with the three seasons of the Egyptian year: shemu (summer), akhet (the flood season), and peret (spring). On the one hand, these reliefs emphasize the sun god's role as the ultimate giver of life and the moving force in nature; on the other, they establish the king's place in the eternal cycle of events by showing his periodic celebration of the sed-festivals. A large mud-brick replica of a bark (boat) of the sun god was built nearby. The temples, therefore, may have been personal monuments to each king's relationship with the sun god. Just like pyramid-complexes, sun-temples were endowed with land, received donations in kind on festival days, and had their own personnel.

The main purpose of Egyptian state religion seems to have been to ensure the continued existence of the state and the kingship. In contrast, individual Egyptians—whose beliefs are preserved in the form of ostraca (inscribed pieces of broken pottery), stelae, and votive offerings—evidently viewed religion primarily as a means of avoiding personal injury or misery. The most popular household gods, such as the dwarf god Bes and the hippopotamus goddess Taweret, were credited with particular protective powers over childbirth. Since it was also believed that neglect of the gods, or blasphemy against them, could lead to punishment, there are also various stelae describing the consequences of such sins (these often stress, however, that penitence could save wrongdoers). Although concerned with maintaining *maat,* Egyptian religion generally was not overtly directed toward the personal morality that was implicit in upholding *maat.* However, the so-called wisdom literature (many surviving examples of which were composed in the Middle Kingdom, c. 2055–1650 B.C.) provides insights into the Egyptians' views on morality, and some of the same concepts are reflected in the funerary texts of the New Kingdom (c. 1550–1069 B.C.).

During the Middle Kingdom, a crucial religious development was the emergence of the cult of Osiris (effectively the "Great God" of all cemeteries). This cult owed its popularity to the enormous interest in it shown by rulers of this time, who were determined to associate themselves with Osiris in order to ensure their survival in the afterlife. In the case of the thirteenth-dynasty rulers, it seems likely that their devotion to the cult was also an attempt to compensate for their nonroyal background. Indeed, the spread of the Osirian cult into the funerary cults of large numbers of Middle Kingdom nonroyal individuals, described by some scholars as a "democratization of the afterlife," was the catalyst for many changes in funerary practices at all levels of society. One of the most prominent changes was the writing of verses from the royal Pyramid Texts on the coffins of nonroyal people; these are therefore known as the Coffin Texts. It was also in the Middle Kingdom that relief carvings—previously found only in Old Kingdom mortuary complexes—began to be used to decorate the walls of the temples of the principal gods.

The vast religious complex of Karnak, initiated during the Middle Kingdom, was associated with a number of deities, but it was dedicated above all to one deity whose influence pervaded the society and politics of Egypt throughout the New Kingdom, Third Intermediate Period and Late Period: Amun-Ra. This super-deity was a fusion of the sun god Ra and the ram god Amun ("the hidden one"), who is first attested in the fifth-dynasty Pyramid Texts but was vigorously promoted as the principal state god from the twelfth dynasty on. Apart from the brief aberration represented by the Amarna Period, the steady rise of the cult of Amun-Ra and the ever-increasing wealth of his temples and priesthood are the most obvious features of the New Kingdom.

Few Middle Kingdom temples have survived, and so our knowledge of religious architecture in the pharaonic period is based almost entirely on New Kingdom examples. The typical New Kingdom temple consisted of four sections: the ceremonial gateway, one or more colonnaded courts, one or two hypostyle halls, and the shrine or sanctuary. There were two types of sanctuary: the cult shrine, where the principal statue of the deity was placed, and the bark shrine, where more portable statues were temporarily deposited during processions. In most major New Kingdom temples, the first and second courts were decorated with scenes of military success and the presentation of spoils to the gods, as well as depictions of the king being recognized by the gods as rightful ruler. The one or two hypostyle halls tended to be decorated with scenes reflecting the three types of rituals carried out there: those relating to the foundation of the specific temple (usually in the first hypostyle hall), those concerning the procession to the sanctuary or chapels, and those relating to kingship (in the second hall).

The sanctuaries or chapels were often built in a form resembling the ancient hut shrines of the Predynastic Period, with curved ceilings. They generally contained depictions of the divine bark and scenes of the daily temple ritual. Various episodes in the daily ritual were shown, beginning with the king or chief priest entering the chapel by breaking the clay seal on the shrine door and drawing back the bolt. He then made a preliminary offering and entered the outer shrine. There was a ritual purification of the bark and the divine image; then the image was removed from the boat and its clothing was changed, and new unguents were poured over its face. Insignia such as the *wesekh* collar were then placed on the image in a specific order. Sand was then scattered around the chapel, the image received the final robing ceremony, and a final prayer was uttered by the king or chief priest. Finally, the king or chief-priest left the sanctuary by the east door and performed a purification rite outside the door, resealing it until the next day.

The floor level of the temple gradually rose from the outer courts through to the sanctuary. The sanctuary of every temple was thought to be the equivalent of the primeval mound where the first god appeared. But as well as being a building housing the image and essence of one or more deities, the temple was also, in a sense, an organism in its own right, and the ritual of the Opening of the Mouth could be used to bring the figures on its walls to life. A similar ritual was used to animate the bodies or statues of the dead. Outside the temple were the sacred lake, the storehouses, the palace, and the priests' houses. Small bark shrines were scattered along the sacred processional ways through temples and between one temple and another in order to provide ritual temporary resting places for the bark as it was carried along.

A temple was not simply the home of the god or gods but also a set of rooms connected with the performance of rituals and festivals. In a sense, the temples served as a means of channeling and recording the movements of the divine images from one shrine to another, with each temple playing a particular mythological role. Thus, at Luxor, the function of the temple was to enable the celebration of the Ipet (or Opet) festival, during which the images of Amun, Mut, and Khonsu were brought from Karnak to Luxor in the second month of the inundation season every year (see chapter 12).

The temple was also a microcosm both of the universe and of the process of creation. The sanctuary is usually regarded as representing the primeval marsh, and the outer courts the emerging facets of the natural world. The bases of walls are decorated with plants and flowers, and the columns in the hypostyle halls represent palms, lotuses, and reeds. Once a temple had been established, its sacred spot usually continued as a religious site through the centuries, with the original shrine gradually being covered up by new buildings. The sacred nature of the stone blocks and statuary, however, meant that they seem often to have been reused as rubble, either within pylons or beneath floors, as the temple was gradually rebuilt and expanded.

By the New Kingdom, accommodation for professional priests was being deliberately incorporated into the temple plan. In the Old and Middle Kingdoms, the priests were largely lay part-time officials, but by the New Kingdom they made up a full-time professional group with various grades and specialities, including singers, musicians, cooks, butchers, and gardeners. One role of the personnel was to deal with the constant flow of offerings into the temple. In order to support the infrastructure and staff of a temple, it had to stand at the center of an economic network. Thus, as in earlier periods, the temples were provided with endowments and estates, the details of which are sometimes preserved in the form of lists of revenue or decrees. The stone temples were invariably surrounded by mud-brick storerooms to hold the proceeds of their various agricultural and mineral assets, which are particularly well-preserved at two Theban mortuary temples, the Ramesseum and Medinet Habu.

FUNERARY BELIEFS AND PRACTICES

The ancient Egyptians believed that each human individual consisted of several other entities apart from the physical body *(khet);* these were the *ka,* the *ba,* the *akh,* the shadow, and the name. Many of the Egyptians' funerary beliefs and customs centered on the important task of sustaining and enhancing thesefacets of the individual.

Ka is an almost untranslatable term used by the Egyptians to denote the creative life-force of each individual, whether human or divine. The *ka,* represented by a hieroglyph consisting of a pair of arms, was considered to be the essential ingredient that differentiated a living person from a dead one. It came into existence at the same moment that the individual was born, subsequently serving as his or her "double." Funerary statues were regarded as images of the *ka* of the deceased, and sometimes these too incorporated the *ka* symbol; for instance, an image of the thirteenth-dynasty ruler Hor from Dahshur (c. 1750 B.C.) depicts the deceased with the *ka* hieroglyph in the form of a headdress. When an individual died, the *ka* was thought to require the same sustenance as the human being had enjoyed in life. For this reason, it was provided either with genuine food offerings or with representations of food depicted on the wall of the tomb, all of which were activated by the offering formula, addressed directly to the *ka.* It appears that the *ka* was not thought physically to eat the offerings but rather to assimilate their life-preserving force. In giving food or drink to one another in normal daily life, the Egyptians sometimes used the formula "for your *ka*" in acknowledgment of this life-giving force.

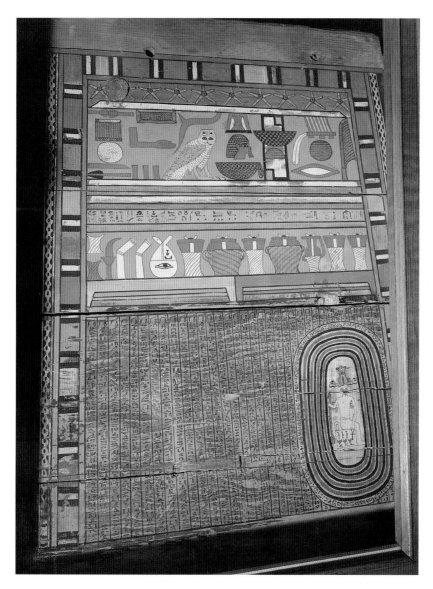

In the Middle Kingdom many people gained access to funerary texts and equipment that had previously been reserved for royal burials. The decoration on this coffin, which belonged to Sepy, a twelfth-dynasty provincial governor buried at Deir el-Bersha in Middle Egypt, includes a depiction of the so-called *Book of Two Ways*, a funerary text designed to help the deceased find his way through the netherworld. The enthroned figure at the bottom right is the god Osiris, whose cult was closely associated with the resurrection of the dead.

The *ba* has similarities with our concept of "personality" in that it comprised all those nonphysical attributes that made one human being unique. However, the concept of *ba* also referred to power, and it could be extended to gods and to inanimate objects. Therefore, *ba* was also the term used for what might be described as the physical manifestations of certain gods, so that the Memphite Apis bull was the *ba* of Osiris, and the four sons of Horus were his *ba*.

It was necessary for the deceased to journey from the tomb to rejoin his *ka* if he was to become transformed into an *akh* (see below), and since the

By the New Kingdom many individuals were buried with papyri bearing texts and vignettes chosen from a corpus of funerary spells called the *Book of Coming Forth by Day* (now known as the *Book of the Dead*). This example belonged to a nineteenth-dynasty official, Hunefer, who was buried in western Thebes (c. 1300 B.C.). The part of the papyrus shown here depicts the "judgment of the dead," in which Hunefer's heart is weighed against a feather in order to determine whether he has lived a sufficiently virtuous life to allow him to pass through to the afterlife.

physical body could not do this, it was the duty of the *ba*. The Egyptian names for the Jabiru stork and the ram both had the same phonetic value as *ba,* and so the hieroglyphic signs for these creatures were used to refer to it in writing. It is possible that this accidental phonetic association with the stork led to the depiction of the *ba* as a bird with a human head and often with human arms. The Egyptians regarded migratory birds as incarnations of the *ba,* flying freely between tomb and underworld. However, it was also believed that the *ba* could adopt any form it wished, and there were numerous funerary spells to assist this process of transformation.

In order for the physical bodies of the deceased to survive in the afterlife, they had to be reunited with the *ba* every night. Chapter 89 of the *Book of the Dead* recommends that a golden *ba*-bird be placed on the chest of the mummy in order to facilitate this reunion. The *ba*-bird was also incorporated into the decoration of nonroyal coffins from the twenty-first dynasty on. Far from corresponding to the modern Western concept of a "spirit" (as it is sometimes translated), the *ba* was closely linked to the physical body, to the extent that it too was considered to have physical needs for such pleasures as food, drink, and sexual activity.

The *akh,* one of the five principal elements that the Egyptians considered necessary to make up a complete personality, was believed to be both the form in which the blessed dead inhabited the underworld, and also the result of the successful reunion of the *ba* with its *ka*. Once the *akh* had been created by this reunion, it was regarded as enduring and unchanging for eternity. Although the physical form of the *akh* was usually portrayed as a mummiform figure, the word *akh* was written with the sign of the crested ibis (Geronticus eremita).

Egyptians set great store by the naming of people and objects, and the name was regarded as an essential element of every human individual, just as necessary for survival as the *ka, ba,* or *akh.* The symbolic importance of the name meant that the removal of personal or royal names from monuments or statuary was considered to be equivalent to the destruction of the very memory and existence of the person to whom the name referred. Conversely, the addition of a new name to a relief or statue (an act usually described by Egyptologists as the "usurping" of a work) was considered to imbue it with the essence and personality of the new owner, regardless of its actual physical appearance. From a more negative point of view, it was felt that the hieroglyphic names of gods, people, and animals were as capable of posing a threat as the living entity itself; for this reason, many of the signs in the Pyramid Texts were deliberately abbreviated and mutilated in order to neutralize potential dangers within the royal tomb.

The importance of the brain was apparently not recognized, and instead the heart was regarded as the most important physical part of an individual. To the Egyptians, the heart (*haty* or *ib*) was the source of human wisdom and the center of the emotions and memory. Its function in the circulation of the blood was not understood, although one religious treatise states that the movement of all parts of the body was determined by the heart. Because of its supposed links with intellect, personality, and memory, it was considered the most important of the internal organs.

Because it was felt that the heart could reveal a person's true character, even after death, it was left in place during mummification, and if accidentally removed would be sewn back into place. There was some concern that the heart might testify against its owner and so condemn him at the judgment; in order to prevent this, a heart scarab was commonly wrapped within the bandages. The inscription on this scarab usually consisted of chapter 30 from the *Book of the Dead:* "Oh my heart which I had from my mother; Oh my heart which I had upon earth, do not rise up against me as a witness in the presence of the lord of things; do not speak against me concerning what I have done, do not bring up anything against me in the presence of the great god of the west." From the New Kingdom on, "heart amulets" taking the form of a vase with lug handles (perhaps representing the blood vessels) were introduced into the funerary equipment. The heading of chapter 29b in the *Book of the Dead* states that such amulets should be made of *seheret* stone (cornelian), but many surviving examples are made from other materials, such as glass.

In the portrayal of the final judgment—a popular vignette in copies of the *Book of the Dead*—the heart of the deceased is shown being weighed against the feather of Maat (the symbol of universal truth and harmony), and the god Anubis is sometimes to be seen adjusting the balance slightly in favor of the deceased to ensure his safe entry into the underworld. The heart of the deceased was thought to be restored to him in the afterlife;

chapters 26–29 of the *Book of the Dead* were therefore intended to ensure that the heart was regained and could not be removed.

The practice of preserving eviscerated organs during mummification is first attested in the burial of Hetepheres, mother of the fourth-dynasty ruler Khufu (2551–2528 B.C.), at Giza. Her viscera were stored in a travertine chest divided into four compartments, three of which contained the remains of her organs soaked in natron, while the fourth held an unidentified dry organic material.

During the First Intermediate Period (2150–2040 B.C.), the so-called canopic jars containing human viscera began to be provided with stoppers in the form of human heads, and at this time the canopic bundles were some-times also decorated with human-faced masks. By the late Middle Kingdom, a typical set of canopic equipment usually comprised two chests (a stone-carved outer container and a wooden inner one) holding four jars furnished with stoppers in the form of human heads. In the early eighteenth dynasty, the stoppers were still human-headed, as in the canopic equipment of Tutankhamun, but from the later eighteenth dynasty on it became more common for the stoppers to take the form of the characteristic heads of each of the four anthropomorphic genii known as the Sons of Horus, who were themselves protected by tutelary deities guarding the four cardinal points. The human-headed Imsety, linked with Isis and the south, protected the liver; ape-headed Hapy, linked with Nephthys and the north, cared for the lungs; jackal-headed Duamutef, linked with Neith and the east, guarded the stomach; and falcon-headed Qebehsennuef, linked with Serket and the west, looked after the intestines.

In the Third Intermediate Period (1070–712 B.C.), mummified viscera were usually returned to the body, sometimes accompanied by models of the relevant genii, but empty or dummy canopic jars were occasionally still included in rich burials. Canopic equipment has been found in Ptolemaic tombs, but it had ceased to be used by the Roman Period. The last known royal canopic jars belonged to Apries (589–570 B.C.), and one of these sur-vived through its reuse as a vessel containing the body of a mummified hawk at Saqqara.

The Rediscovery of Ancient Egypt

The archaeological remains of pharaonic Egypt span three millennia (c. 3100–332 B.C.) and encompass a diverse body of artifacts, architecture, texts, and organic remains. Museums throughout the world contain millions of Egyptian antiquities, and an even greater number of remains are still *in situ,* ranging from the temples, tombs, and cities of the Nile Valley and Delta to rock in-scriptions carved on remote crags in the Libyan Desert, the Eastern Desert, or the Sinai Peninsula. Three principal factors have facilitated the survival of an unusual wealth of detail concerning pharaonic Egypt: a penchant for grandiose and elaborate funerary arrangements, arid conditions conducive to preservation, and the use of writing on a wide variety of media.

It is difficult to be precise about the point at which a simple enthusiasm for Egyptian antiquities was transformed into something resembling the modern discipline of Egyptology. Most histories of Egyptian archaeology, however, see the Napoleonic expedition at the beginning of the nineteenth century as the first systematic and scientific attempt to record and describe the standing remains of pharaonic Egypt. The importance of the *Description de l'Egypte,* the multivolume publication that resulted from the expedition, lay not only in its high standards of draftsmanship and accuracy but also in the fact that it constituted a continuous and internally consistent appraisal by a single group of scholars, providing the first real assessment of ancient Egypt in its totality.

However, the beginning of Egyptology as a complete historical discipline, comprising the study of both texts and archaeology, was made possible by the more desk-bound endeavors of Jean-François Champollion. His decipherment of Egyptian hieroglyphs in 1822, closely followed by Thomas Young's decipherment of the demotic script in the late 1820s, transformed Egyptology almost overnight from prehistory into history. The translation of a whole range of documents, containing such information as the names of gods and kings as well as the details of religious rituals and economic trans-

The process of recording the monuments of ancient Egypt began in earnest with the Napoleonic expedition in which a team of scholars compiled the *Description de l'Egypte,* a majestic multivolume work that documented many of the major temples and tombs, as well as the flora and fauna of the Nile valley. The *Description* is still a valuable piece of work, because it sometimes provides information on monuments that have disintegrated or disappeared.

25
—

actions, soon enabled the field of Egyptology to take its place alongside the study of the Classical civilizations. Champollion's discovery, however, had also set in motion an inexorable process of academic divergence between linguists and excavators, and between historians and anthropologists. The purely archaeological view of Egyptian culture, as it was preserved in the form of buried walls, artifacts, and organic remains, would henceforth always have to be seen in the context of a richly detailed corpus of texts written on stone, papyrus, and potsherds.

Although the greatest individual achievement in the history of Egyptology was undoubtedly the decipherment of hieroglyphs by Champollion, the birth of Egyptian archaeology owes a great deal to the work of another French Egyptologist, Auguste Mariette. As a result of his prolific archaeological work at many different sites (including Giza, Abydos, Thebes, and Elephantine), Mariette was appointed in 1858 as the first director of the Egyptian Antiquities Service (now known as the Supreme Council of Antiquities). This post enabled him to reduce the plundering of Egyptian antiquities and to create the nucleus of a national archaeological collection, housed initially in a disused warehouse at Bulaq and most recently at the Egyptian Museum in the center of Cairo. During the next twenty years, Mariette excavated at about thirty-five different sites and gradually expanded the national museum.

Between the period of organized plundering undertaken by such men as Belzoni and Drovetti in the early nineteenth century and the excavations of Émile Amélineau and Jacques de Morgan in the 1890s there was surprisingly little development in the techniques employed in Egyptian archaeology. Change came with the arrival of two innovative workers: Flinders Petrie from Britain, and George Reisner from the United States. At a time when methods of fieldwork were still in their infancy throughout archaeology, the ground-breaking methods of Petrie and Reisner set new standards for the discipline as a whole. Petrie created a new style of fieldwork in which close attention was paid to every detail of the archaeological deposits, rather than simply concentrating on the large monumental features of sites. Whereas his predecessors tended to clear large tracts of archaeological material relatively indiscriminately, Petrie dug selectively, excavating trenches in strategically selected parts of each site and thus building up an overall picture of the remains without destroying the entire site in the process. At Tell el-Amarna, for instance, he obtained a good overview of a huge, complex urban site in a single season by excavating a range of different types of structures in various parts of the city.

Petrie was the first Egyptologist to begin to make sense of Predynastic chronology when he invented his "sequence dating" system. In 1890, he showed in his excavation of the complex stratigraphy of Tell el-Hesy in Palestine that careful artifactual synchronisms could be drawn between the various strata and Egyptian historical phases. About ten years later, he ap-

(A)

(B)

Modern Egyptologists use various techniques to uncover new archaeological remains or record those that are already known. (A) Ian Mathieson, mapping the cemetery at Saqqara on behalf of the British Egypt Exploration Society, employs satellite technology to survey the tombs with GPS equipment. (B) The traditional epigraphic techniques in Egypt involved tracing of decorations either by placing paper or film against the monument or copying photographs, but Peter Der Manuelian of the Museum of Fine Arts, Boston, has pioneered a "digital epigraphy," in which a combination of digitized photographs and computer drawing programs are used to document the decoration in the mastaba-tombs of high officials surrounding the fourth-dynasty pyramids at Giza. Here the computer screens show a color scan of a scene from the tomb of Tepemankh, and a digital drawing of the same scene, with the photograph removed.

plied the same basic process to the assemblages at Egyptian Predynastic funerary sites, which were difficult to date because cemeteries tend to develop horizontally across the ground rather than forming vertically arranged stratigraphic layers like settlements such as Tell el-Hesy. Because virtually all the Predynastic sites discovered by the end of the nineteenth century were cemeteries, the whole period was very difficult to date. Petrie's use of sequence dates, consisting initially of the matching of many different slips of paper bearing the details of individual funerary assemblages, allowed him to assign relative dates to each grave within the Predynastic cemetery at Diospolis Parva. He was thus able to create a relative chronology for the newly discovered Predynastic Period, which later was broadly confirmed both by stratigraphic excavation and radiocarbon dating.

Although Reisner did not begin to excavate in Egypt until about twenty years after the arrival of Petrie, he made a comparable impact on the field. Like Petrie, he worked with enormous attention to detail, but he was the first archaeologist in Egypt to recognize the need to provide such detailed records of his surveys or excavations that any future researcher would be able to reconstruct both the site and the process by which it was originally examined. The principal drawback of his painstaking approach was the inherent slowness of preparing the reports for publication, which resulted in much of his work remaining unpublished at his death (cynics might add that this was another aspect of his work in which he was ahead of his time). It was Reisner who introduced the systematic use of the section drawing into Egyptian archaeology, some forty years after such stratigraphic analysis had been pioneered by Giuseppe Fiorelli at Pompeii. Reisner was also one of the earliest archaeologists to take genuinely multidisciplinary teams to Egypt: at the Predynastic site of Naga ed-Der, for instance, he was accompanied by the anatomist Grafton Elliot Smith, whose detailed observations on the material from cemetery N7000 have provided modern researchers with an extremely reliable anthropological database.

As a result of the application of scientific methods of survey and analysis, along with the assimilation of ideas and information from subjects as diverse as linguistics, geophysics, and art history, the field of Egyptology has expanded into a sprawling multidisciplinary monster extending from bioanthropology and geophysics to philology and sociology. Even though this diversification sometimes threatens the integrity of the subject as a whole, it is also increasingly its strength, in that each of the many different academic disciplines utilizing Egyptological data provides fresh sources of stimulation and new directions for future research.

Hierakonpolis

C. 3200–2600 B.C.

The earliest Egyptian city: Maceheads

and elephant bones

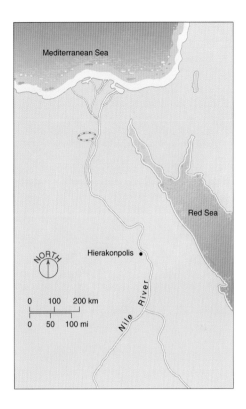

In the last few centuries of the prehistoric period, Egypt began to change from a very fragmented collection of farms and villages into a highly centralized and sophisticated state. The period from about 3200 to 2900 B.C., spanning the late Predynastic Period and the beginning of the Early Dynastic Period, is sometimes called the "Protodynastic." We can tell from the gradually increasing depictions of battles that the late Predynastic was a time of growing conflict within Egypt, as local chiefs and their villages grew stronger and expanded. Eventually, it appears, three main areas—Naqada, Hierakonpolis, and This—were struggling for power.

All three of these regions are in Upper (southern) Egypt, and it is possible that the emergence of kingdoms in Upper Egypt earlier than in Lower Egypt was determined at least partly by physical geography. In Upper Egypt, the relatively narrow confines of the Nile Valley may have created the political and demographic "pressure cooker" that was needed to encourage the growth of city-states. In contrast, the settlements in the north of Egypt, in the Nile Delta, were scattered over a much wider expanse of fertile land and therefore may have been less prone to military conflict and resulting political unification. It is also possible that the strength and precocity of Upper Egyptian states was connected with their exploitation of gold mines and trade routes through the Eastern Desert.

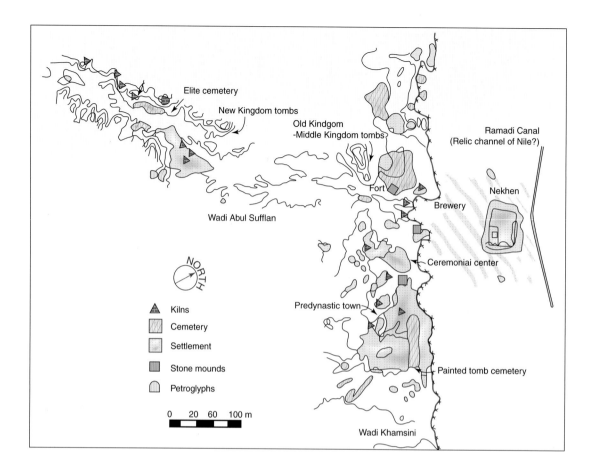

Map of Hierakonpolis (after
Renée Friedman).

With each local victory, the political geography of Upper Egypt was gradually being altered, until, on the brink of unification, it must have consisted
of a series of large regions rather like the provinces, or "nomes," of the
pharaonic period. These provinces were vying for supremacy. Around this
time, Egyptian artisans produced a significant set of votive maceheads and
palettes, which served as vivid symbols of power.

The ancient city of Nekhen—or Hierakonpolis, as it was known in
Greek and Roman times—was the cult center of the hawk god, Horus.
The town and its surrounding cemeteries, situated 50 miles (80 kilometers)
south of Luxor, may well have been the first significant urban center in the
Nile Valley. Certainly the earliest pharaonic settlement remains at Naqada,
Koptos, and Abydos cannot compare with Nekhen either in their extent
or in the diversity of finds and monument types. The Nekhen region as a
whole covers an area of almost 40 acres (15 hectares), comprising the
pharaonic town and temple near the floodplain, as well as various areas of
earlier settlement, cemeteries, and rock carvings in the desert to the west.

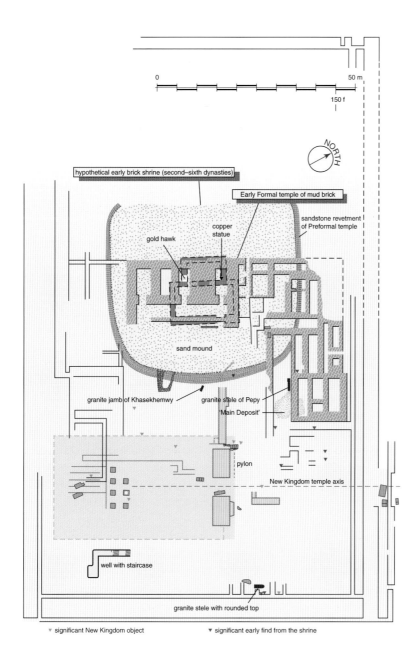

0   50 m

150 f

NORTH

hypothetical early brick shrine (second–sixth dynasties)

Early Formal temple of mud brick

sandstone revetment of Preformal temple

copper statue

gold hawk

sand mound

granite jamb of Khasekhemwy

granite stele of Pepy

'Main Deposit'

pylon

New Kingdom temple axis

well with staircase

granite stele with rounded top

▽ significant New Kingdom object   ▼ significant early find from the shrine

31

It reached its peak during the late Predynastic and Early Dynastic periods (c. 4000–2649 B.C.). A fairly small heap of settlement remains covered with red pottery and burnt earth at the northern end of the site has given the site its modern name, Kom el-Ahmar ("red mound"); the most substantial surviving part of the Early Dynastic city, however, is now known as Kom el-Gemuwia.

Early Religious Buildings and Votive Artifacts

Archaeological research at Kom el-Gemuwia and other parts of Hierakonpolis began in 1898 with the excavations of the British Egyptologists James Quibell and Frederick Green in a temple founded in the late fourth millennium B.C., when Egyptian civilization was just emerging from prehistory.

Quibell had gained his first experience of digging by accompanying Flinders Petrie (the first truly scientific excavator to work in Egypt) on his excavations at Koptos, Naqada, and Ballas, where many of the remains were comparable in date with Hierakonpolis. Green had also served a valuable apprenticeship with Petrie. Despite their training, however, neither Green nor Quibell made a very successful job of their two seasons at Hierakonpolis. Even by the standards of their time, and taking into account the fact that this was a comparatively difficult site to excavate, their recording methods have left some of the important finds difficult for modern archaeologists to analyze or reinterpret.

Quibell and Green found a large number of votive objects in the early temple, including one significant group in a part of the site that they described as the Main Deposit. This was a stratum, or layer of archaeological material, situated between two walls relating to the Old Kingdom temple complex. Despite the likely Old Kingdom date of the stratum itself, its contents seem to have consisted primarily of ceremonial objects dating to the late Predynastic and Early Dynastic periods (c. 3100–2700 B.C.), including ceremonial cosmetic palettes, maceheads, and carved ivory figurines. These artifacts have proved to be some of the most important pieces of evidence for our understanding of the beginnings of the Egyptian state. Unfortunately, because we lack accurate published plans and stratigraphic sections from the site, the full significance and the true date of this crucial Protodynastic assemblage remain unclear. The mixture of objects of different dates suggests that they constituted a series of royal gifts to the temple, but we have no way of knowing whether each piece was brought to the temple in person by a number of rulers from the late Predynastic through to the Old Kingdom, or whether they were all dedicated en masse by a later ruler in the Old or Middle Kingdom.

Three of the objects in particular are thought to shed interesting light on the nature of Egyptian culture and society in the early pharaonic period. These are the Narmer Palette, the Narmer Macehead, and the Scorpion Macehead. The only one of these to have survived almost intact is the Narmer Palette, a shield-shaped ceremonial cosmetic palette carved from dark grey siltstone, with delicately carved raised relief decoration on both sides. One side bears a depiction of a king, identified as Narmer by two hieroglyphic symbols above him, wearing the tall "white crown" of Upper Egypt and smiting a foreign captive in the presence of the hawk god. The other side shows the same king in the "red crown" of Lower Egypt, apparently taking part in a procession with standard-bearers, moving toward rows of decapitated prisoners, perhaps in a victory celebration.

Until the 1980s, the Narmer Palette was widely regarded as a memorial related to a series of specific military successes over Libyans or northern Egyptians, or both, accomplished by the king of Upper Egypt in the course of unifying Egypt. There are still some adherents to this view, but it now seems more likely that the decorations on the Narmer Palette and some contemporary votive objects are either general iconographic "summaries" of the role of the king, or simply lists of rituals undertaken in the year during which the object was presented to the temple. Whatever the historical significance of its reliefs, though, the Narmer Palette is crucially important for our understanding of the initial development of Egyptian art in the dynastic period. It effortlessly combines certain elements of Predynastic art with the more rigid set of official conventions and proportions that established the tone for the artistic style of the historic period.

The Narmer Palette was not found within the Main Deposit itself, but somewhere nearby. Attempts to establish its original location more precisely have been frustrated by the vagueness and contradictions of the two excavators' notes: Quibell's published report in 1900 claimed that it was found in the Main Deposit, whereas Green's publication in 1902 described its find-spot as a Protodynastic level of the temple (and his field notes say that it was found a yard or two away from the Main Deposit). If Green's version is correct—and his description is at least partially backed up by his original notes—then it is quite likely that the palette was dedicated during the reign of Narmer himself, around 3100 B.C.

Part of the temple adjacent to the Main Deposit may have been a series of storerooms. In these buildings excavators discovered two almost identical seated statues of the second-dynasty ruler Khasekhemwy, one carved in siltstone and the other in limestone—the earliest examples of Egyptian royal sculpture in three dimensions. There were also two unique metal statues of a sixth-dynasty king, Pepy I (2321–2287 B.C.), constructed by hammering and joining sheets of copper alloy. The object that offers the most important clue about the function of the temple at Hierakonpolis is a golden falcon's head that may have been part of one of the cult statues of the god, placed in his innermost shrine. Few such statues have survived from any of the temples of pharaonic Egypt.

While the objects from the Main Deposit relate primarily to the role of the pharaonic period temple at Hierakonpolis, excavations in another part of the town in 1985 provided vital information on the emergence of prehistoric religious architecture. At "Locality Hk29A," the American archaeologist Michael Hoffman found a large parabolic clay-paved courtyard of the Naqada II period. At its southern end is a stone-filled post-hole in which there must originally have stood a massive pole, perhaps surmounted by some kind of fetish or totem. This is thought to be the earliest temple yet excavated in Egypt. The presence of numerous bones of fish and animals (ranging from goats to crocodiles) suggests that the ritual slaughter of living creatures was already part of Egyptian religion as early as the mid-fourth millennium B.C.

The Painted Tomb

In the 1899 season at Hierakonpolis, Green concentrated on the Predynastic cemetery, the less plundered westerly section of which had been examined by Quibell in the first season. He came across a group of five unusually large late Gerzean (mid- to late fourth millennium B.C.) tombs, which would immediately have reminded him of the elite tombs in Cemetery T, excavated six years earlier by Petrie at Naqada and dated to the very end of the Predynastic (the so-called Dynasty 0). One of Green's tombs is a rectangular brick-lined excavation (5.85 by 2.85 meters in area and 1.5 meters deep). Like some of the graves in Petrie's Cemetery T, it is divided into two sections by a free-standing brick wall extending about halfway across the width of the tomb, from the northeastern wall to the center. Much of the mud plaster covering the walls was damaged, but the southwestern wall had survived better than the rest and was decorated with paintings executed mainly in black, gray, and brown on an ocher background. Dated stylistically to the mid-fourth millennium B.C., these are still the only wall-paintings found in an Egyptian Predynastic grave. Like the decoration on the painted vessels of the late Predynastic period, the images in Tomb 100 can be interpreted in several different ways. One possibility is that they are simply faithful depictions of life along the Nile Valley, including boats, religious images, and hunting and trapping scenes in the desert.

There has been some debate concerning the date of this grave and its contents. Although both the tomb's architecture and some of the images in the paintings are similar to the elite "Dynasty 0" tombs in Cemetery T at Naqada, many grave goods found inside Tomb 100 have been conclusively shown to date to the Naqada IIc Period, about three hundred years earlier. It is possible that further light may be shed on this chronological enigma in the future, either through a fresh examination of the tomb or, more likely, through excavations of other tombs in the vicinity.

An Unexpected Burial

From 1967 on, new excavations were undertaken at Hierakonpolis by an American team directed by Walter Fairservis and Michael Hoffman. Their multidisciplinary project set out to understand the environmental and cultural context of the site by employing thorough and painstaking techniques that had not previously been applied to a prehistoric site in the Nile Valley. Initially, they made a large-scale general survey of the region, then followed this up with a series of sondages (test pits) in various "localities." The results of this combination of survey and excavation have led to a hypothesis that

A watercolor copy of the main painted wall of Tomb 100 at Hierakonpolis. The decoration is dominated by a group of six immense boats, but there are also many other smaller scenes evidently dealing with the themes of hunting and warfare. These images are comparable not only with the images depicted on Naqada II pottery vessels but also with the later scenes on the decorated ceremonial palettes of Dynasty 0.

the population of the Hierakonpolis region slowly moved eastward over the course of hundreds of years (c. 3800–3100 B.C.), eventually concentrating near the river. According to Hoffman, several environmental and cultural factors can explain the topographical development of the settlement.

In the early 1980s, Hoffman excavated a part of Hierakonpolis denoted Locality 6, covering an area of about 700 by 300 feet (210 by 90 meters), about 1.5 miles (c. 2.5 kilometers) into the desert west of the main town site. He found eleven graves, eight of which contained elite human burials; the rest held the remains of dogs, baboons, and cattle. Some of the graves dated to the early Predynastic Period (the Naqada I and IIa phases), and others to the late Predynastic (Naqada III). None appeared to date to the height

The Narmer Palette.

This votive palette, excavated from the Old Kingdom temple at Hierakonpolis, was made at the end of the fourth millennium B.C., when the most characteristic elements of Egyptian culture were emerging. Both faces are decorated with relief scenes showing the pharaoh, Narmer. On one side he is shown wearing the White Crown of Upper Egypt as he smites a foreigner with a mace in the presence of the falcon-god Horus. On the other side, above a depiction of intertwined mythical beasts, he is shown in the Red Crown of Lower Egypt, taking part in a procession and reviewing the beheaded bodies of his enemies. The Narmer Palette has usually been interpreted as an historical document recording a number of military successes over Libyans or Lower Egyptians by means of which the first unification of the Egyptian state was achieved. More recently, however, it has been suggested that the reliefs simply depict a number of rituals (probably relating to the kingship) enacted in the year that this palette was brought as an offering to the temple.

of the Predynastic (the so-called Gerzean Period, c. 3500–3200 B.C.), perhaps indicating that the cemetery was abandoned during this time.

When the British archaeologist Barbara Adams resumed excavation at Locality 6 in 1997, her primary aim was to find out what had happened to this cemetery in the middle of the Predynastic Period—the phase for which Hoffman had found no evidence. As happens so often in archaeology, what she actually found had nothing to do with the problem she was trying to solve. Adams began near the middle of the cemetery, uncovering two further graves (labeled Tombs 13 and 14) containing early Predynastic potsherds and the remains of two young men and at least seven domestic dogs. Tomb 14, how-

By the end of the Predynastic Period, the motifs on painted pottery were only one element in an ambitious array of artistic developments, including the carving of complex and elaborate figurative scenes on ceremonial stone palettes, maceheads, and ivory knife-handles. The cache of ritual items excavated from beneath the floor of the early temple at Hierakonpolis included a number of objects that were probably created as votive offerings dedicated to the gods. Among them were the palette and macehead of King Narmer, who was probably the first ruler of a united Egypt.

Some of the narrative-style scenes on the palettes and maceheads from Hierakonpolis and other late Predynastic sites were once widely regarded as renditions of actual events (the military defeat of the northerners, in the case of the Narmer Palette). Now, however, there is good reason to assume that they represent purely mythological events and ritual acts. The difficulty of distinguishing among history, myth, and dramatic ritual is a continual problem throughout the study of ancient art.

The decoration of the palettes, maceheads, and carved ivories of the late Predynastic Period has to be seen as a reflection of the desire to communicate the "context" of the object in terms of event and ritual. The Canadian Egyptologist Nicholas Millet has demonstrated this well in his analysis of the Narmer Macehead. The analysis of the scenes and texts on these objects is complicated by our modern desire to distinguish between real events and rituals; whereas the ancient Egyptians seem to have blended these categories deliberately to create a unified narrative of myth and history.

Late Predynastic lapis lazuli female figurine from Hierakonpolis, now in the Ashmolean Museum, Oxford.

ever, also contained some large bones belonging neither to men nor dogs. A large toothless jawbone was eventually identified, showing that the first animal buried in the tomb was a young African elephant. Although Hoffman had found a few fragments of elephant bone on the surface at the Locality 6 cemetery, this elephant burial is the earliest ever found in Egypt. We cannot tell why the people of Hierakonpolis in the early fourth millennium B.C. went to such great effort to bury an elephant, unless this was part of some hunting ritual. Ongoing excavations at the site may eventually indicate whether this grave is unique or simply the first one to be discovered. Meanwhile, the question of the abandonment of the cemetery remains unanswered.

One of a pair of highly unusual Predynastic pottery masks excavated at Abydos. Details of the hair, eyebrows, eyes, mouth, and beard are depicted in red paint.

Further Reading

The earliest publications dealing with Hierakonpolis are the two volumes published by James Quibell and Frederick Green (Hierakonpolis, London, 1900–02). Renewed interest in Hierakonpolis followed a meticulous account of the site published by the German archaeologist Werner Kaiser in 1961 (in volume 17 of the German Egyptological journal *Mitteilungen des Deutschen Archäologischen Instituts, Abteilung Kairo*). Further information deriving from Quibell and Green's excavations, together with much data from the unpublished work of John Garstang and Harold Jones in the "Fort Cemetery" (some 188 Predynastic graves excavated in 1905–1906), has been collated and reexamined by Barbara Adams in *Ancient Hierakonpolis* (Warminster, 1974), *The Fort Cemetery at Hierakonpolis* (London, 1987), and *Ancient Nekhen: Garstang in the City of Hierakonpolis* (New Malden, 1995). Both Barry Kemp and J. C. Payne reanalyzed the Painted Tomb in articles published in volume 59 (1973) of the *Journal of Egyptian Archaeology*. Reports on the most recent excavations at the site include Michael Hoffman, *The Predynastic of Hierakonpolis: An Interim Monograph* (Giza and Macomb, Ill., 1982), and Renée Friedman and Barbara Adams (eds.), *The Followers of Horus: Studies Dedicated to Michael Hoffman* (Oxford, 1992). A comprehensive description of the late Predynastic palettes and maceheads is found in Whitney Davis's *Masking the Blow: The Scene of Representation in Late Prehistoric Egyptian Art* (Berkeley and Los Angeles, 1992), along with an intriguing, if somewhat controversial, discussion concerning their meaning and function.

Further Viewing

Various Early Dynastic artifacts discovered by Quibell and Green in the early temple at Hierakonpolis can be seen in the Egyptian Museum, Cairo (the Narmer Palette, the Pepy I statues, the golden hawk's head, and the limestone statue of Khasekhemwy), in the Ashmolean Museum, Oxford (the Scorpion and Narmer maceheads, many ivories, and the schist statue of Khasekhemwy), and in the Petrie Museum, University College, London. Some of the objects from John Garstang's excavations at Hierakonpolis are on display in the museum of the School of Archaeology, Classics and Oriental Studies at the University of Liverpool.

CHAPTER

TWO

———

Abydos

c. 3000 B.C.

Graves of the first pharaohs

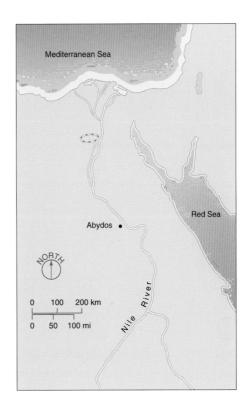

In a land where most sites had some kind of religious association, Abydos was perhaps the most sacred place of all. Situated in a large bay in the cliffs on the west bank of the Nile, about 30 miles (48 kilometers) south of modern Sohag, the area first became prominent as the burial place of the earliest Egyptian rulers (Dynasty "0" and the first and second dynasties). These kings' power base probably centered on the nearby town of This, which is now buried under cultivation, like many other early Egyptian settlements. Abydos retained great significance throughout the pharaonic period as the center of the cult of the god Osiris, who was identified with the dead king, and one of the early royal tombs eventually came to be regarded as the tomb of Osiris himself. The earliest temple at the site was dedicated to the canine god Khentimentiu, who later was absorbed into the cult of Osiris as Osiris-Khentimentiu.

Because of the importance of Osiris with regard to the royal funerary cult—and therefore, by transference, in the hopes for the afterlife among all the king's subjects—Abydos was a popular place for pilgrimage, burial, and the dedication of funerary stelae. Over the surface of the desert between the Early Dynastic cemetery and the cultivated fields were scattered graves and cenotaphs (tomb-like structures that contained no actual body but were intended to ensure that the person for whom they were erected received some of the benefits of the cult of Osiris), as well as animal burials.

Map of the site of Abydos.

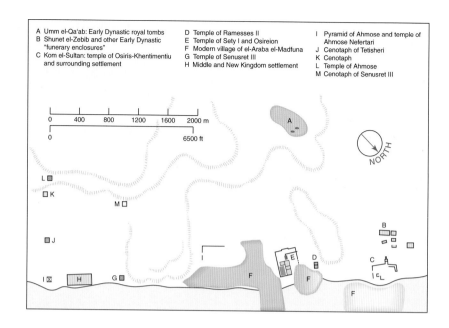

A Umm el-Qa'ab: Early Dynastic royal tombs
B Shunet el-Zebib and other Early Dynastic "funerary enclosures"
C Kom el-Sultan: temple of Osiris-Khentimentiu and surrounding settlement
D Temple of Ramesses II
E Temple of Sety I and Osireion
F Modern village of el-Araba el-Madfuna
G Temple of Senusret III
H Middle and New Kingdom settlement
I Pyramid of Ahmose and temple of Ahmose Nefertari
J Cenotaph of Tetisheri
K Cenotaph
L Temple of Ahmose
M Cenotaph of Senusret III

0 400 800 1200 1600 2000 m
0   6500 ft

NORTH

Parts of the pharaonic town at Abydos have survived in the modern mound known as Kom el-Sultan, but the site as a whole is now dominated by the New Kingdom temples of Sety I and his son Ramesses II. The cult temple of Sety I is an L-shaped limestone building. The iconography of its exquisite painted reliefs has been used to interpret the procedures of the religious rituals that were enacted there. In one scene, Ramesses II is shown reading out the names of previous kings from a papyrus roll, in the presence of his father. The contents of the document are carved on the adjacent wall; this "king-list" (along with a similar list from the temple of Ramesses II) has made an important contribution to Egyptian chronology.

Behind the temple of Sety I is the Osireion, a subterranean building constructed of huge granite blocks, which has been interpreted as a kind of cenotaph of the god Osiris. The structure is entered via a long descending gallery and is decorated with excerpts from the *Book of Gates* and the *Book of the Dead* (New Kingdom texts and paintings concerning the afterlife), as well as with cosmological and dramatic texts. It was once thought to be an Old Kingdom building because of the grandiose scale of the masonry, but it has now been dated to the reign of Sety I; the style is now generally presumed to have been an attempt at archaizing by New Kingdom architects.

The Discovery and Excavation of the Royal Tombs at Umm el-Qa'ab

The Abydos cemeteries, including the Early Dynastic necropolis now known in Arabic as Umm el-Qa'ab ("mother of pots," from the large numbers of

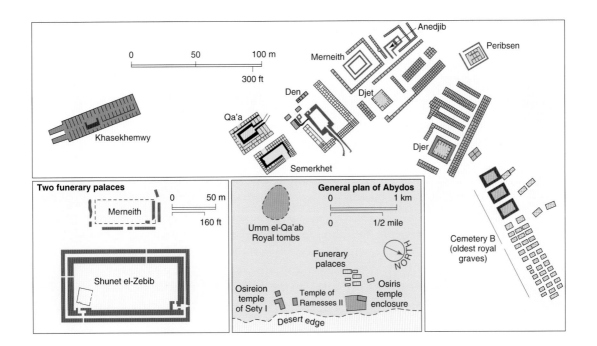

Plan of the Early Dynastic royal tombs at Abydos, with inset plans of the royal "funerary palaces" of Merneith and Khasekhemwy.

potsherds covering the desert surface), were excavated in the late nineteenth and early twentieth centuries, mainly by two French archaeologists, Auguste Mariette and Émile Amélineau, and two British archaeologists, Flinders Petrie and Eric Peet.

Mariette excavated at Abydos in the 1850s, clearing part of the Middle Kingdom cemeteries as well as the temples of Sety I and Ramesses II. He obtained a large number of statues and stelae from these graves, and it was presumably the promise of such rich finds that persuaded Amélineau to begin excavation at the Umm el-Qa'ab cemetery in December 1895.

Over a period of four years, Amélineau cleared the "royal tombs" more than a mile away from the cultivated land. The royal cemetery consists of two distinct areas: the Umm el-Qa'ab, burial chambers of important individuals with tumulus superstructures, stelae, and subsidiary burials, dated as early as the beginning of the fourth millennium B.C.; and the North Cemetery, paneled mud-brick enclosures and subsidiary burials. Although Amélineau's methods were much criticized by other archaeologists at the time, particularly by Gaston Maspero and Flinders Petrie, and the standards of his work have been described by one modern scholar as "a verbose and unfocused antiquarianism," his techniques were probably no worse than those of most others working in the late nineteenth century (indeed, close examination of the French scholar's careful publications shows that he was somewhat unfairly maligned by Petrie and his colleagues). More frustrating, perhaps, is the fact that the artifacts excavated by Amélineau from the royal tombs have not survived as an intact collection: they were sold off as separate lots at a Paris auction in 1904.

Each of the royal tombs at Abydos seems to have been originally marked by a pair of stone slabs carved with the "Horus name" of the king. The stele belonging to King Djet of the first dynasty (c. 3000 B.C., limestone, h. 143 cm), whose name is written with the "serpent" hieroglyph, is aesthetically the best of those that have survived.

Each of the Abydos royal tombs originally incorporated two large stone tablets sculpted with the relief form of a palace façade surmounted by the name of the king and the Horus falcon. The finest of these stelae is the one found by Amélineau in the tomb of King Djet ("Serpent"). The original positions of the stelae are not known because none of them has been found exactly *in situ,* but virtually all were found in the immediate vicinity of the tombs, and Amélineau wrote that he excavated the Djet stela from a niche inside a room he identified as the burial chamber (Petrie later described it as a kind of store-room). It is clear from the finds made both by Amélineau and Petrie that the store-rooms in the Abydos royal tombs still contained large numbers of funerary objects.

In 1896, Jacques de Morgan excavated Predynastic graves at Abydos, identifying both these and the ones excavated by Petrie at Naqada in the same year as remains dating from the time before the dynastic period began. These excavations were extremely useful for the development of the study of Egyptian prehistory, but the small area covered by the Predynastic cemetery suggests that the settlement of Abydos was relatively limited until the late Predynastic and Protodynastic periods.

When Amélineau finally gave up the Abydos concession, it was left to Petrie to sift through the remains and to attempt to reconstruct the royal cemetery at Umm el-Qa'ab, after it had been plundered by both the Copts and Amélineau. After five years' work from 1899 to 1903, Petrie had begun to make sense of the Early Dynastic remains. Compared with Amélineau, he paid more attention to the fine details of the funerary architecture and the more ephemeral aspects of the funerary equipment. He found that, beginning in the reign of the early first-dynasty ruler Djer (c. 3000 B.C.), each tomb contained a number of chambers in which different types of grave goods had been placed, including stone vases sealed with golden lids, copper bowls, gold bracelets, food, weapons, tools, and furniture made from ivory and ebony. Petrie managed to find several still intact chambers within the first-dynasty tombs of Queen Merneith and King Qa'a, both of which had supposedly been completely excavated by Amélineau.

In an area of desert a short distance to the east of the Early Dynastic cemetery, a set of graves known as Cemetery U was first excavated by Amélineau in the late nineteenth century, and later by Peet in the early twentieth. In the 1980s and 1990s, this part of Abydos was reexamined by the German Archaeological Institute; the new excavations uncovered hundreds more tombs, in addition to the 150 found by Amélineau and the 32 found by Peet. The German excavation team, directed by Günter Dreyer, obtained evidence to suggest that there are strong cultural links between Petrie's royal graves (traditionally dated to the "0" and first dynasties, the very beginning of the Early Dynastic phase at Abydos) and the adjacent late Predynastic Cemetery U. They argue, therefore, that the line of powerful rulers buried at Abydos

Several of the Abydos royal tombs have recently been meticulously re-excavated by the German Archaeoloical Institute in Cairo; the tomb of the first-dynasty ruler Den was the first to incorporate steps leading down into the tomb from ground level (visible in the foreground).

may now be pushed further back into what was previously considered to be "prehistory."

U-j is the largest tomb in Cemetery U, measuring 9.1 by 7.3 meters; the brick lining of the walls has survived, as well as wood, matting, and brick from the roof or superstructure. It contained hundreds of Egyptian wavy-handled pottery vessels, as well as beer jars, bread molds, and plates dating to the Naqada IIIa2 phase of the late Predynastic Period (c. 3200 B.C.). Many of the Egyptian vessels bear inscriptions in black ink, including depictions of a scorpion, which was perhaps the name of the early king buried there. One chamber of Tomb U-j was filled with about 400 Palestinian-style vessels that probably originally contained wine. Very few of these vessels have been identified with specific types of Early Bronze Age vessels found in southern Palestine, raising the possibility that these were produced specifically to contain goods being exported to Egypt. We cannot be sure by what route they arrived in Egypt. It is possible that they were brought across the northern part of the Sinai Peninsula and down through the eastern Nile Delta, eventually being conveyed up the Nile to Abydos by boat, but they may also have arrived from the east via the Red Sea and along one of the early trade routes crossing the Eastern Desert.

The funerary equipment in an earlier tomb (U-127) included a fragment of an ivory knife-handle bearing a carved depiction of a row of offering-bearers, and two other fragments decorated with rows of bearded captives and animals. Perhaps most significant, tomb U-j contained a large model ivory heka-scepter, an essential part of the traditional Egyptian royal regalia, which was evidently in use at least 200 years before the date when it was once thought that the first pharaohs reigned.

What Did the Tombs Originally Look Like?

Petrie's excavations showed that most of the Early Dynastic royal tombs at Abydos consisted of a pit reinforced with mud-brick walls; the center was usually lined with cedar wood or stone. The whole of each pit was originally roofed with wooden planks supported by wooden pillars. Although only a few traces of the superstructures had survived, Petrie was able to judge from the remains that the mud-brick retaining walls had risen above ground level to surround a low, benchlike plastered mound of rubble.

Petrie's ideas concerning the outward appearance of the royal tombs have been expanded and refined in the course of the recent German work at the site. The study of traces of retaining walls within and beside the tombs suggests that the entire burial pit was initially covered by a smaller subterranean mound, and that this was later covered by a much larger rectangular mound clearly visible above the surface.

A stairway leading down into the tomb was introduced in the reign of Den, both in his own tomb at Abydos and in Tomb 3035 (Hemaka's) at Saqqara. This refinement would have allowed the tomb, theoretically at least, to have been filled up with grave goods during the king's own lifetime, perhaps acting as a storehouse for surplus produce. Twenty ivory and ebony labels have survived from the tomb of Den, eighteen of which were found by Petrie in Amélineau's spoil heaps.

Stelae from first-dynasty subsidiary tombs were excavated by Petrie. There are many rows of smaller subsidiary tombs around the massive royal tombs, and some of them were apparently covered by a common roof. Amélineau and Petrie excavated more than 200 stelae from the subsidiary burials. These stelae, inscribed with the name and sometimes the occupation or title of the deceased, show that the tombs belonged to various members of the royal

Hypothetical reconstruction of the superstructure of the tomb of the first-dynasty ruler Djer, showing the brick-lined substructure surmounted by two mounds, one below ground level and the other above. The illustration also shows the possible position of Djer's funerary stele.

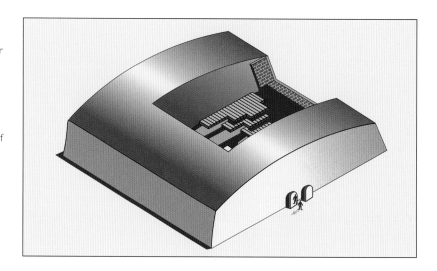

court: women of the royal harem, palace officials, royal dwarfs, and even favorite dogs (four of the 45 stelae excavated by Amélineau were those of dogs).
As with the royal stelae, it is not certain precisely where these were placed,
but we know that the nonroyal second-dynasty tombs at Helwan often contained stelae attached to the ceiling of the burial chamber. There is no direct
evidence of how these retainers died, but it seems fairly likely that a few of
them died just before the royal burial itself; that is, they were killed deliberately in order to join the king in the afterlife. The custom of human sacri-
fice apparently reached its peak in the time of Djer, who had more than 580
retainers buried around his tomb and funerary palace.

What Was the Shunet el-Zebib?

Modern visitors to Abydos tend to concentrate on the temples of Sety I and
Ramesses II, who reigned about 1,500 years later than the Early Dynastic
rulers, but many of those who visit the temple of Ramesses II notice a huge
gray rectangular building on the desert horizon to the north. This impressive mud-brick enclosure, measuring 410 by 215 feet (123 by 64.5 meters)
in area and still reaching a height of 40 feet (12 meters) in places, is known
locally as the Shunet el-Zebib ("storehouse of grapes") because of its resemblance to some kind of massive storage structure. A little farther to the
north is a similar structure, not quite so well-preserved, which is now known
as Deir ("monastery") owing to its reuse as a Coptic settlement.

For a long time, archaeologists assumed that these two structures were ancient fortifications of some kind. In 1921, however, Petrie excavated the surrounding area and discovered that the Shunet el-Zebib and the Deir were
part of a group of Early Dynastic rectangular enclosures surrounded by rows
of tombs belonging to various servants and officials of the first- and second-
dynasty rulers. It was only through the survival of these so-called tombs of the
courtiers that the outlines of most of the other enclosures could be discerned.

The enclosures were evidently contemporary with the surrounding graves,
and indeed linked with them in some way, but their purpose remained unclear until the 1960s. Then Barry Kemp, a British Egyptologist, reexamined
the site as a whole and reanalyzed the results of the excavations conducted
by Petrie and Peet. Kemp suggested that the Shunet el-Zebib was simply
the best-preserved of a row of large ritual enclosures, each of which was
linked with one of the Early Dynastic royal tombs at Umm el-Qa'ab to the
west. These buildings, which he described as "funerary palaces," might well
have been the prototypes of the mortuary temples and valley temples in Old
Kingdom pyramid complexes.

In 1991, the excavations of David O'Connor, an American Egyptologist,
provided further support for Kemp's theory in the form of a number of Early
Dynastic wooden "boat-graves" close to the Shunet el-Zebib "funerary
palace." These boat-graves resemble a model boat burial in association with

an Early Dynastic tomb up at Saqqara; and, more important, they parallel the two dismantled wooden boats found buried beside the fourth-dynasty pyramid of Khufu at Giza, one of which was so well preserved that it was able to be entirely rebuilt (see chapter 4).

The Stele of Weni

In February 1860, Mariette was excavating on a small hill at the northern end of Abydos when he came upon a single-room tomb chapel, one wall of which was made up of an inscribed yellowish limestone slab over 3 feet (1 meter) high, nearly 10 feet (3 meters) wide, and about 1 foot (30 centimeters) thick. The inscription on this slab identified it as the funerary stele of Weni, a high official who had risen rapidly through the ranks of officialdom during the reigns of Teti, Pepy I, and Merenra, toward the end of the Old Kingdom (c. 2345–2287 B.C.). Because Abydos was full of cenotaphs as well as genuine tombs, it was once not certain whether Weni was actually buried at Abydos or somewhere in the cemeteries serving the administrative center of Memphis. However, excavations conducted in 1999 and 2000 have proved beyond any doubt that this was Weni's burial place.

The "autobiographical inscription" was one of the most common types of text in nonroyal tombs from the Old Kingdom onward. The earliest examples appear in the fourth dynasty in the Memphite necropolis, among the rows of mastaba-tombs surrounding the pyramids. In these earlier tombs, there was simply a relief image of the deceased and a prayer for offerings and a good burial; the later tombs with "autobiographies" used the literary styles of narration and declaration to add to the basic prayer a record of the essentials of the tomb-owner's life and achievements, concluding with a warning to visitors not to desecrate the tomb. The two main themes were career and moral character, both of which resulted directly from the individual's role in life—particularly from his relationship with the king, which was usually the means by which he gained his finely equipped tomb in the first place. The main topics therefore tended to be the enactment of tasks on behalf of the king and the rewards that the individual was consequently granted by the king.

The text on the stele of Weni, inscribed from right to left and consisting of one horizontal line along the top (a prayer for offerings) and 51 vertical columns, is the longest "literary" record of the Old Kingdom. Because it describes the principal events in the career of Weni, it is important not only for its status as a very early work of literature but also for the light it sheds on sixth-dynasty history, society, and administration. Taking the form of a kind of biography, it can be broken down into typical Old Kingdom themes: Weni's career as a bureaucrat in the palace administration; his procurement of a stone sarcophagus and masonry for his tomb; his military campaigns in the Eastern Desert and Palestine; a hymn of victory, including a stereotypical description of an Asiatic country; his organization of quarrying expeditions to Hatnub and Aswan; and

For many years, scholars assumed that the Sumerian cuneiform writing system emerged at an earlier date than Egyptian hieroglyphs, and that the relatively sudden appearance of writing in Egypt at the end of the fourth millennium B.C. was probably the result of increased contact with Near Eastern peoples. Although it seemed unlikely that the Egyptian writing system had evolved out of cuneiform, many scholars believed that the basic idea of pictographic writing might have come from Mesopotamia. However, archaeological discoveries at Abydos during the 1990s have begun to provide insights into the emergence of the Egyptian writing system, suggesting that the origins of the script were almost certainly much earlier than was previously thought.

The excavations of the German Archaeological Institute at tomb U-j, the impressive burial of "King Scorpion" described earlier in this chapter, have revealed one room containing numerous small labels carved from wood and bone that appear to bear clearly recognizable hieroglyphs representing numbers, commodities, and possibly also place-names or royal agricultural estates. The importance of these hieroglyphic labels is that they are probably not just pictorial signs ("ideograms"), which would represent a much more basic stage in the history of the script; many of them are representations of sounds in the spoken language ("phonograms"), a stage in the development of the script that was not thought to have occurred until at least the first dynasty. The German philologists who studied the labels were able to identify them as phonetic symbols because they often spell out the names of well-known towns frequently mentioned in later inscriptions, such as Buto and Bubastis.

It therefore appears that the bureaucrats employed by the earliest rulers at Abydos—at least 200 years before the first dynasty—were already using a sophisticated form of Egyptian script involving phonetic signs as well as ideograms. The fact that this writing often seems to refer to Lower Egyptian place-names as the sources of goods placed in an Upper Egyptian ruler's tomb is very strong evidence that the northern and southern halves of Egypt were already closely connected economically, and perhaps politically too. Thus, many of the factors associated with fully developed states—such as writing, bureaucracy, monumental architecture, and complex systems of exchange and economic control—were evidently in place in Egypt much earlier than previously thought.

Many small inscribed bone and ivory labels, bearing early hieroglyphic inscriptions, were found in tomb U-j at Abydos (c. 3200 B.C.), suggesting that a fully developed phonetic system was already in use about 150 years earlier than once thought. The signs on the two labels in the bottom left-hand corner spell out *grḥ dju* ("mountains of darkness") and the signs on the three in the bottom right-hand corner spell *akh dju* ("mountains of light"), perhaps referring to the mountains to the west and east of the Nile, respectively.

his creation of a new river channel through the First Cataract at Aswan. The literary style of the text derives partly from early religious inscriptions (particularly the Pyramid Texts), but it is innovative in its attempts to combine prose narrative with poetic material. One extraordinary element of Weni's biography is a reference to secret legal activities concerning Weretyamtes, a wife of Pepy I, which some Egyptologists have interpreted as evidence that he witnessed the trial of a queen accused of conspiracy against the king himself.

Further Reading

The work of Auguste Mariette in the cemeteries of Abydos was published as *Abydos: Description des fouilles exécutées sur l'emplacement de cette ville,* 2 vols. (Paris, 1869–1880). Amélineau' s work was published very rapidly in the three volumes of *Les nouvelles fouilles d'Abydos* (Paris, 1895–1904). Flinders Petrie's excavations in the Early Dynastic royal cemetery are described in *The Royal Tombs of the Earliest Dynasties* (London, 1900–1901). The recent work of German excavators at Abydos has been published annually in the journal *Mitteilungen des Deutschen Archäologischen Instituts, Abteilung Kairo* from 1979 on, and also in a series of monographs. The work of David O'Connor in the vicinity of the funerary palaces is the subject of a 1991 article, "Boat Graves and Pyramid Origins: New Discoveries at Abydos, Egypt" (*Expedition* 33.3: 5–17). Barry Kemp's carefully argued discussion of the arguments for Abydos rather than Saqqara being the early royal cemetery can be found in volume 41 (1967) of the journal *Antiquity* (pp.22–32). The funerary inscription of Weni has been translated by Miriam Lichtheim in *Ancient Egyptian Literature, vol. 1* (Berkeley, 1973, pp.18–23), and the recent reexamination of his tomb is published in the Spring 2000 and Fall 2001 issues of the *Kelsey Museum Newsletter.*

Books on the temple of Sety I include Amice Calverley and Myrtle Broome, *The Temple of King Sethos I at Abydos,* 4 vols. (London and Chicago, 1933–1958), and Rosalie David, *A Guide to Religious Ritual at Abydos* (Warminster, 1981). The Osireion is discussed by Henri Frankfort in *The Cenotaph of Seti I at Abydos* (London, 1933).

Further Viewing

There are further impressive mud-brick Early Dynastic tombs at other sites, including Saqqara, Helwan, and Abu Rawash. Funerary material from the Early Dynastic royal tombs at Abydos, as well as stelae and other items of various dates, can be seen in a number of museums, including the Louvre, the British Museum, the Petrie Museum (University College, London), and the Egyptian Museum, Cairo. The last collection also includes the funerary stele of Weni. A substantial part of the king-list of Ramesses II from his temple at Abydos is displayed in the British Museum.

Saqqara

c. 2650 B.C.

Steps to heaven: The first pyramid

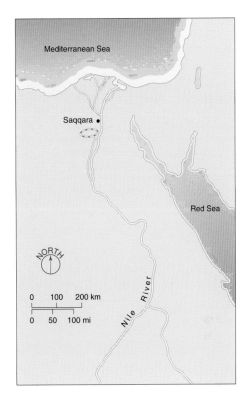

Saqqara, a vast field of ruins situated about 10 miles (16 kilometers) from Giza, a suburb of Cairo, was the principal necropolis of Memphis, the ancient Egyptian capital city for much of the pharaonic period. It was in use as a cemetery almost continuously from at least the end of the fourth millennium B.C. until the Christian period (395–540 A.D.). The total length of the necropolis is about 3.75 miles (6 kilometers), with a maximum width of about a mile (1.6 kilometers). In a sense, it is just one link in a long chain of elite cemeteries that extends from Abu Rawash in the north down to Dahshur in the south, a distance of more than 13 miles (20 kilometers).

Saqqara, however, is both the densest and the earliest part of the Memphite city of the dead. Although much of the modern-day desert surrounding the pyramids looks placid and undisturbed, thousands of shafts and tunnels were long ago cut into the sand and rock of the plateau, forming a vast labyrinth in which Early Dynastic human burials and Ptolemaic and Roman galleries full of mummified animals are inextricably interlinked. The burials are crowded together, and many tombs were reused repeatedly in ancient times, sometimes making it difficult to work out the date at which they were originally created. Most of the tombs have also been plundered again and again.

The first-dynasty ruler Narmer is the earliest king whose name is known from Saqqara. His actual burial was almost certainly in tomb B17–18 of the Umm el-Qa'ab at Abydos (see chapter 2), but

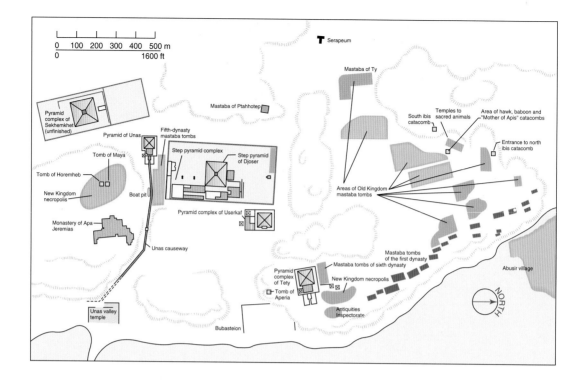

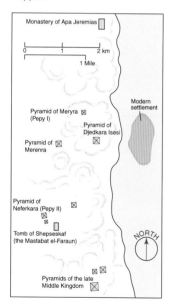

Map of northern and southern
Saqqara.

a stone bowl bearing his name was discovered in one of the extensive store-
rooms beneath the Step Pyramid of Djoser (r. 2630–2611 B.C.). It is not impossible that there was originally a monument of the reign of Narmer at
Saqqara, since slightly later first-dynasty mastaba-tombs are well attested at
the site, forming a distinct group along the northeastern edge of the plateau.

It is thought likely that the original site of the White Wall (one of the
ancient names for Memphis) was probably near the modern village of Abusir,
which is situated at the northeastern corner of the site, close to the first- and
second-dynasty tombs. Mastaba-tombs were constructed at Saqqara for the
Memphite elite during the Old Kingdom, many of them centered closely
on the pyramids of the kings, which range in date from the third-dynasty
complex of Djoser to the thirteenth-dynasty monument of Khendjer. The
fifth-dynasty pyramid of Unas is the earliest known to be inscribed with
the Pyramid Texts, while the pyramid complex of the sixth-dynasty ruler
Pepy II (2278–2184 B.C.) is the last major funerary monument of the Old
Kingdom at Saqqara. The remains of the tiny mud-brick pyramid of the obscure eighth-dynasty ruler Ibi aptly symbolize the decline in the political and
economic system from the Old Kingdom to the First Intermediate Period.

Although Thebes was probably the religious capital of the New Kingdom,
Memphis retained a great deal of its administrative importance and for most
of Egyptian history it was the real seat of government. Many important
officials of the New Kingdom resided in the city, and although their rulers

chose to be buried in the Valley of the Kings at Thebes (see chapter 13), many nobles constructed elaborate temple-style tomb chapels for themselves at Saqqara, usually surrounded by the smaller tombs of their servants and family. There was also New Kingdom activity in northwestern Saqqara, in the form of the hypogea of the sacred Apis bulls, which were buried in the underground galleries of the Serapeum from at least the time of Amenhotep III (1391–1353 B.C.) until the Roman period.

From the Late Period (712–657 B.C.) on, sacred animals were buried in huge quantities in the vast underground catacombs at the north end of the site; these mummified animals and birds included cows identified as the "Mothers of Apis," as well as Cynocephalus baboons, hawks, and ibises. The area was probably chosen for a sacred animal necropolis because of its traditional connection with Imhotep, the architect of Djoser's Step Pyramid, who became identified with Thoth, a god particularly associated with baboons and ibises. The texts suggest that rams sacred to the god Banebdjedet and the calves of the Apis bull may also have been buried in this area, although the actual galleries have not yet been located. Farther to the east, there were burials of dogs or jackals connected with the Anubieion, and of cats connected with the Bubasteion. So many cats were buried in this part of Saqqara that their mummified remains were deposited in many of the earlier nonroyal funerary monuments, including the nearby tomb of Aperia.

Tombs dating to periods later than the New Kingdom were also constructed at Saqqara, most of them near the Step Pyramid complex. Near the pyramid of the fifth-dynasty ruler Userkaf there are deep shaft tombs of the twenty-sixth dynasty. Tombs of the twenty-sixth and twenty-seventh dynasties are also located near the pyramid of Unas. Many of the artists decorating tombs of the twenty-sixth dynasty deliberately copied a great deal of

By the end of the fourth millennium B.C., the early towns of northern and southern Egypt were united culturally and politically. By then, one city had become preeminent. It was situated just south of the apex of the Nile Delta, in the ideal geographical position to control both halves of the newly united state, and at first was known as Ineb-hedj ("White wall"). The precise location of its earliest stage is uncertain, although the results of excavations during the 1990s suggest that it may have been close to the modern village of Abusir, toward the northeast of the desert plateau where the pyramid of Djoser would later be constructed.

From this time on, the expansion of the city seems to have been influenced primarily by the locations of the royal pyramids in the Saqqara necropolis extending along its western side. As construction began on each new pyramid, the geographical focus of the town slowly shifted. By the sixth dynasty, Ineb-hedj seems to have been eclipsed in importance by a set of suburbs farther to the south, centering on Djed-isut, the town and palace associated with the pyramid of King Tety. Eventually, however, it was Men-nefer (later rendered into Greek as "Memphis"), the part of the city associated with (and named after) the pyramid of Pepy I, that provided the name by which the whole urban area was known for the rest of its history. From at least the New Kingdom on, a vast temple dedicated to the god Ptah lay at the center of Memphis; little of this, however, has survived, particularly compared with the Karnak temple of Amun, at the heart of Thebes, which it must have rivaled.

Like many other Egyptian settlements, Memphis was occupied virtually continuously throughout the pharaonic, Ptolemaic, and Roman periods. The archaeological site covers almost four square kilometers. Modern excavations suggest that the houses and temples gradually spread southward and eastward as the Nile retreated eastward toward its modern location.

the earlier funerary art at Saqqara. Tombs of the thirtieth dynasty and the Ptolemaic and Roman periods are clustered mainly on the northern side of the Step Pyramid, and toward the Serapeum.

Because many of the tombs at Saqqara were constructed from unusually small stone blocks (particularly during the New Kingdom), they could be dismantled easily to provide a ready source of stone for later building operations. For instance, much of the monastery of Apa Jeremias, south of the Unas causeway, was constructed from such reused blocks. During the time of the monastery, a small Coptic settlement was established to the southeast, close to the valley temple of Unas.

The Step Pyramid Complex

The whole site of north Saqqara is overshadowed by the massive rectangular stone-built step pyramid of the third-dynasty ruler Djoser. During the first two dynasties, as more and more important officials exercised their right to build large mastaba-tombs along the plateau edge, the people of Memphis may have found it increasingly difficult to distinguish any particular tomb among the great mass on the edge of the plateau. Some researchers have suggested that it was the desire for greater visibility that caused Djoser's funerary monument to develop into such an innovative structure. This was the first time that stone architecture had been used on such a large scale in Egypt. Not surprisingly, therefore, many of the details of the architecture were still rooted in the building traditions connected with mud brick and organic materials; the "palace façade" style of decoration continued to be used, and wooden columns were simply copied in stone.

Only the king's "Horus name," Netjerykhet, appears in third-dynasty inscriptions associated with the pyramid, and it is purely through a piece of New Kingdom graffiti mentioning Djoser (inscribed on a wall by a scribe called Ahmose about a thousand years after the construction of the monument) that a link has been established between Djoser and the Step Pyramid. A number of fragments of statuary representing Netjerykhet-Djoser were recovered from the pyramid complex, including an almost life-size seated statue from the serdab (statue-room). On the walls of one of the subterranean galleries to the east of the burial chamber are three reliefs depicting the king enacting various rituals. Djoser's pyramid seems initially to have taken the form of a huge mastaba-tomb, built in stone rather than mud brick, but it was gradually extended and elaborated until it became a pyramidal superstructure consisting of six massive steps and reaching a height of 200 feet (60 meters), making it highly visible from the capital city of Memphis. A passage from the north side led to the subterranean royal burial chamber and to eleven subsidiary chambers for other members of the family. A series of ancillary chambers and corridors was decorated with elaborate blue faience tiles and relief sculpture showing the king performing rites at his royal jubilee.

This—the first pyramid ever to be constructed—is thought to have been designed by a man called Imhotep, an architect and vizier whom the historian Manetho credited with the invention of building in dressed stone. Imhotep is also said to have written a number of "instructions" (a kind of wisdom text similar to the biblical Proverbs), although none of them has survived. About two thousand years after his death, the first evidence appears of his deification—a great rarity for nonroyal individuals in ancient Egypt. His own tomb has still not been discovered (despite the strenuous efforts of the British Egyptologist Bryan Emery during the 1960s), although it has been suggested that it may be the large uninscribed Mastaba 3518 in north Saqqara. As well as having a cult center at Saqqara, Imhotep was also worshipped at Karnak and Philae. In the Ptolemaic temple to Hathor at Deir el-Bahari, on the Theban west bank, he was venerated alongside Amenhotep, son of Hapu, an important architect of the eighteenth dynasty.

The recessed, "palace-façade" architectural style characteristic of the superstructures of Early Dynastic nonroyal tombs at Saqqara was used to decorate the great enclosure wall surrounding the Step Pyramid and its ancillary buildings. It therefore seems likely that the complex was a combination of royal tomb and "funerary palace" (like the second-dynasty Shunet el-Zebib at

53
—

Abydos; see chapter 2). To the east of Djoser's pyramid was an open area surrounded by rows of solid "dummy" buildings apparently intended to replicate various provincial shrines. This part of the complex was almost certainly connected with the celebration of the sed-festival (royal jubilee), although it is not clear whether the ritual itself would have been enacted there during the king's lifetime.

A possible mortuary temple, now badly ruined, stood on the north side of the pyramid, and a large rectangular structure known as the "south mastaba" lay at the south end of the enclosure, perhaps serving as a cenotaph balancing the main pyramid, so that the two "tombs" may have symbolized the king's rule over both Upper and Lower Egypt. The complex as a whole seems to have been simultaneously a permanent monumental equivalent of the sed-festival and a celebration of the royal funerary cult. As later pyramids (such as those at Giza) became more concerned with the king's solar connections, the importance of the sed-festival as an element of the funerary complex appears to have diminished correspondingly.

The remains of the unfinished step pyramid complex of one of Djoser's successors, Sekhemkhet, lie a short distance to the southwest of the Step Pyramid. A few other surviving traces of enclosure walls at the western side of the Saqqara necropolis, including the so-called Great Enclosure (recently investigated by a team from the Royal Museum of Scotland), suggest that further third-dynasty rulers probably erected step pyramids similar to those of Djoser and Sekhemkhet. It is also worth pointing out that the use of steps in pyramid building never truly died out, in that some "true pyramids" continued to consist of a stepped structure, which was simply transformed in the final stages of construction by the application of a smooth outer casing. The late third-dynasty (or early fourth-dynasty) pyramid at Meidum was originally conceived as a step pyramid; we know this because the smooth outer casing eventually collapsed, thus revealing the original stepped core of the superstructure.

What Does the Step Pyramid Tell Us about Early Egyptian Kingship?

On the eastern side of the Step Pyramid complex was an elaborate architectural setting for the royal jubilee (sed-festival), including the remains of a double pavilion that would have held two thrones like the ones shown on an ebony label from the tomb of the first-dynasty ruler Den at Abydos. It is presumed that the king would have sat on one throne and then the other, dressed in the Upper and Lower Egyptian regalia, respectively, symbolizing his dominion over the "two lands" of Egypt.

The sed-festival was a ritual of renewal and regeneration, intended to be celebrated by the king only after a reign of thirty years had elapsed. In practice, the surviving inscriptions and monuments associated with this festival seem to show that many kings whose entire reigns were much shorter than thirty years left evidence of celebrating their sed-festivals. There are two possible interpretations of this situation: first, many kings may actually have celebrated the sed-festivals well before the requisite thirty years had elapsed; or second, they may have ordered the depiction of the ritual in anticipation of its happening later in the reign.

Documented from a very early stage in Egyptian history, the sed-festival (which derives its name from a wolf-god called Sed, closely related to the jackal-god Wepwawet of Asyut), is inextricably linked with the Egyptian perception of kingship. The two essential elements of the ceremony—the paying of homage to the enthroned king, and the ritual of territorial claim—are depicted on the aforementioned ebony label from the tomb of King Den at Abydos. The right-hand corner of the label shows the king first seated inside one of the special festival pavilions, wearing the double crown, and second, running between two sets of three cairns or boundary markers that probably symbolize the borders of Egypt. The two scenes are framed by the king's name in a *serekh* panel (a rectangular shape perhaps representing a palace gateway) on the left, and the hieroglyphic sign for a regnal year on the right.

In the adjoining court to the south of the Step Pyramid, traces were found of boundary markers like those between which the king was required to run. A relief from the subterranean chambers of the pyramid shows Djoser himself running between two sets of cairns; this dynamic image of the running pharaoh (often holding strange implements) continued to be depicted in sed-festival reliefs throughout the pharaonic period, as in the case of one of the blocks from the red chapel of Queen Hatshepsut (c. 1473–1458 B.C.) at Karnak temple.

The Seven Mysterious Small Step Pyramids

As well as the large-scale step pyramid of Djoser and the unfinished step pyramid of Sekhemkhet, there is also an enigmatic set of seven small step pyramids located at various sites in Upper Egypt, as well as one in the Delta. The sites of these miniature step pyramids are Seila, Zawiyet el-Mayitin, Abydos, Naqada, el-Kula (Hierakonpolis), Edfu, and Elephantine. Most of them are on the west side of the Nile, the exceptions being Zawiyet el-Maitin and Elephantine. All stand in isolation, with no adjacent temples or other buildings, and all are built of the locally available stone (granite at Elephantine, sandstone at Edfu, and limestone at the other five). Most originally consisted of three steps, but the one at Zawiyet el-Maitin had four, and that at Seila had five. They vary in height from about 13 feet (4 meters) in the case of Abydos to about 30 feet (9 meters) at el-Kula. All of them are oriented with one side parallel to the river, except for the one at Seila, the sides of which are oriented toward the four cardinal points. Architecturally,

Map showing the locations of the step pyramid at el-Kula and the other six small step pyramids of the late third dynasty.

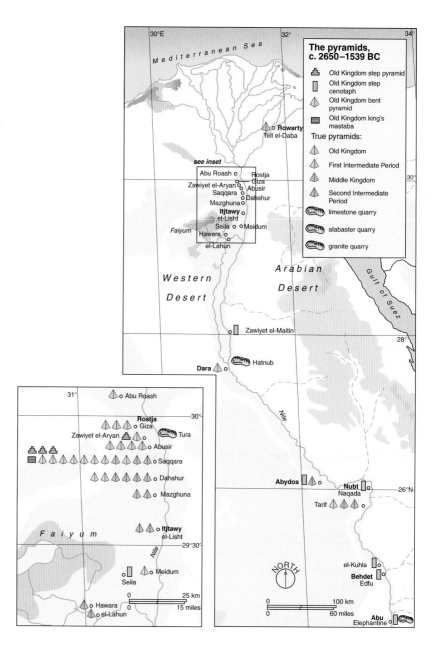

they all appear to be similar in date to the step pyramids of Djoser and Sekhemkhet, and since they are square at the base (rather than oblong), they are perhaps more likely to date from the reign of Sekhemkhet and later.

Three of the pyramids have yielded more detailed information. The one at Naqada was excavated by Flinders Petrie, revealing a pit below it, which he interpreted as the remains of a grave that had been robbed before the pyramid itself was built. The one at Elephantine was excavated by a French expedition beginning in 1909; Joseph Gautier found a large granite cone nearby, inscribed on its base with the name of the late third-dynasty ruler Huni. The Seila pyramid was excavated from 1981 on by a team from Brigham Young University, who found fragments of a white calcite statuette and two round-topped stelae, each about 5 feet (1.5 meters) high, buried in rubble in front of the east side of the pyramid; one stele is uninscribed, but the other bears the names and titles of the first fourth-dynasty ruler, Sneferu, suggesting that this pyramid may have been the last in the sequence.

The purpose of these small pyramids remains uncertain, although there is no shortage of theories. The French archaeologist Jean-Philippe Lauer suggested that they were third-dynasty queens' cenotaphs, each erected at the individual's place of birth, while her real burial would presumably have been near the king in the Memphite necropolis. Dieter Arnold argues that they were set up as representations of the "primeval mound" or site of the Creation, at settlements that claimed to be where the original primeval mound had first appeared. In 1979, Werner Kaiser and Günter Dreyer carried out a survey of seven of the pyramids and concluded that they were either royal cenotaphs or symbols of royal power set up by King Huni, the last ruler of the third dynasty, in the neighborhood of his provincial residences in order to "fly the flag" outside the capital. Kaiser's and Dreyer's theory is quite persuasive but is flawed by the fact that the Seila pyramid is fairly close to Memphis (actually within sight of the Meidum pyramid, which may have been built for Huni by his successor, King Sneferu).

The Pyramid of Unas and the Emergence of the Pyramid Texts

Just south of the Step Pyramid complex is the fifth-dynasty Pyramid of Unas, the earliest royal tomb to contain wall inscriptions relating to the king's death and afterlife. The Egyptians' composition of funerary texts probably stretched back to an original preliterate oral tradition, traces of which have survived only in the form of certain poorly understood funerary artifacts and sculptures.

The Pyramid Texts comprise about 800 spells, or "utterances," written in columns on the walls of the corridors and burial chambers of nine pyramids of the late Old Kingdom and First Intermediate Period. The earliest surviving Pyramid Texts are inscribed in Unas's pyramid (2375–2345 B.C.), but the examples inscribed in the pyramid of Pepy I (2321–2287 B.C.), a short distance to the south, were the first to be discovered, by the brothers Émile and Heinrich Brugsch in 1881. Texts of this type were inscribed in the pyramids of six kings altogether, all buried at Saqqara between the sixth and eighth dynasties, as well as in the three pyramids of Pepy II's queens (Neith, Iput, and Wedjebten). No single pyramid contains the whole collection of spells; the maximum number is the 675 utterances in the pyramid of Pepy II (2246–

The Saqqara Serapeum, the burial place of the sacred Apis bulls, consists of a series of catacombs northwest of the Step Pyramid of Djoser. The term "serapeum" was applied to a number of buildings associated with the cult of the Apis bull or with the later syncretic god Serapis. Funerary processions originally would have approached the Serapeum via a dromos (sacred way) running from the city of Memphis to the Saqqara plateau.

The catacombs were first excavated in 1851 by Auguste Mariette, who was led to the site through his discovery of traces of some of the sphinxes lining the dromos, which are faithfully described by the Greek writer Strabo (c. 64 B.C.–21 A.D.). The catacombs date back at least as early as the reign of Amenhotep III (c. 1390–1352 B.C.) and con-

Portico of the "Khaemwaset monument" overlooking the Serapeum, showing the bases of two rows of lotiform columns.

2152 B.C.). New texts have continued to be found during the 1980s and 1990s as a result of Jean Leclant's excavations among the pyramid complexes of south Saqqara.

What Was the Purpose and Meaning of the Pyramid Texts?

The constant references to the cult of the sun-god in the Pyramid Texts suggest that they were probably composed by the priests of Heliopolis ("sun city"), which was situated a few kilometers northeast of Memphis. Heliopolis, originally known as Iuru, was the site of the first temple dedicated to the sun-god Ra-Horakhty and continued to be the main focus of the sun cult in later periods. Its site is now largely covered by the northwestern suburb of Cairo, but excavations have revealed the tombs of the sixth-dynasty chief priests of Ra.

There appear to have been several basic categories of utterances among the Pyramid Texts, including what might be described as "magical" spells

tinued in use until the Ptolemaic Period (c. 332–30 B.C.). They contain many massive granite sarcophagi, each weighing up to 80 tons, although all but one had been robbed of their burials. Mariette also claims to have found the burial of Khaemwaset, a son of Ramesses II, who was responsible for constructing some of these vaults. Khaemwaset had inscriptions carved on some of the Old Kingdom monuments in the Memphite necropolis indicating that he devoted considerable effort to restoring the pyramid complexes, some of which were already more than a thousand years old.

In 1991, an expedition from Waseda University discovered a stone-built monument about a mile (1.6 kilometers) northwest of the Serapeum that was apparently erected by Khaemwaset. Most of the main blocks had been removed by robbers, leaving just the floors and foundations, but about a thousand small fragments of relief in limestone or granite remained. The main building consists of three elements arranged on an east-west axis. First there is a portico, probably originally 66 feet (20 meters) long with 16 columns, similar to the chapels of the New Kingdom tombs south of Unas's causeway, such as the tomb of Horemheb. This leads to a rectangular room, essentially just a passage measuring 7 by 16 feet (2 by 5 meters), followed by a cult room measuring about 7 feet square.

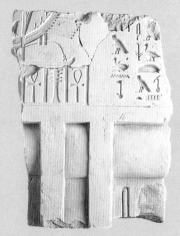

Part of a granite false door, bearing a depiction of a seated figure of Khaemwaset, was found on the floor of the cult room. About fifty limestone fragments have been pieced together to form a second false door. The presence of late New Kingdom hieratic inscriptions on some of the blocks suggests that the building was actually constructed by Khaemwaset, rather than being a posthumous cult building of later date. From the vantage point of this cult temple, it is possible to look out across the whole of the Memphite necropolis except for the southernmost cemetery, Meidum. This has led some scholars to suggest that the building may have been the spot from which Khaemwaset coordinated his various restoration projects.

Fragment of a false-door stele from the "Khaemwaset monument."

aiming to prevent harm to the deceased; these often use archaic language, perhaps indicating the Predynastic origins of the ideas. Another type of utterance seems to consist of the texts of various rituals that would have been performed at the royal funeral, with the deceased addressed as Osiris. This type of spell, which includes texts dealing both with offerings and with the resurrection, was inscribed in the burial chamber itself, no doubt the most sacred part of the pyramid. The Opening of the Mouth ceremony is first recorded in these ritual texts, along with the early offering ritual. Another category of spell, generally inscribed on the walls of the antechamber and corridor, seems to have been intended to be uttered by the tomb owner himself.

In modern texts and translations of the Pyramid Texts, the individual utterances are conventionally numbered in a sequence relating to their usual position in the pyramid, progressing from the burial chamber outward, although it has been suggested that the opposite order (from the entrance to the burial chamber) may be a more logical sequence. Siegfried Schott, for

The Pyramid Texts in the burial chamber of the pyramid of Unas.

instance, has argued that the texts make up a ritualistic description of the funereal progress of the king's dead body from its arrival in the valley temple to its deposition in the burial chamber (although many other scholars have refuted this theory).

Sometimes the Pyramid Texts seem to refer to aspects of the funerary cult that were no longer current at the time that the pyramids were built, as in the case of utterances 273–274 (the "Cannibal Hymn"), which appear only in the pyramids of Unas and Tety. These utterances describe the king "eating the magic" and "swallowing the spirits" of the gods. It is difficult to know in this instance whether the concept of the king eating the gods was purely metaphorical, or a reference to some early sacrificial act. For the Protodynastic and Early Dynastic periods, there may be archaeological indications of the funerary sac-

A fragment of Pyramid Texts from the pyramid of Unas, now in the Petrie Museum, University College London.

rifice of servants. It has been argued that the apparent shared roof covering many "subsidiary burials" surrounding the tombs of certain first-dynasty rulers at Abydos and Saqqara indicates that large numbers of royal retainers were killed simultaneously in order to accompany the pharaoh into the afterlife.

Further Reading

The excavations of Early Dynastic tombs at Saqqara were published by Bryan Emery as the three-volume work *Great Tombs of the First Dynasty* (Cairo and London, 1949-1958), but *Archaic Egypt* (Harmondsworth: Penguin, 1962) presents an account of his findings aimed at a more popular audience. Djoser's Step Pyramid is described by Cecil Firth, James Quibell, and Jean-Philippe Lauer in *The Step Pyramid,* 2 vols (Cairo, 1935-1936); this monument is also the focus of more recent works by Lauer, such as *Saqqara: The Royal Cemetery of Memphis: Excavations and Discoveries since 1850* (London, 1976). The later pyramids at the site, as well as the seven mysterious small step pyramids, are discussed by Iorwerth Edwards in *The Pyramids of Egypt* (5th ed., Harmondsworth: Penguin, 1993), and by Mark Lehner in *The Complete Pyramids* (London and New York: Thames and Hudson, 1997). Chris Eyre provides a fascinating study of the cultural context and meanings of the Pyramid Texts and Coffin Texts in *The Cannibal Hymn* (Liverpool, 2002).

Both the New Kingdom Tombs and the Sacred Animal Necropolis have been published by Geoffrey Martin in *The Hidden Tombs of Memphis* (London, 1991) and *The Sacred Animal Necropolis at North Saqqara* (London, 1981). The post-pharaonic animal cults at the site are discussed by John Ray in "The World of North Saqqara," *World Archaeology,* vol, 10 (1978), pp. 149-157.

Further Viewing

Artifacts from the excavation of the high officials' tombs of the Early Dynastic period at Saqqara can be viewed in a number of museums; the largest collections are in the Egyptian Museum at Cairo and at the British Museum. The former also has the statue of King Djoser from the serdab of the Step Pyramid (the one visible at the site is a modern plaster cast). Items from the New Kingdom tombs are spread through a wide variety of museum collections, including the Egyptian Museum at Cairo, the British Museum, the Berlin Museum, the Rijksmuseum van Oudheden in Leiden, the Ny Carlsberg Glyptotek in Copenhagen, and the Brooklyn Museum.

Giza

c. 2600–2500 B.C.

The pyramids and the Sphinx

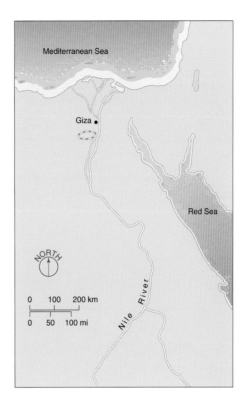

It is one of the more surprising facts of modern archaeology that the Giza plateau—site of the Great Pyramid and perhaps the best-known group of archaeological remains in the world—has still not been fully mapped and explored. Despite millennia of speculation about the meaning and purpose of the pyramids, Giza itself has been the site of relatively little serious excavation.

The necropolis is situated in the immediate vicinity of the southwestern suburbs of modern Cairo. Like Saqqara, it forms part of the long sequence of cemeteries known collectively as the Memphite necropolis. Giza is dominated by a group of pyramid complexes built by three rulers of the fourth dynasty (2575–2465 B.C.): Khufu (also called Cheops), Khafra (or Chephren), and Menkaura (or Mycerinus). The earliest known monument at the site is a tomb known as Mastaba V, which probably dates to the reign of the first-dynasty ruler Djet (c. 2950 B.C.). The name of the owner of the tomb is unknown, although the presence of the graves of fifty-six retainers suggests that he or she was an important member of the Early Dynastic elite. Jar sealings bearing the name of the second-dynasty ruler Nynetjer have also been found in a tomb to the south of the main necropolis.

Khufu built the largest surviving pyramid, now usually known as the "Great Pyramid" but originally called "Khufu is the one belonging to the horizon." His father, Sneferu, had erected the first true

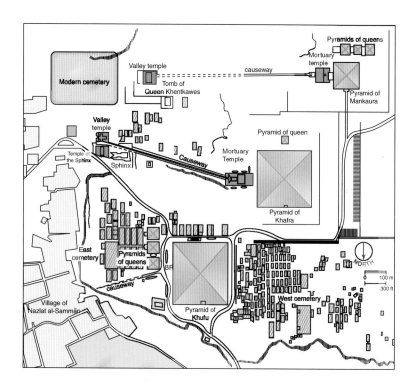

pyramid at Dahshur (just south of Saqqara), as well as the so-called Bent Pyramid at Dahshur, and perhaps also the pyramid at Meidum. Sneferu, therefore, undoubtedly wins the prize for the largest quantity of time, effort, and materials expended on funerary monuments. It is his son, however, who has come to be regarded as the consummate pyramid-builder; his reputation has been enhanced not only by the monument itself but also by the account given by the Greek historian Herodotus, who, writing in the fifth century B.C., claimed that Khufu's daughter was prostituted once for each of the stone blocks in the pyramid.

Less shocking statistics have been recited by generations of tour guides: a height of 481 feet (147 meters), a base length of 756 feet (230 meters), an orientation only 3′6″ off true north, and raw materials comprising 3,200,000 blocks of limestone weighing an average of 2.5 tons apiece. The Great Pyramid differs from most pyramids in having two burial chambers within the built structure, as well as a third unfinished chamber below ground. From each of the two upper chambers, narrow sloping tunnels were constructed; these so-called air shafts probably had little to do with ventilation, and for some time it has been accepted that they may have some astronomical function. In 1993, a German team led by Rudolf Gantenbrink and Rainer Stadelmann, using a robot camera, discovered a sealed stone door in one of the shafts leading from the Queen's Chamber. In 2002 a camera was inserted through a hole drilled in the "door," revealing only another stone door beyond it.

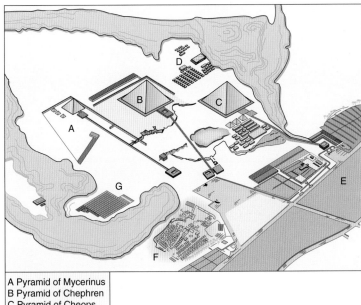

Reconstruction of the Giza plateau as it may have looked at the end of the fourth dynasty.

A Pyramid of Mycerinus
B Pyramid of Chephren
C Pyramid of Cheops
D West cemetery
E Royal palace
F Pyramid town
G Workers' village

It has been suggested that the original design of the Great Pyramid called for a subterranean burial chamber, but that this must have been abandoned at an early stage of the work, because it is only partly hewn. When first recorded, the chambers were found empty, perhaps having been robbed as early as the First Intermediate Period (2150–2040 B.C.), when the central government that had been responsible for their construction and upkeep went into decline for over a hundred years. Like the other true pyramids at this site and elsewhere, the superstructure of the Great Pyramid would not originally have been uneven but covered by a layer of smooth white Tura limestone, and probably crowned by gold sheet at the apex. This good-quality stone was stolen in later times for reuse in the medieval mosques and mausoleums of Cairo.

Although Khufu's immediate successor, Radjedef (2528–2520 B.C.), began to construct a pyramid complex at Abu Rawash, 5 miles (8 kilometers) north of Giza, he may have been responsible for some quarrying at Giza. Some scholars have attributed work on the Great Sphinx to him, although this sculpture is usually assigned to the reign of Khafra (2520–2494 B.C.), builder of the second of the Giza pyramids. The Sphinx is carved from a knoll of rock in a quarry beside Khafra's causeway, which leads from his well-preserved granite valley temple to the mortuary temple on the eastern side of his pyramid.

66

Khafra's pyramid is built on a slight eminence; for this reason, and because it still preserves some of its limestone casing at the apex, it actually appears to be larger than that of Khufu. Known in ancient times as "Great is Khafra," this monument is more typical of Old Kingdom pyramid design, with its subterranean burial chamber. On the north and west sides, it shows clear evidence of the quarrying necessary to level the site, the removed stone being used for the construction itself.

Khafra's granite valley temple is the best-preserved temple among the three Giza complexes. The smallest of the three is that of Menkaura (2490–2472 B.C.). Unlike that of his predecessor, the valley temple was not built of granite but was finished in mud brick. However, it was here that a series of superb schist triad-statues was discovered by the Harvard-Boston expedition in 1908. They represent the king with Hathor, goddess of Memphis, and various nome deities. Like the pyramid of Khafra, that of Menkaura had its lowest courses cased in red granite, and, like its predecessor, it had the chambers below the built structure. Unlike the other pyramids at Giza, "Menkaura is Divine" had palace-façade carving on its interior walls. This pyramid was the subject of Saite interest in the twenty-sixth dynasty, when a new wooden coffin was placed in the burial chamber. In 1838, the original granite sarcophagus was lost at sea while being transported to England, although the wooden coffin lid is now in the British Museum.

The pyramid complexes are surrounded by groups of mastaba-tombs in which members of the royal family and high officials were buried. The most extensive mastaba cemeteries are arranged in regular "streets" to the west, south, and east of the pyramid of Khufu, all tombs being similar in size. The earliest nonroyal tombs at Giza are cut into the quarry faces surrounding the pyramids of Khafra and Menkaura.

Early Exploration of the Giza Pyramids

Not surprisingly, many Classical writers provided descriptions of the Giza pyramids, and there is no shortage of fanciful tales purporting to explain how and why they were built. It was the Jewish historian Josephus, in the late first century A.D., who first suggested that the enslaved Hebrews had been employed for the pyramids' construction, although it is now evident that the Old Kingdom pyramids were built more than a thousand years before the first historical references to the Hebrews. The conviction that the pyramids were built not as tombs but as vast granaries was first set out by the fifth-century Roman writer Julius Honorius; this idea was still current in the Middle Ages, as illustrated in a twelfth-century mosaic inside St. Mark's Cathedral at Venice that shows workers extracting sheaves of corn from one of a group of steep-sided pyramids.

According to the Roman geographer Strabo (c. 25 B.C.), there was a movable block of stone covering the entrance to the "descending passage," located halfway across one of the faces of the Great Pyramid. The British archaeologist Flinders Petrie was sufficiently intrigued by this account to posit the existence of some kind of pivoting entrance stone, on the basis of possible pivot holes that he had discovered in the blocks flanking the entrance to the slightly earlier Bent Pyramid of Sneferu at Dahshur.

It is difficult to know precisely when the majority of the fine outer casing stone was removed from the Giza pyramids, but a description written in the twelfth century A.D. by the Arab scholar Abd el-Latif implies that the pyramids were covered in writing (presumably graffiti) and, therefore, probably still retained much of their casing. The same writer, however, also noted that several of the pyramids (including that of Menkaura) had begun to be dismantled during the reign of Saladin (1183–1193 A.D.), indicating that by then the process of "quarrying," whereby blocks were detached from the pyramids and reused in the buildings of Cairo, was already well under way.

European travelers to Egypt from the fifteenth century on brought back accounts of the pyramids and the Sphinx, often illustrating them with wildly inaccurate depictions. It was not until the arrival of the Napoleonic expedition at the end of the eighteenth century that the archaeological remains at Giza began to be scientifically documented. The scholars accompanying Napoleon's armies included skilled architects and artists who depicted the monuments of Giza in faithful detail. Some travelers in the seventeenth and eighteenth centuries had entered the pyramids, but Napoleon's architects and engineers, including Jean Lepère and Edmé Jomard, not only meticulously measured the exteriors of the pyramids but also made precise studies of the passages inside Khufu's tomb. Ironically, Lepère also contributed to the ongoing disintegration of the monuments by removing some of the blocks from one of Menkaura's queens' pyramids in a fruitless search for a possible intact burial.

Napoleon's scholars were followed by a number of other pioneering Egyptologists, including the Italians Giovanni Caviglia and Giovanni Belzoni; the former was the first archaeologist to undertake full-scale excavations at Giza. In the late 1830s, two Englishmen, the army officer Howard Vyse and the engineer John Perring, undertook valuable documentation of the pyramids, but Vyse's frequent use of dynamite and boring rods did little to ensure the long-term conservation of the monuments.

Reisner and the Tomb of Hetepheres

It was not until 1925 that one of the most spectacular modern discoveries at Giza took place. The renowned American Egyptologist George Reisner was excavating in the vicinity of the row of queens' pyramids beside the Great Pyramid. Reisner himself was temporarily absent from the site, on a trip back to the United States, when his photographer found that a leg of his tripod was sinking into the ground north of the queen's pyramid known as GI-a. This incident led to the discovery of a tomb-shaft crammed with fragments of stone masonry. The empty shaft and burial chamber of pyramid GI-a itself had been known for many years, but the pit found under the photographer's tripod was a new shaft, raising the possibility that someone else had been buried close to Khufu's pyramid.

After spending weeks clearing the stone out of the 89-foot (27-meter) shaft, Reisner reached a small rectangular chamber. There he found an empty travertine sarcophagus and, in a niche in the western wall, a travertine canopic chest containing the remains of a set of internal organs—the earliest surviving instance of this funerary practice. There were also the remains of broken pottery vessels, boxes of linen, and pieces of wooden and metal funerary furniture scattered around the burial chamber. Reisner was undoubtedly the most painstaking excavator working in Egypt at this date, and so the air of disarray, together with the fact that the items seemed to be situated almost in reverse order compared with other tombs that he had excavated, suggested to him that this material was not originally intended to be placed in the chamber where he found it, and that the objects had for some reason been hastily reburied.

Much of the equipment could be reconstructed. The inclusion of such items as silver bracelets, a kind of sedan chair, and a magnificent canopy (which would have fitted exactly into one of the three queens' pyramids' burial chambers) suggested that the occupant of this tomb was a member of the fourth-dynasty royal family. This impression was swiftly confirmed by the survival of a number of royal names and titles on some of the items of funerary regalia, as well as on seal impressions (pieces of clay impressed with official seals when various items were ceremonially closed up). The name of Hetepheres, described both as "mother of the king" and "daughter of the god," occurred several times, suggesting that she was the wife of Sneferu and the mother of Khufu (or perhaps the mother of one of his three older step-brothers, who died before him). But why had the sarcophagus and equipment been reburied, and why was the queen's body missing?

Reisner speculated that Hetepheres might originally have been buried near one of the two pyramids of her husband Sneferu at Dahshur, several miles south of Giza, but that the tomb might have been plundered and her body violated, perhaps without the reigning king's knowledge, and that the remaining parts of her burial might then have been reinterred at Giza. Since no tomb of Hetepheres has ever been found at Dahshur, the American archaeologist Mark Lehner has made the alternative suggestion that the shaft-tomb discovered by Reisner was actually the queen's original burial, but that her body had been reburied in a new sarcophagus and with fresh equipment in the burial chamber under the newly constructed pyramid GI-a, from which it might later have been stolen. Lehner's theory may also explain the damage inflicted on the sarcophagus, pottery, and furniture of the original tomb. It is still not known, however, why the canopic chest (containing the queen's intestines) was not removed along with the body, although it is possible that the shaft-tomb was felt to be so close to the queen's pyramid that the canopic equipment did not need to be transferred. Ironically, it was probably the lack of a superstructure that helped to preserve the contents of the shaft-tomb found by Reisner, whereas pyramid GI-a was presumably robbed in ancient times.

Khufu's Solar Boat

The Great Pyramid is surrounded by several huge, roughly boat-shaped pits, each of which was intended to contain a ceremonial wooden boat: two to the east of the main pyramid, one by the causeway, and two others among the subsidiary pyramids. The two pits to the south of the main pyramid, unlike the others, are not at all boat-shaped but simply rectangular. However, in 1954 two rectangular pits were discovered immediately to the south of the pyramid. When the easternmost of these was excavated by the Egyptian archaeologist Kamal el-Malla, it turned out to contain one of Egypt's most astonishingly preserved finds: 1,244 pieces of cedar wood making up a dismantled boat 142 feet (43.3 meters) in length. It took fourteen years for an Egyptian conservator, Hag Ahmed Yusuf, to complete the careful and extremely impressive restoration of this massive boat, which is currently displayed in its own museum directly beside the site of the discovery.

The second of the southern boat pits was not investigated until 1985, when an American expedition inserted a tiny camera through a hole drilled into the limestone roofing blocks. It was hoped (perhaps somewhat optimistically) that the tight casing might have sealed in a capsule of original fourth-dynasty air, but it became apparent from extensive insect damage to the wooden boat that the contents of this pit were actually more poorly preserved than their neighbor; they have therefore been left undisturbed.

Although no such boats have yet been found in any of the other Old Kingdom pyramid complexes, most had several boat-shaped pits in the vicinity, suggesting that there was a strong tradition that the dead king should be provided with boats. David O'Connor's discovery of rows of model boats alongside the Early Dynastic funerary palaces at Abydos (see chapter 2) indicates that this tradition has a very long history, stretching back many hundreds of years before the time of Khufu. Some scholars have argued that the boats formed part of the royal funerary ceremonies, and that perhaps one of them bore the king's body to the valley temple. However, it is equally likely that they performed a more symbolic role as part of the funerary equipment provided for the travels of the deceased king with the sun god. Just as the images of gods were carried between temples or shrines in ceremonial barks (boats), so the sun god and the deceased pharaoh were believed to sail through the netherworld in a "solar bark." There were two different types of solar bark, that of the day (Mandet) and that of the night (Mesektet); this may explain the fact that Khufu was provided with a pair of dismantled boats, when one might have been thought sufficient.

What Can Khafra's Pyramid Complex Tell Us about Royal Funerary Practices in the Old Kingdom?

Just as the fully developed Old Kingdom mastaba-tomb had three basic elements—the burial chamber, the superstructure, and the offering chapel—so the pyramid complexes consisted of several main components. From the Step Pyramid onward, the pyramids were not isolated structures but parts of large funerary complexes dedicated to celebrating the cult of the dead king. A typical Old Kingdom complex consisted of five elements (1) a pyramid containing the tomb shaft and burial chamber; (2) a mortuary temple attached to the pyramid's eastern face; (3) a smaller pyramid to the southeast, which was probably intended for the king's mummified entrails; (4) a so-called valley temple, closer to the Nile and sometimes connected with it by a canal; and (5) a causeway that led from the mortuary temple down to the valley temple. During the king's funeral, several important rites were carried out—perhaps in the valley temple—including the ritual purification of the body and its embalming. Most royal pyramid complexes were also closely surrounded by the tombs of contemporary courtiers and nobles. The pyramid complex of Khafra comprises several good examples of the buildings within which the royal funerary cult was celebrated.

The basic components of the Old Kingdom mortuary temple were the entrance hall, a columned court, five niches for royal statues, various storerooms, and a sanctuary. Khafra's mortuary temple—excavated by the German archaeologist Uvo Hölscher in 1909–1910—has all these components, as well as being surrounded by five boat-pits. The entrance hall is preceded by a transverse corridor with various chambers leading from it, each interpreted by Herbert Ricke (another German archaeologist who undertook many excavations in the Memphite necropolis) as possible shrines for the king's viscera. On either side of the entrance hall are two long chambers, interpreted by Hölscher as serdabs (special rooms for the king's statuary) and by Ricke as containers for models of the southern and northern barks of the sun god. Beyond the entrance hall is a courtyard paved in travertine and surrounded by a colonnade, as in Khufu's mortuary temple.

The presence of a drain in the middle of Khafra's court suggests that there may originally have been an altar there, from which the drain would have taken away the sacrificial blood and the liquid spilled in the course of libations. Twelve seated statues of the king were attached to the piers surrounding the court, and above each statue were carved pairs of vultures representing Nekhbet, the mother goddess who was thought to preside over the Upper Egyptian half of the king's domain. The inner walls of the court were decorated with limestone reliefs above a granite dado; one fragment of relief excavated by Hölscher depicts part of a bound Asiatic captive. Opposite each of the five openings on the west side of court was a deep niche that probably contained a statue of the king, perhaps corresponding to the king's five names or to his association with five different cult symbols. This open court seems to have marked the limit beyond which only priests could pass to the sanctuary, which consisted of a false door and a low altar on which the priests placed daily offerings.

Khafra's causeway was walled but, unlike Khufu's, there is no evidence that it was roofed. If Herodotus is correct in stating that the walls of Khufu's causeway were decorated (and by no means all of Herodotus's history of Egypt is as apocryphal as his tale of Khufu's daughter), then it would almost certainly have needed some kind of roof to protect the painted scenes. It is also possible that roofs might have been introduced to keep the king's coffin hidden and to preserve its purity while in transit. The earlier causeways at Meidum and Dahshur apparently were neither roofed nor decorated.

The valley temple of Khafra, excavated by Mariette in 1860, is the best-preserved building in any Old Kingdom pyramid complex. It has an almost square ground-plan comprising thick walls of coarse local limestone, faced inside and outside with ashlar blocks of red granite; each wall has a pronounced batter on the outside. A stone kiosk, perhaps intended to hold a royal statue, stood outside the east wall. The long transverse antechamber could be entered via two vestibules, each with a doorway to the east, around which were carved the king's names and titles. After the antechamber there was a T-shaped hall, against the sides of which twenty-three diorite gneiss, siltstone, and travertine statues once stood. In a deep pit in the long antechamber of the valley temple, Mariette found a set of diorite gneiss and siltstone sculptures of the king. Among them is probably the most famous Egyptian statue, the gneiss figure of Khafra with the hawk Horus behind his head. This group of statues is now split between the Egyptian Museum in Cairo and the Nubia Museum in Aswan.

What was the purpose of the valley temple? Some of the inscriptions and reliefs associated with Old Kingdom pyramids and mastaba-tombs suggest that the valley temple was essentially concerned with purification and embalming. According to Reisner, it was a stone version of an earlier pavilion-style edifice made from poles and matting. The Georgian archaeologist Bernard Grdseloff, however, identified the valley temple with the Egyptian architectural term *seh-netjer* ("pavilion of the god") and suggested that it might have been a combination of two buildings commonly associated with Old Kingdom mastaba-tombs: the *ibu* ("purification tent") and the *wabet* ("house of embalming"). He thought that the *ibu* was a tent on the roof (perhaps indicated by the round holes still visible in the upper side of the roof of Khafra's temple), and that the antechamber was to be identified with the *wabet*, thus making it the place where the king's body was embalmed. Conversely, the French Egyptologist Étienne Drioton thought that the antechamber was the *ibu* and that the embalming took place on the roof. Herbert Ricke argued that the processes of purification and embalming probably took place in mud-brick buildings elsewhere, and that the valley temple was simply used as a context for the ritual reenactment of these actions. Ricke suggested that the symbolic rites of purification took place on the terrace in front of the temple, and that the symbolic embalming occurred in the transverse part of the T-shaped hall.

It was also suggested that the valley temple was concerned with the ritual of the Opening of the Mouth. According to Ricke and Schott, this ritual, which was regarded as an essential means of instilling life into mummies or statuary, could have been performed on each of the twenty-three statues that originally stood in Khafra's valley temple. The statues would have been dressed in royal regalia; the mouth of each would have been touched with both an adze and a chisel, and then milk would have been rubbed onto the lips. Ricke and Schott further suggested that each of the statues might have represented one of the deities who protected each of the twenty-six different parts of the king's body (they pointed out that only twenty-three statues would have been needed because three of the deities were associated with not one but two parts of the body). The king's coffin could have been placed in the hall while the ritual was taking place, and the king's viscera kept in four of the rooms to the south. A small chamber at the end of the corridor leading up from the valley temple to the causeway was interpreted by Hölscher as a kind of sentry-box for a porter, while Grdseloff suggested, perhaps more plausibly, that it was a place where food offerings were stored for use in the various valley temple ceremonies.

How Were the Pyramids Built?

Judging from surviving tools, Egyptian architects, surveyors, and builders used two particular implements to lay out the foundations of the pyramid complexes: the *merkhet* and the *bay*, which are mentioned in contemporary texts.

These allowed them to lay out straight lines and right angles and to orient the sides and corners of structures in accordance with astronomical alignments. Iorwerth Edwards argued that true north could have been found by measuring the place where a particular star rose and fell in the west and east, then bisecting the angle between these two points. The observation could have been made with a *bay*, and the two points marked out with a *merkhet* along a circular wall constructed around the site of the monument, with the surveyor standing at the center. More recently, the British Egyptologist Kate Spence has suggested that the architects of the Great Pyramid almost certainly aligned the monument by sighting on two stars rotating around the position of the North Pole (b-Ursae Minoris and z-Ursae Majoris). These two stars would have been in perfect alignment around 2467 B.C., when Khufu's pyramid is thought to have been constructed, and the orientations of earlier and later pyramids can be correlated closely with the degree to which the alignment of the two stars deviates from true north.

Diagrams of the *merkhet* (left) and the *bay* (right), the two basic implements used by Old Kingdom architects for surveying and astronomical alignment of the pyramids (after L. Borchardt).

Both practical and ritual acts of measurement had to be undertaken. We know something about the rituals, both from contemporary textual sources such as the Pyramid Texts (see chapter 3) and from much later depictions of similar processes, such as the "foundation scenes" in the First Hypostyle Hall of the temple of Sety I at Abydos. The latter show the acts of measuring and "stretching the cord" being performed by the king and by the goddess Sefkhet' Abwy. One of these scenes, which could be construed as a depiction of the king lassoing the temple, actually shows him throwing gypsum into a surrounding trench as part of the foundation ceremony.

The builders' first task was to strip off the surface layer of sand and gravel to get down to bedrock. This was followed by a procedure of leveling and smoothing the rock. In the case of the Great Pyramid, the resulting surface was so level that the perimeter of the base differs from a level plane by less than half an inch (1 centimeter), the difference between the heights of the southeastern and northwestern corners. Edwards suggests that this process of leveling could have been achieved by surrounding the whole area with banks of mud, filling it with water, and cutting a network of trenches all of which had their bottoms equidistant from the water level; these trenches could then be joined up to form the new surface.

During the 1980s, Mark Lehner undertook a very detailed survey of the Giza plateau. One of its aims was to examine the areas around the three Giza pyramids—including the mapping of various holes and trenches cut into the bedrock—with a view to reconstructing the methods used to level and orient the pyramid. Lehner pointed out that the ancient builders' process of fine leveling was not spread over the whole area, but simply along narrow perimeter strips around the edges of the pyramids on which the lowest course of casing would be placed; this was no doubt because the Giza pyramids each contain a core massif of bedrock, visible at a number of points in the internal passages, including the so-called service shaft of the Great Pyramid, which runs from the bottom of the Grand Gallery to the Descending Passage. These rock cores also meant that diagonals could not be measured to achieve a perfect square.

The baseline of the pyramid was formed gradually as each casing block was lowered into position and trimmed to conform with the bedding and slope lines. The lines of holes, the trenches, and the troughs carved into the bedrock formed an outside reference scheme for both the orientation and the leveling. Lehner pointed out that the original bedrock level around the Khafra pyramid was about 33 feet (10 meters) higher than the current level of the court surrounding it. Probably the long trenches at the corners of the court helped to provide the first approximation of the square, and the rows of holes closer to the pyramid later provided a much closer definition by the measuring of offsets. He also makes the practical suggestion that wooden stakes placed in the holes would have allowed the water level to be marked permanently (either by marking the stakes or by cutting them off at the right level), so that the builders could remove the bedrock down to the correct level without having to work actually in the water. These same holes might later have served as sockets for scaffolding set up in order to dress the enclosure wall or finish off statues within the court.

According to Dieter Arnold, a German Egyptologist, the archaeological evidence shows that various systems of ramps were used to build different types of pyramids. He therefore argues that all-embracing theories about the type of ramp used to build "the pyramids" are likely to be too generalized and fail to take into account such factors as changing technology and adaptations to local situations. There are at least five different theories about the systems of ramps that may have been used to convey the blocks from ground level to their required position in the pyramid. First, a "linear" ramp, the most

Reconstruction drawings of different types of ramp that may have been used for building pyramids: (A1) the inclined plane, (A2) the linear ramp, (B) the staircase ramp, (C) the spiral ramp, (D) the interior ramp, (E) the reversing ramp on one side of the pyramid.

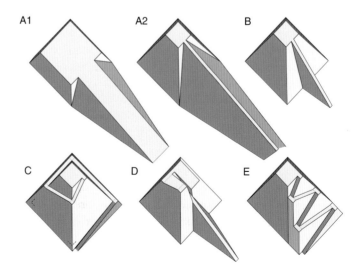

obvious and potentially the easiest method, was probably used for the un-finished third-dynasty step pyramid of Sekhemkhet, but it has been suggested that linear ramps generally needed to be too wide to make them really feasible. Second, traces of a narrower "staircase" ramp, with a much steeper angle of ascent than the linear type, may have survived at the Sinki, Meidum, Giza, Abu Ghurob, and Lisht pyramids. Third, the use of a "spiral" ramp may be described in the nineteenth-dynasty Papyrus Anastasi, but it is unclear what a ramp of this type would have rested on; furthermore, it is likely that it would have covered the whole of the pyramid, thus hindering the calculating of distances between the corners of the pyramids. Fourth, it is possible that some kind of "reversing" or "switchback" ramp was used, creating a zigzag path up one face of the pyramid; this would probably have been most useful on step pyramids, but it is noticeable that there are no indications of its use at Saqqara, Sinki, and Meidum. Fifth, an "interior" ramp would probably have worked quite well, and there are examples at the pyramids of Sahura, Nyuserra, Neferirkara, and Pepy II; eventually, however, an exterior ramp would still have been needed after the interior was filled in.

Debate has also focused on the means by which blocks were transported from the quarries to barges, from the barges to the ramps, and then up the ramps onto the pyramid. One possibility is that large wooden cradles or "rockers" were used to roll or rock the blocks along. Although no full-scale examples of such cradles have survived, there are a number of small models of wooden semicircular devices that might have been used for this purpose. Probably wooden and copper levers were used to maneuver the blocks into position.

In the study of the mathematical basis of pyramid construction, it is best to restrict the mathematics to what can be proven to have been known in ancient Egypt, such as the calculation of the volume and the *seked* (slope) of the pyramids, especially on the basis of the Rhind and Moscow "mathematical papyri." Thus, for instance, the Bent Pyramid of Sneferu at Meidum can be studied in terms of three fundamental stages of the project, each being a mathematical solution with common parameters rather than simply a series of unrelated attempts to achieve a "true" pyramid. The evolution of the standard pyramidal shape and slope can be boiled down to a series of simple mathematical (rather than engineering) choices.

A mathematical approach has also been used by an American Egyptologist, Stuart Kirkland Wier, to calculate the likely size of the work force employed by Khufu to build the Great Pyramid. Wier calculated the volume of stone in the pyramid (2,595,600 cubic meters) and the energy required to extract the blocks from quarries, transport them to the pyramid, and lift them into position. Assuming that the construction process was spread over the entire known reign of Khufu (23 years, or 8,400 days), Wier arrived at a volume of 315 cubic meters per day to be extracted, transported, and erected, employing a total of 69 to 87 million man-days; this allowed him to calculate that the Great Pyramid could have been built either by a steadily diminishing work force, beginning at around twelve thousand and gradually decreasing to around four thousand when the pyramid had reached a height of about 400 feet (120 meters), and only forty-one workers when the full height of 483 feet (145 meters) was reached. Alternatively, and perhaps more likely, he estimated that a work force of between eight and ten thousand could have been employed throughout the project. This manpower (slightly less than 1 percent of the estimated entire population of Egypt in the mid-third millennium B.C.) is very close to the figure independently assessed by Lehner in his population estimate for the workmen's settlement currently being excavated at Giza (see below).

The Search for the Men Who Built the Pyramids: Who Were They, and Where Did They Live?

When Petrie was excavating the area to the west of the pyramid of Khafra in 1881, he uncovered part of a long row of about one hundred rectangular rooms, which he interpreted as workmen's barracks. However, these buildings contained several fragments of royal statues and yielded very few traces of the kind of domestic refuse that would be expected at a settlement of any size (such as pottery and organic remains), so it seems more likely that these were either storerooms or the workshops of royal craftsmen. The latter interpretation was supported by excavations undertaken by Mark Lehner in 1988–1989, when tiny fragments of gemstones and copper were found. There were also a few sculptors' trial-pieces, including a small limestone statuette depicting a king, which appears to have been produced as a prototype of a particular kind of statue known from Khafra's mortuary temple and the Sphinx temple.

In the early 1970s, a group of archaeologists from Cairo University directed by Abdul Aziz Saleh found a set of remains in the southeastern corner of the enclosure surrounding the pyramid of Menkaura. These comprised part of a courtyard surrounded by rows of structures possibly identifiable as houses. Like the galleries excavated by Petrie and Lehner, the artifacts excavated in these buildings suggest that it was a workshop complex concerned with the processing of travertine and copper, including several hearths where copper tools may have been produced or perhaps simply sharpened. Intriguingly, the Austrian archaeologist Karl Kromer found a large pile of settlement debris just a short distance farther to the southeast, outside Menkaura's enclosure. However, this confused pile of material seems to have been dumped there in ancient times, probably after the demolition of a settlement actually situated somewhere else (perhaps in the spot where the pyramid of Menkaura itself was to be built).

Because neither the galleries beside Khafra's pyramid nor the workshops in Menkaura's complex appear to fit the bill for a workers' settlement,

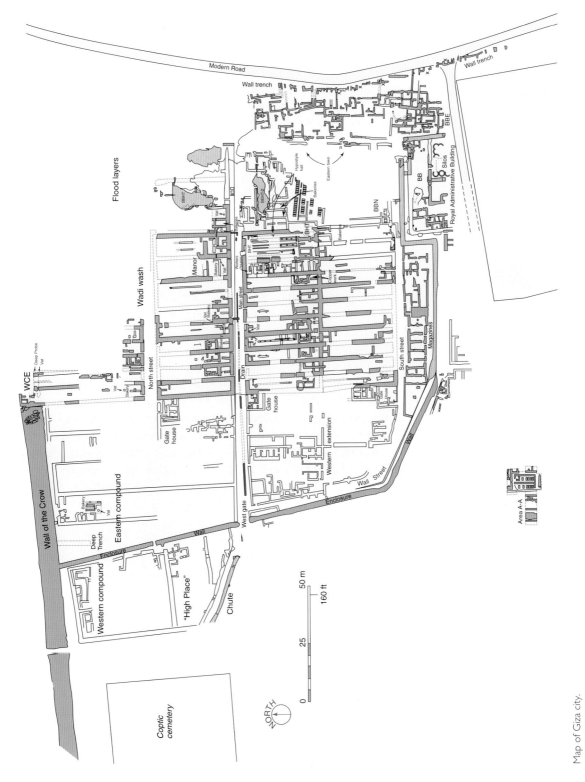

Map of Giza city.

Modern Road

Flood layers

Wadi wash

Wall trench

Wall trench

BBE

Royal Administrative Building

Silos

BB

BBN

Hypostyle hall

Eastern town

Bakeries

Bakery

BBHT

BBHT

BHT

Manor

Bakery

Vat

Workers houses

Bakery

Copper work

Bakery

Vat

Vat

North street

Bakery

Main street

Vat

Vat Bakery

Magazines

South street

Wall

WCE

Deep Probe

Vat

Vat

Bakery

Vat

Gate house

Enclosure

Eastern compound

Bakery

Vat

Deep Trench

Gate house

Western extension

Gate house

Wall Street

Enclosure

Wall of the Crow

Western compound

"High Place"

Chute

Enclosure Wall

West gate

Drain

Coptic cemetery

NORTH

0   25   50 m

160 ft

Area A-A

77

GIZA

attention has turned to the far southeastern corner of the plateau, beyond a large and enigmatic stone construction known as the Heit el-Ghourab ("wall of the crow"). Lehner's excavations here since 1988 have uncovered many substantial mud-brick buildings, some of which were clearly used as bakeries for the large-scale production of loaves cooked in bell-shaped pottery molds. However, just as the Khafra galleries and Menkaura workshops seem to have been more concerned with craft production than with housing the work force, so only a small section of the "settlement" excavated by Lehner is so far recognizable as a conventional set of houses or barracks. Most of the site appears to be a production and storage area concerned with feeding the pyramid-builders.

How Old Is the Sphinx?

Giza is famed not only for its pyramids but also for the largest colossal statue in the world: the Great Sphinx, whose Arabic name is Abu el-Hol, "father of terror." Situated beside the causeway of the pyramid of Khafra (c. 2500 B.C.), the Sphinx is 243 feet (73 meters) long and reaches a maximum of 67 feet (20 meters) in height. The idea for sculpting the monument may well have emerged simply as a convenient way of utilizing a knoll of rock left behind after quarrying local stone for the pyramids. This same stone was also used in the fourth dynasty to begin to build a temple (never completed) immediately in front of the monument. Both the Sphinx and the temple were probably intended for the worship of three divine forms of the sun: Khepri in the morning, Ra at midday, and Atum in the evening. Much later in its history, in the New Kingdom, the Sphinx was identified with the god Horemakhet ("Horus in the horizon"), perhaps because the monument—continually engulfed by sand from the surrounding desert—often looked like the head of a great king emerging from the horizon. Even before the work of archaeologists in the nineteenth and twentieth centuries, there are several ancient reports of the clearing of sand away from the Sphinx, the most famous instance being the "Dream Stele" erected directly in front of the Sphinx by Thutmose IV (c. 1400 B.C.). In the text inscribed on the stele, Thutmose recounts how he dreamed that the Sphinx offered him the kingship if he would free it from its covering of sand.

Because the Sphinx is surrounded both by fourth-dynasty royal pyramid complexes and by the tombs of royal officials of similar date, most scholars have automatically assumed that it was sculpted around the same time, especially given the fact that its nemes headcloth, its uraeus (the royal snake at its brow), and its facial features are generally regarded as typical of this epoch. Khafra seems the most likely fourth-dynasty ruler to have ordered its carving, since the inscription on the Dream Stele includes a possible reference to him; and perhaps more significant, the Sphinx and its temple are immediately adjacent to Khafra's valley temple.

In the fourth-dynasty nonroyal tombs at Giza, there appears to have been an unusual concern with the preservation of the head by use of a type of funerary sculpture consisting of a limestone human head, usually with excised (or unsculpted) ears and enigmatic lines carved around the neck and down the back of the cranium. About thirty examples of these so-called reserve heads are known, all deriving from mastaba-tombs in the Old Kingdom Memphite necropolis (principally at Giza) primarily from the reigns of Khufu and Khafra.

The term "reserve head" (and the German equivalent, Ersatzkopf) arose from the early theory that this sculpture was intended to act as a substitute for the deceased's real head in the afterlife. The fact that the reserve heads were placed in the burial chamber close to the corpse, whereas other statues were usually placed in the chapel or the serdab, was regarded as proof of this unusually close connection with the physical body of the deceased. Although the facial features are in many respects just as idealized as in other forms of statuary, there is a commonly held view that they were somehow intended to be a more precise personal portrait than was typical. The Belgian Egyptologist Roland Tefnin has presented an alternative hypothesis that the heads had a more complex religious function, simultaneously serving as a means by which the spirit could identify its own body and as a symbol of the ritual decapitation and mutilation of the deceased, thus protecting the living from the ill will of the dead.

The Great Sphinx at Giza.

In 1992, however, an American geologist, Robert Schoch, announced that he had found evidence suggesting that the Sphinx and its surrounding enclosure had been eroded by considerable amounts of rainwater. He argued that the history of Egypt's climate showed that such rainfall could have taken place only in the Neolithic period, between 5000 and 7000 B.C., thousands of years earlier than Khafra and the rest of the fourth-dynasty rulers. Predictably enough, a debate ensued between Schoch and Egyptologists defending the traditional fourth-dynasty date. Perhaps the most crucial contribution to the argument, however, came from another American geologist, James Harrell, who made the alternative suggestion that the erosion could have resulted either from a constant covering of saturated sand or from the annual floodwaters of the Nile. Harrell argued that the landscape of the Giza plateau tended to funnel water naturally down toward the monument, so that even the relatively low levels of rainfall in the Old Kingdom might have been enough to keep the sand saturated.

Harrell's geological arguments were backed up by archaeological data provided by Mark Lehner and Zahi Hawass, the two Egyptologists who spent the most time studying the site during the last two decades of the twentieth century. It was pointed out, for instance, that a large stone block intended for the Sphinx temple had been discovered in a stratigraphic position above a layer containing fourth dynasty potsherds.

Lehner's study of the Sphinx has led to a much better understanding of the successive stages in which it was built and restored in ancient times. Many tales have been told about secret chambers under the Sphinx, including the accounts given by two Arab writers, al-Makrizi and al-Kodai, concerning a chamber beneath the Sphinx from which passages extended to each of the three Giza pyramids. Lehner, however, has located only three passages cut into the Sphinx. One of these is a small, well-documented shaft drilled into the top of the neck by Vyse in the mid-nineteenth century; the two others, one in the tail of the Sphinx and the other in its north flank, have yielded neither significant artefacts nor inscriptions.

Further Reading

A fascinating early view of Giza is provided by John Perring's *The Pyramids and Temples of Gizeh* (London, 1839–1842) and Howard Vyse's *Operations Carried On at the Pyramids of Gizeh in 1837* (London, 1840), but the first truly scientific description is given in Flinders Petrie's *The Pyramids and Temples of Gizeh* (London, 1883). Hermann Junker's twelve-volume report *Giza* (Vienna, 1929–1955) is also important, as is George Reisner and William Stevenson Smith's *A History of the Giza Necropolis* (Cambridge, Mass., 1942–1955), the second volume of which is the original report on Hetepheres's tomb. This burial has been reassessed by Mark Lehner in *The Pyramid Tomb of Hetep-heres and the Satellite Pyramid of Khufu* (Mainz, 1985).

The results of Lehner's extensive survey and excavation work have been published mainly in articles in various specialized journals, such as "A Contextual Approach to the Giza Pyramids," *Archiv der Orientforschung* 32 (1985), 136–158, but he has also discussed many of his results and interpretations in *The Complete Pyramids* (London, 1997).

The first attempt to present a comprehensive archaeological description of the Great Sphinx was Selim Hassan's *The Sphinx: Its History in Light of Recent Excavations* (Cairo, 1949). A more up-to-date account, including full discussion of the dating controversies of the 1990s, is Paul Jordan's excellent *Riddles of the Sphinx* (New York, 1998).

Further Viewing

The small statuette of Khufu that is the only known surviving three-dimensional representation of the builder of the Great Pyramid was found not at Giza but at Abydos, and is currently displayed in the Egyptian Museum, Cairo. Statues of Khafra and Menkaura can be seen in the Egyptian Museum, Cairo, and at the Museum of Fine Arts, Boston. Khufu's solar boat is preserved almost in situ in its own museum at Giza. The carefully restored finds from the tomb of Queen Hetepheres can be seen in the Egyptian Museum, Cairo; they represent some of the best evidence for the nature of elite funerary equipment during the Old Kingdom, providing insights into the likely wealth of a full royal burial of the period. Fragments of the Sphinx's beard are preserved in the British Museum and in the Egyptian Museum, Cairo.

As far as modern interpretations of pyramid architecture are concerned, there are numerous celebrated twentieth-century examples that can be visited: the so-called Rainforest Pyramid at Galveston, Texas, a glass-and-steel edifice 125 feet (38 meters) high covering an indoor tropical rain forest; the Luxor Hotel at Las Vegas, a structure fronted by a double-sized replica of the Great Sphinx with a height of 365 feet (111 meters); and the three-sided glass "pyramids" created by I. M. Pei around the entrance to the Louvre in Paris.

Abusir and Abu Ghurob

c. 2500–2345 B.C.

Papyri, priests, and sun temples

The sites of Saqqara and Giza described in earlier chapters have provided a great deal of evidence about the origins of pyramid-style tombs and the techniques used to build them, but the archaeological remains at the Abusir necropolis, situated midway between Giza and Saqqara, are undoubtedly our best source of information concerning the day-to-day functioning of Old Kingdom pyramid complexes. At least four fifth-dynasty pharaohs (Sahura, Neferirkara, Neferefra, and Nyuserra) chose Abusir as the location for their funerary monuments. The ancient names given to their pyramids were "The *ba* of Sahura rises," "Neferirkara has become a *ba*," "The *ba*s of Neferefra are divine," and "The places of Nyuserra are enduring." In addition to these four pyramids, there was an unfinished complex at the northeastern end of the site that may have belonged to Nyuserra's ephemeral successor, Shepseskara.

In 1838, the pyramids of Sahura, Neferirkara, and Nyuserra were first surveyed and partially cleared by John Perring, who reached the burial chamber of Sahura, finding only part of a basalt sarcophagus. Five years later, the pioneering German Egyptologist Richard Lepsius undertook further survey work at Abusir. His compatriot Ludwig Borchardt fully excavated the three funerary complexes between 1902 and 1908. Some indication of Borchardt's archaeological background can be gleaned from the following description of the German excavations at the site of Olympia in Greece: "Nothing was superficially

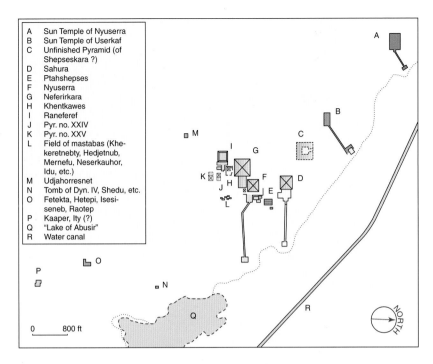

A Sun Temple of Nyuserra
B Sun Temple of Userkaf
C Unfinished Pyramid (of
   Shepseskara ?)
D Sahura
E Ptahshepses
F Nyuserra
G Neferirkara
H Khentkawes
I Raneferef
J Pyr. no. XXIV
K Pyr. no. XXV
L Field of mastabas (Khe-
   keretnebty, Hedjetnub,
   Mernefu, Neserkauhor,
   Idu, etc.)
M Udjahorresnet
N Tomb of Dyn. IV, Shedu, etc.
O Fetekta, Hetepi, Isesi-
   seneb, Raotep
P Kaaper, Ity (?)
Q "Lake of Abusir"
R Water canal

0   800 ft

NORTH

worked, but each spot and each building received careful attention. Each detail was carefully noted, and all the finds were systematically arranged, so as to afford a general view for eventual reconstruction; preservation and arrangement involved reconstruction, quite a new and salutary proceeding" (A. Michaelis, *A Century of Archaeological Discoveries,* London, 1908). This meticulous approach and architectural bias shine through in Borchardt's detailed plans of the three pyramid complexes that he excavated at Abusir.

The Fifth-Dynasty Pyramid Complexes

The funerary monument of Sahura (2458–2446 B.C.), the most complete of the four king's burials at Abusir, is the quintessential fifth-dynasty pyramid complex, consisting of valley temple, causeway, mortuary temple, and pyramid. The imposing portico of the mortuary temple gave access to a large courtyard with a well-preserved basalt-paved floor and a colonnade consisting of sixteen red granite palm columns that are now largely destroyed. Beyond the colonnade were a series of storerooms surrounding the "statue chamber," where the king's statues stood in niches, and immediately adjacent to the pyramid was the sanctuary with its travertine altar. In the southeastern corner of the complex stands a small subsidiary pyramid.

When Borchardt excavated Sahura's complex, he discovered that many of the rooms had been decorated with extensive painted reliefs, although he later estimated that only a trifling 150 square meters had survived out of a

The pyramid complex of Sahura at Abusir (called "Sahura's *ba* shines"), with the mortuary temple in the foreground, excavated by Ludwig Borchardt between 1902 and 1908. The main courtyard of the temple was paved with basalt slabs and surrounded by sixteen granite columns.

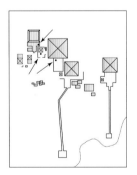

Map of the pyramids of Neferirkara, Neferefra, and Khentkawes at Abusir showing the findspots of the caches of papyri.

likely original total of about 10,000 square meters. The remaining reliefs included a scene of the king smiting his enemies, the earliest surviving instance of this classic image portrayed in a temple. There were also scenes of the king hunting wild game and surveying the arrival of Asiatic traders by boat. The corridor surrounding the palm-columned court was decorated with unusual depictions of the cat goddess Bastet; in the New Kingdom this corridor seems to have been reroofed and used as a sanctuary for a local form of the lion goddess Sekhmet. Borchardt transferred the remains of the original limestone walls, with their fine painted decoration, to the Egyptian Museum in Cairo and to the Berlin Museum.

The complexes of Neferirkara (2446–2426 B.C.) and Nyuserra (2416–2392 B.C.) are both unfinished and poorly preserved. Neferirkara's tomb, undoubtedly intended to be larger than that of Sahura, is now best known for the cache of papyri discovered in its mortuary temple, which provide valuable evidence on the organization of royal funerary cults in the Old Kingdom (see below). The pyramid seems to have been intended initially as a six-tier step pyramid, but there are enough traces of subsequent masonry to suggest that the builders began to fill in the steps in order to convert it into a true pyramid, and probably later attempted to encase it in granite. The bad quality of the rubble core used in all the Abusir pyramids has left them in poor condition, especially since virtually all of the fine blocks of outer casing have been plundered. Neferirkara's causeway was evidently usurped by Nyuserra, who diverted it to his own mortuary temple. It has been suggested that the pyramid complex of Nyuserra incorporated the earliest known example of a "pylon," a form of massive ceremonial gateway that eventually became one of the most characteristic features of Egyptian temples.

To the northwest of the pyramid of Sahura are the remains of another unfinished pyramid complex, which probably belonged to Shepseskara (2426–2419 B.C.), the successor of Nyuserra. At the opposite end of the site are two badly preserved monuments that probably were once small pyramids, perhaps built for female relatives of Nyuserra. The finest of the many mastaba-tombs surrounding the pyramids at Abusir is that of the fifth-dynasty vizier Ptahshepses, a close relative of Nyuserra, which incorporates two boat-shaped rooms presumably meant to hold full-sized boats, an unusual feature for a nonroyal tomb.

Since the 1970s, the work of a team of Czech archaeologists under the direction of Miroslav Verner has revealed the mud-brick mortuary temple of Neferefra (2419–2416 B.C.), whose unfinished pyramid was evidently transformed into a mastaba-tomb. Their excavation of the mortuary temple resulted in the discovery of a collection of cult objects, as well as the most important surviving group of fifth-dynasty royal sculpture, including a painted limestone statue of Neferefra with a Horus falcon embracing the back of his head, and several wooden statuettes of foreign captives that are thought to derive from the base of a large statue of the king worshipped in Neferefra's mortuary temple. In 1988–1989, Verner's team excavated the shaft-tomb of the important Persian Period "chief physician," Udjahorresnet, who served as chancellor to Cambyses I and Darius I (525–486 B.C.).

Was Queen Khentkawes a King?

In the 1978–1979 excavation season, the Czech archaeologists uncovered a small pyramid complex belonging to Khentkawes, a female member of the fifth-dynasty royal family. It was initially argued that this 57-foot-high (17-meter) pyramid was probably a cenotaph, because the mastaba-tomb of a woman called Khentkawes, assumed to be the same person, had previously been found between the causeways of Khufu and Khafra at Giza. However, many scholars now think that these were two different individuals: the Giza woman (denominated Khentkawes I) a late fourth-dynasty queen, and the Abusir woman (Khentkawes II) the mother of the two fifth-dynasty kings Nyuserra and Neferefra and the wife of Neferirkara.

Khentkawes I and II (assuming that they are two separate people) have several things in common besides their names: they both hold the same unusual title, "King of Upper and Lower Egypt, and the mother of the King of Upper and Lower Egypt"; and they are both depicted with the royal uraeus at their brows. These titles and uraei imply that both were not only royal mothers and daughters but were also rulers in their own right. This would add one or both of these women to the very small group of females, including twelfth-dynasty Sobekneferu and eighteenth-dynasty Hatshepsut, who are known to have held the Egyptian kingship.

The fact that the axis of Khentkawes II's mortuary temple is oriented east-west—which appears to be characteristic of royal funerary complexes, as opposed to the tomb-chapels of their officials—is a third indication that she may have risen to the throne at some point during the fifth dynasty. Certainly we know from the dates of papyri found in one of the rooms of her mortuary temple that the cult of Khentkawes II was celebrated in this pyramid complex for at least three centuries after her death.

The Discovery and Significance of the Abusir Papyri

In 1893, local villagers picking over the unexcavated remains of Neferirkara's pyramid complex found a large number of fragments of papyri, which they sold to antiquities dealers. These documents ended up in four collections: the Egyptian Museum in Cairo (via the Giza Museum), the Petrie Museum of University College, London (via Flinders Petrie), the British Museum (via Edouard Naville), and the Louvre (via Urbain Bouriant). In 1903, a further set of papyri (now in the Berlin Museum) was excavated by Borchardt from the same location, and one of the new finds was found to match up with an earlier one, confirming their provenance.

For over sixty years, few attempts were made to tackle the archive as a whole, partly because of the great difficulties of piecing together many tiny fragments and partly because their "old hieratic" script is unusually difficult to decipher. Eventually, however, translations of most of the papyri were published by the French Egyptologist Paule Posener-Kriéger between 1956 and 1976.

A large quantity of flint blades were found in one of the chambers of the mortuary temple of Neferefra, which was almost certainly known as the "sanctuary of the knife," judging from the frequent repetition of this phrase on inscribed potsherds from the temple. The line drawings (above) are the hieratic signs for "knife" (nemet).

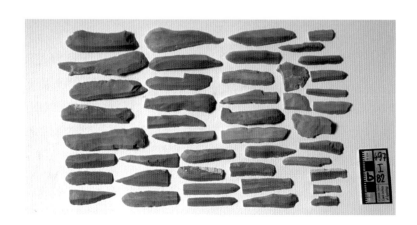

The documents from Neferirkara's temple turned out to date mainly from the reign of Djedkara-Isesi to that of Pepy II, a period of more than two centuries (2414–2184 B.C.). They are concerned mainly with the daily life of the temple and its economy, including lists of people engaged in certain tasks necessary for the running of the temple, registers of income and expenses, records of inspections of temple equipment, lists of officials, and even copies of letters sent between the priests. Our best sense of the economic functioning of the temple is provided by the papyri bearing accounts of products and materials supplied to it. There are also a few documents related to the architecture of the pyramid complexes, describing such things as building repairs and regular maintenance.

The Czech finds at Abusir in the 1970s included two more papyrus archives: one in the mortuary temple attached to the small pyramid of Queen Khentkawes II, and the other in one of the mud-brick store-rooms in the mortuary temple of Neferefra's unfinished pyramid. The contents of the Neferefra archive are similar to those of Neferirkara, but they include more royal decrees and have proved very helpful in archaeological terms. They often refer, for example, to the "sanctuary of the knife," a place within the mortuary temple of Neferefra where animals were ritually slaughtered; just such a complex, incorporating the remains of many flint knives, was found by the Czech excavators within the temple itself.

It is unlikely that other papyrus archives of this type have survived, because they seem usually to have been located among the dwellings of priests centering on the valley temples, most of which now lie beneath the groundwater level, where the papyri would have been soaked and destroyed. It is pure luck that Neferirkara's causeway was usurped by Nyuserra, thus severing Neferirkara's mortuary temple from his valley temple, and causing his priests, along with their papyri, to focus their day-to-day activities on the mortuary temple instead. In the case of Neferefra's archive, the fact that the pyramid was never completed must have meant that no causeway or valley temple was even begun, leaving the unusual L-shaped mortuary temple as the only place for the priests to celebrate and document the king's funerary cult. Similarly, Khentkawes II's complex was probably never intended to consist of anything more than the main pyramid, mortuary temple, and a small satellite pyramid, once again restricting priestly activity to the drier part of the necropolis. Even in these two cases, however, it is obvious that only small fractions of the total archives of papyri have survived.

The Sun Temples of Abu Ghurob: The Cult of the Sun in the Old Kingdom

It became common in the fifth dynasty for the rulers to expend resources not only on the construction of their own funerary complexes but also on the building of huge temples to the Heliopolitan sun god, Ra. Abu Ghurob, originally known to travelers as the "Pyramid of Righa," is dominated by the remains of a sun temple erected by Nyuserra. This temple is the better preserved of the only two surviving examples (the other is that of Userkaf, midway between Abusir and Abu Ghurob), although at least six temples of this type are mentioned in contemporary texts, including the Abusir papyri. The temple of Nyuserra was excavated between 1898 and 1901 by the German scholars Borchardt, Heinrich Schäfer, and Friedrich von Bissing. They sent many of the reliefs to museums in Germany, where several were unfortunately destroyed by bombing during World War II.

The central feature of the temple was a large, squat monument with proportions midway between a *benben*-stone and a true obelisk. Both the "obelisk" and the tapering platform on which it stood were masonry constructions rather than monolithic. In front of the monument (of which only the core of the plinth remains) is a large open court, and in the center of this open area is a massive travertine altar comprising a disk surrounded by four carved examples of the hieroglyphic sign *hetep* ("offering"), giving the whole an unusual cruciform shape. The altar is flanked on the north by a slaughter area and by temple store-rooms. To the south of the temple was a brick-built imitation of the bark of the sun god.

The entrance to the temple is linked with a "valley building" by a covered causeway like those connecting pyramids with their valley temples. On reaching the temple proper, the causeway becomes a corridor running down

The travertine altar in the main courtyard of the sun-temple of Nyuserra at Abu Ghurob takes the form of a huge disk surrounded by four *hetep* signs (the hieroglyph for "offering").

the east side of the courtyard and along the south side. This corridor, which contained reliefs of the sed-festival (royal jubilee), led to the "Room of the Seasons" (containing painted reliefs depicting the three seasons of the Egyptian year) and ended in a chapel decorated with scenes of the dedication of the temple. Although these are evidently important scenes, they were carved on poor stone enhanced with a coating of lime plaster; such economies perhaps illustrate the strain placed on the finances of the Egyptian elite in the late Old Kingdom by the need to build both pyramids and sun temples.

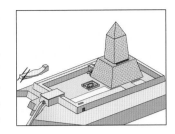

Reconstruction drawing of the sun-temple of Nyuserra at Abu Ghurob, which focussed on a vast masonry obelisk, only the base of which now survives.

What Do We Know about Old Kingdom Priests?

In chapter 4 (Giza), we discussed the architecture and possible functions of different parts of the mortuary and valley temples. The Abusir papyri and other texts also provide evidence concerning the activities and rituals that took place in these buildings during the hundreds of years that the kings' cults generally survived. Some of the texts inscribed on the walls of the sun temple of Nyuserra list the vast amounts of produce flowing into the temple from the agricultural estates with which it had been endowed, including an annual donation of more than 100,000 rations of bread, beer, and cakes, 1,002 oxen and 1,000 geese. The Abusir papyri indicate that such quantities were also typical of the materials flowing into pyramid complexes during the time that their cults flourished. Such large-scale movements of produce suggest that Old Kingdom temples were important elements of the national economy, requiring vast numbers of staff to supervise the practicalities of gathering, transporting, and preparing the food and to oversee the rituals surrounding the items' progress through the temple. In addition, the temple staff were heavily involved in the guarding and maintenance of numerous items of equipment owned by the temple. The large daily offerings, presumably not physically consumed by the dead king or the deity in question, were regularly distributed as rations to the temple officials and servants.

Each pyramid complex or temple had at least one town associated with it, where the officials charged with upholding the cult—priests, guards, and servants—were housed. Archaeological traces of such residential areas have survived at a number of sites, including the small mud-brick houses built in front of the valley temple of Menkaura at Giza and nine or ten dwellings inside Neferirkara's mortuary temple at Abusir. Even the pyramid of Queen Khentkawes I at Giza had an associated terrace of small houses for priests.

We know from references to temple officials in the papyri and from the titles of individuals buried in mastaba-tombs around the pyramids of the Memphite necropolis that the religious officials were organized in a strict hierarchy. In the early part of the Old Kingdom, this was a fairly simple arrangement. At the top of the priestly pyramid was the *imy-r* (overseer); below him were groups of *wab* ("purification") priests and *hery-heb* ("lector," or reader) priests; and the third tier consisted of a mass of *hemu-netjer* ("god's servants"), who may have been recruited from among the craftsmen and agricultural workers living near the pyramid or temple. By the time that the royal funerary cults at Abusir and Saqqara were flourishing, in the fifth and sixth dynasties, the hierarchy had become more complex. The pyramid of Neferirkara had one set of permanent staff, comprising *wab* priests, *hery-heb* priests, scribes and craftsmen, and another set of part-time officials, including "inspectors," "assistants," *hemu-netjer*, and a new category of workers known as *khentyu-she* ("those foremost in the royal precinct"). The part-time staff were organized into a number of groups known as "phyles," each supervised by an inspector and his assistant. The phyles operated according to a shift system, allowing large numbers of "priests" to continue to make a normal living outside the confines of the pyramid complex and its town. The total number of part-time and full-time staff employed by Neferirkara's cult was probably between 300 and 350 individuals.

The papyri provide enough information to show us roughly what these officials would have been doing on a typical day at the pyramid. There were ceremonies based around the preparation and consumption of two ritual meals, one in the morning and one in the evening; this ties in with references in the Pyramid Texts to five meals consumed by the dead king each day, three in the heavens and two on earth, the latter being the responsibility of his priests. During the course of the ritual meals, priests performed the Opening of the Mouth ceremony on each of the five principal statues of the king housed in shrines within the mortuary temple. Each shrine had to be ritually opened so that the *khentyu-she* could wash and clothe the statue, while the *hemu-netjer* censed the shrine and statue with incense. Each morning and evening, one of the *hemu-netjer* and one of the *khentyu-she* would walk clockwise around the pyramid, pouring out libations at intervals from a jar containing a mixture of water and natron. After the ceremonies had been performed, the various pieces of equipment, such as basins and balls of incense, had to be replaced carefully in wooden chests. Many of the surviving papyri are concerned with the pedantic details of repair and storage of such ritual items; each phyle evidently had its own set of equipment. As well as the daily rituals, there were occasional festivals lasting several days: one of Neferefra's papyri records a ten-day festival during which 130 bulls were slaughtered.

Further Reading

Ludwig Borchardt published his excavations of fifth-dynasty pyramid complexes at Abusir in three volumes: *Das Grabdenkmal des Königs Ne-user-Re, Das Grabdenkmal des Königs Nefer-ir-ka-Re,* and the two-part work *Das Grabdenkmal des Königs Sahu-Re* (Leipzig, 1907–1913). The Czech excavations since the 1970s are described by Miroslav Verner in *Forgotten Pharaohs, Lost Pyramids: Abusir* (Prague, 1994); Verner deals specifically with the excavation of Queen Khentkawes II's tomb in *The Pyramid Complex of the Royal Mother Khentkaus* (Prague, 1994).

The earlier finds of Abusir papyri have been published in two volumes: Paule Posener-Kriéger and J.-L. de Cenival, *Hieratic Papyri in the British Museum: The Abusir Papyri* (London, 1968); and Posener-Kriéger, *Les archives du temple funéraire de Neferirkare (Les papyrus d'Abousir),* 2 vols. (Cairo, 1976). The more recently discovered papyri are discussed by Verner in *Forgotten Pharaohs, Lost Pyramids: Abusir.*

The excavated remains of the sun temples of Userkaf and Nyuserra are described by Herbert Ricke in *Das Sonnenheiligtum des Königs Userkaf,* 2 vols. (Cairo, 1965; Wiesbaden, 1969), and by Friedrich von Bissing et al. in *Das Re-Heiligtum des Königs Ne-Woser-Re* I (Leipzig, 1905), pp. 8–10, 19–24. The pyramid and sun temple of Nyuserra are also discussed by Dieter Wildung in a catalog accompanying an exhibition: *Ni-User-Ra: Sonnenkönig-Sonnengott* (Munich, 1985).

Further Viewing

Sculpted reliefs and architectural fragments from the pyramids and sun temples at Abusir and Abu Ghurob can be viewed at the Egyptian Museum in Cairo, the Berlin Museum, and the Museum für Völkerkunde in Hamburg. The papyri from the mortuary temple of Neferirkara can be seen at Berlin, the British Museum, the Petrie Museum (University College, London), and the Louvre.

Mediterranean Sea

Red Sea

NORTH

Elephantine •
          • Aswan

0   100   200 km
0   50   100 mi

Nile River

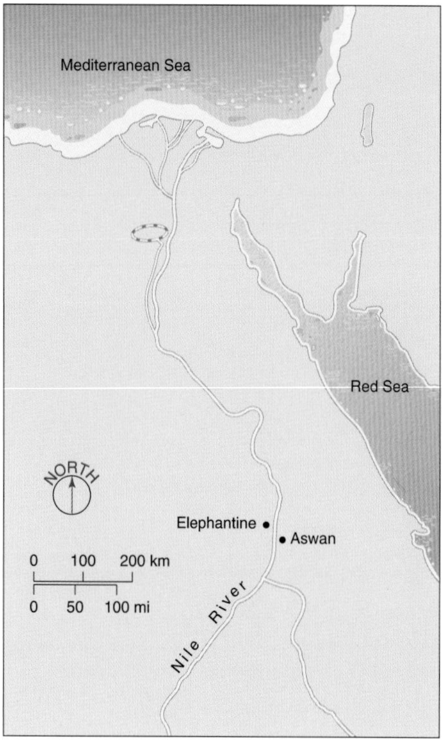

Aswan and Elephantine

c. 2686–1650 B.C.

City of ivory

Aswan, the southernmost city in modern Egypt, is situated immediately north of the First Cataract of the Nile, at the northern tip of Lake Nasser. The ancient remains at Aswan can be divided into three components: the town, temples, and granite quarries of Aswan proper on the eastern bank of the Nile; the rock-cut tombs of Qubbet el-Hawa, on the western bank; and the town, temples, and Nilometer on Elephantine, an island in the center of the river. By the time travelers reach as far south as Aswan, the width of the agricultural land flanking the Nile has dwindled to as little as a mile (1.6 kilometers) on the eastern bank, and the fertile island of Elephantine stands out in stark contrast to the generally arid surroundings. Apart from two small Ptolemaic and Roman temples, there are few surviving remains of Aswan itself because the area has been occupied continuously up to modern times. The tombs of Qubbet el-Hawa, which date mainly to the Old and Middle Kingdoms (c. 2649–1640 B.C.) contain important biographical reliefs and inscriptions.

The ancient names given to Aswan (Sunu, meaning "trading") and Elephantine (the Greek version of Abu, "ivory" or "elephant") evidently emphasized the multiple roles of the First Cataract region as a frontier post in the Early Dynastic period and Old Kingdom; it was an important commercial center and a source of granite and siliceous sandstone. Because this was the point where the Nile entered Egypt proper in the early pharaonic period, the town also became firmly associated with the idea of the divine source of the Nile, which was thought to rise amid two rocks between Elephantine and Aswan.

The two deities most closely linked with the emergence of the Nile at Aswan were the ram god Khnum and his consort, Satet. Khnum eventually became one of the principal creator -gods, but he was originally the divine manifestation of the fountains of the river, mythically located in the whirlpools of the First Cataract. It was the shrine of Satet on Elephantine, however, that seems to have been the site of the earliest known cult of the Nile flood, initially taking the form of a hollow in the rocks beside which a small temple gradually developed (see below). The so-called Famine Stele on the island of Sehel, a short distance south of Elephantine, is a Ptolemaic inscription purporting to be an Old Kingdom account of appeals to Khnum at a time of famine caused by a succession of unusually low annual Nile floods.

The Governors' Tombs: Harkhuf and the Pygmy

The rock-tombs of the provincial governors of the First Upper Egyptian nome and their relatives during the Old Kingdom, First Intermediate Period, and Middle Kingdom lie opposite the northern end of the town on the west bank of the Nile. Dramatically approached via causeways slanting steeply up from the river, this group of tombs is known collectively as the Qubbet el-Hawa ("dome of the wind"), because the cliff into which they are cut is surmounted by a small domed tomb of Islamic date. Interspersed among these tombs are at least three New Kingdom ones, including one at the northernmost tip of the necropolis that belonged to Kakemu, a nineteenth-dynasty chief priest of Khnum.

The design of the tombs follows a standard pattern. The visitor climbs a causeway and then approaches via a narrow courtyard. The tomb entrance is cut through a flat façade, occasionally flanked by small stone obelisks. The interior consists of a wide rectangular room with a false-door stele cut into the rear wall; usually the ceiling is supported by one or more rows of rock-cut columns. Comparatively little of the wall surface is decorated either with images or inscriptions, and most of this decoration is restricted to the entrance, the false door, and the columns.

The best-known of these tombs is that of Harkhuf, a sixth-dynasty "overseer of foreign soldiers" whose official titles include such posts as governor of Upper Egypt, royal seal-bearer, and chief of scouts. The outer façade of his tomb is decorated with a biographical text consisting of fifty-eight lines of hieroglyphs, largely devoted to the description of four expeditions to Nubia, which he led on behalf of the rulers Merenra and Pepy II.

Harkhuf quoted in great detail from an enthusiastic letter sent to him by Pepy II on hearing that he was bringing back a *deneg* (probably a pygmy) acquired on his expedition to Nubia:

> The king's decree to the sole companion, lector-priest, chief of
> scouts, Harkhuf . . . You have said in this dispatch of yours that

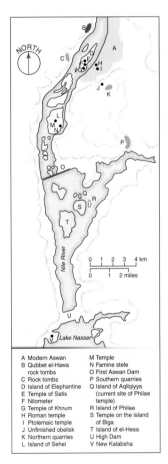

A Modern Aswan
B Qubbet el-Hawa rock tombs
C Rock tombs
D Island of Elephantine
E Temple of Satis
F Nilometer
G Temple of Khnum
H Roman temple
I Ptolemaic temple
J Unfinished obelisk
K Northern quarries
L Island of Sehel
M Temple
N Famine stele
O First Aswan Dam
P Southern quarries
Q Island of Aqilqiyya (current site of Philae temple)
R Island of Philae
S Temple on the island of Biga
T Island of el-Hesa
U High Dam
V New Kalabsha

Map of Aswan and Elephantine.

you have brought all kinds of great and beautiful gifts, which Hathor mistress of Imaau has given to the *ka* of King Neferkara, who lives for ever. You have said in this dispatch of yours that you have brought a pygmy of the god's dances from the land of the horizon-dwellers, like the pygmy whom the god's seal-bearer Bawerded brought from Punt in the time of King Isesi . . . Come north to the residence at once! Hurry and bring with you this pygmy whom you brought from the land of the horizon-dwellers live, hale and healthy, for the dances of the god, to gladden the heart, to delight the heart of King Neferkara who lives forever! When he goes down with you into the boat, get worthy

Detail of the inscription of Harkhuf on the outer façade of his rock-tomb at Qubbet el-Hawa, Aswan. This section comprises part of the letter sent to Harkhuf by King Pepy II, in which he issues instructions for the care of a pygmy brought back from Harkhuf's expedition to Nubia.

men to be around him on deck, lest he fall into the water! When he lies down at night, get worthy men to lie around him in his tent. Inspect ten times at night! My majesty desires to see this pygmy more than the gifts of the mine-land and of Punt!

Another tomb, excavated by the Egyptian archaeologist Labib Habachi, belonged to a man called Setka, who was governor of the region during the so-called Herakleopolitan Period (ninth and tenth dynasties, c. 2160–2025 B.C.). The painted scenes on the walls of his tomb include many original and unusual images, such as a group of Nubian archers in the midst of battle, wearing head-feathers and colored leather kilts typical of those found in burials of the "C Group" people, who populated Lower Nubia from the late Old Kingdom until the New Kingdom (c. 2500–1550 B.C.).

In the 1990s, a set of mastaba-tombs was found at the foot of the cliff. The only one of these that has so far been excavated dates to the sixth dynasty and resembles those found on Elephantine. The date of the others has not yet been determined, and it is not yet known whether they were used for the inhabitants of Elephantine or the people of an unexcavated settlement known from texts to have been situated north of Qubbet el-Hawa.

The Settlement on Elephantine:
A Case Study in Egyptian Urbanization

The earliest archaeological exploration of the island of Elephantine, at the beginning of the twentieth century, was concerned mainly with the search for papyri (see below). In 1969, however, German excavators began a program of excavations intended to chart the development and nature of the town over a period of four thousand years. It is now known that the settle-

Reconstruction of the first-dynasty fortifications at Elephantine, c. 3000 B.C., showing a complex of buildings constructed on the highest part of the island.

One of the few surviving parts of the temple of Khnum on Elephantine is a large monumental gateway.

ment grew from a tiny Predynastic village to a congested Late Period city covering more than 17 acres (7 hectares).

The study of the temple of the antelope goddess Satet, "Lady of the Town," has uncovered a continuous sequence of building stages stretching back to a small late Predynastic (c. 3200 B.C.) mud-brick sanctuary built between three granite boulders. During the first dynasty, a fortified building was constructed near the shore in the eastern part of the settlement, and soon afterward the entire area of housing was surrounded by a mud-brick wall. As the settlement expanded during the Early Dynastic Period and Old Kingdom, the wall was repeatedly enlarged, providing protection for a steadily increasing population. The impression of Elephantine as a fortified frontier outpost is reinforced by the fact that texts in the Old and Middle Kingdoms include the "fortress" sign with the place-name "Abu."

By the sixth dynasty, the mud-brick sanctuary of Satet had been provided with a granite room for the goddess's cult statue, but Old Kingdom rulers dedicated only a few votive offerings to Satet. The eleventh-dynasty pharaoh Intef II was the first king to erect new stone chapels for both Satet and Khnum on Elephantine (commemorating this act with texts inscribed on the door-frames of their temples), and each of Intef's eleventh-dynasty successors followed his example. This sequence of events also seems to have been true for many other temple sites in Egypt. In fact, apart from a few specific exceptions, royal building activity in the provincial temples of Upper Egypt is attested only from the eleventh dynasty on.

At the eastern side of Elephantine is an unusual construction consisting primarily of a set of steps cut into the rock. This is the best surviving example of a "Nilometer" of the pharaonic period. Because Egyptian agriculture

depended crucially on the annual flooding of the Nile, the ancient Egyptians devised various methods for measuring the height of the inundation. These usually consisting of a series of steps against which the increasing height of the inundation, as well as the general level of the river, could be measured. Records of the maximum height of the inundation were kept on such official inscriptions as the Palermo Stone (see the Introduction), but there is no firm evidence that these records were used in any systematic way in the determination of taxation on the amount of agricultural land flooded. The Elephantine Nilometer was rebuilt in Roman times, and the markings still visible at the site date from this later phase. It was most recently repaired in 1870 by the Khedive Ismail.

Elephantine lost some of its importance as a frontier town when the twelfth-dynasty ruler Senusret I conquered Lower Nubia and began the construction of a chain of fortresses stretching along the Nile Valley for about 250 miles (400 kilometers) down to Semna, which represented the new southern border of Egypt. From this period on, Aswan and Elephantine were associated more with commerce and administration than with defense.

The Cult of Hekaib: Egyptian "Deification"

A man called Pepinakht, also known as Hekaib ("ruler of my heart"), was evidently governor of the First Upper Egyptian nome at a time of great crisis in the late Old Kingdom. The "biographical" inscription in his tomb at Qubbet el-Hawa indicates that he held titles connecting him with the maintenance of the pyramid complexes of Merenra and Pepy II at Saqqara. His

Detail of the fifth-dynasty king list known as the Palermo stone.

Statue of the provincial governor Sarenput, from the chapel of Hekaib on Elephantine.

day-to-day activities, however, seem to have been concerned largely with his role as "overseer of foreigners," which meant that he was placed in charge of the mercenary soldiers protecting Egyptian expeditions through Nubia and the Eastern Desert. Most of the military activities that he described simply involved the killing or capture of Nubians and their livestock, but there is one especially intriguing episode: a heroic trip to the Red Sea coast to bring back the bodies of an official called Ankhty and his followers, who had evidently been attacked and murdered while on an expedition to the land of Punt (see chapter 10).

Hekaib was so highly regarded after his death that he became the object of a religious cult on the island of Elephantine by the eleventh dynasty. Only a very few nonroyal Egyptians—for example, Imhotep, the third-dynasty architect of the Step Pyramid at Saqqara, and Amenhotep son of Hapu, Amenhotep III's chief of works—ever developed sufficiently high reputations to justify religious veneration in their own right, the ancient Egyptian equivalent of sainthood. Hekaib's cult center (a so-called ka-chapel) was established at the beginning of the Middle Kingdom to the northwest of the temple of Satet. It was rebuilt in both the late eleventh and early twelfth dynasties, eventually leading the late Middle Kingdom governors to emulate it by setting up their own cult chapels in the vicinity, in addition to their rock-cut tombs at Qubbet el-Hawa. At this date, lesser officials also set up stelae and statues near Hekaib's sanctuary; excavations at the site in the late 1940s revealed twelve shrines, twenty-six stelae, and more than fifty statues of officials. When the local population celebrated the annual festival of the god Sokar, a statue of Hekaib was carried through the streets in procession.

The Jewish Settlement on Elephantine

Between 1890 and 1893, the American Egyptologist Charles Wilbour bought nine sealed papyrus rolls and some fragments of papyri from local women at Elephantine, who showed him that they had found them under the floors of ancient mud-brick houses on the island. Although Wilbour's initial assumption was that these documents were inscribed in some kind of Phoenician script, he eventually deduced that they were written in Aramaic. His main interest was in hieroglyphic and hieratic texts, so he put these papyri into storage, and they came to light only many years later when Wilbour's daughter bequeathed them to the Brooklyn Museum in New York.

The first Aramaic papyri and ostraca documenting the Jewish community that lived on the island during the Late Period were published in 1903 by a British papyrologist, Sir Arthur Ernest Cowley, and a French scholar, Julius Eutling. In subsequent years, more and more papyri from Elephantine appeared on the antiquities market, and the Brooklyn papyri found by Wilbour were eventually published by Emil Kraeling. These documents have proved to be one of the most useful sources of information on life in Egypt during the First Persian Period; indeed, many details concerning the Achaemenid Empire as a whole have emerged from studies of the Elephantine papyri. The three main archives of papyri came from the households of three men called Mibtahiah, Ananiah, and Jedaniah.

There were two fortresses at Aswan in the Persian period, one on Yeb (Elephantine), and the other on the east bank in the city of Syene (Aswan). The Jews assigned to these two fortresses were soldiers and their families, employed by the Persian rulers of Egypt to guard their southern frontier during the fifth century B.C. It is not clear whether the Jews were descendants of refugees or merchants, but they certainly seem to have been living at Aswan for at least two hundred years before the Persian conquest. The *hayla* ("garrison") was manned not just by Jews but also by a variety of other ethnic groups, including Babylonians, Persians, and Caspians. Judging from a set of Aramaic papyri found at Ashmunein in Middle Egypt, there was a similar Jewish colony living somewhere in the vicinity of the ancient city of Hermopolis Magna at around the same time.

One of the Aramaic papyri from Elephantine.

The detailed information provided by the papyri has been supplemented by the results of German and French excavations on Elephantine in the early 1900s. Because the primary aim of both of these projects was to obtain papyri and inscribed ostraca, the digging was not of great quality by modern standards, generally resulting in a rather confused mass of mud-brick walls of many different levels and dates. The Elephantine settlement had risen upwards over the centuries like a typical tell (settlement mound) site, with the houses of one era becoming the foundations and cellars of later residences. The houses of the Aramaic-speaking community were evidently fairly distinctive: many of the rooms were very long, narrow, and thick-walled because of the use of barrel-vaulted brick-built roofs rather than wooden roof-beams. The objects found in these houses included terracotta statuettes and wooden figurines, the latter usually consisting of a woman and child, a motif with a long history in Egypt, where it probably was a means of encouraging fertility and helping in childbirth.

The French excavations, directed by Charles Clermont-Ganneau, focused on the search for the Jewish temple dedicated to Yahu (i.e., Yahweh, the God of the Bible), which is mentioned in several of the papyri. His efforts were somewhat frustrated, however, by the artificial line drawn between the German archaeological concession and his own. His researches convinced him that a pile of huge granite blocks excavated by the Germans (and interpreted by them as the remains of some kind of fortress) might have been the platform on which the temple had been constructed. Since this "platform" was on the German side of the line, his efforts were restricted to a futile attempt to excavate what he hoped to be the northeastern corner of the platform, which protruded just into his own side of the concession line. In a letter written in 1908, Clermont-Ganneau graphically described his problems: "I see the promised land. I almost touch it with my hand. And it is

The unfinished granite obelisk at Aswan probably dates to the Thutmosid period; it seems to have been abandoned when cracks in the rock indicated to the quarriers that it could not be removed intact.

not given to me to enter there. It is truly provoking." Eventually, in 1918, an expedition sent by the Pontifical Biblical Institute at Rome excavated the "platform," but they found only debris and a jar containing the body of a child. The location of the temple of Yahu still remains a mystery.

The Unfinished Obelisk: Hard-Stone Quarrying in the Pharaonic Period

Undoubtedly the most important source of knowledge on Egyptian granite quarrying is the so-called unfinished obelisk, which lies in the northern quarries a few miles southeast of the center of modern Aswan. Work on this obelisk, which is nearly 138 feet (42 meters) in length and probably eighteenth dynasty in date, was abandoned at a very late stage in the process of its extraction when significant flaws must have suddenly become apparent. If it had been completed, it would have weighed almost 1,200 tons (1180 metric tons) and would have been about 33 feet (10 meters) higher than the largest surviving complete obelisk (originally set up by Thutmose IV at Karnak, but now standing in the Piazza San Giovanni in Laterano, Rome). Careful studies of the partly worked monument have given us a better understanding of some of the methods of hard-stone quarrying in the New Kingdom.

The quarriers first removed the weathered surface of the granite, then marked out the shape of the obelisk with a deep trench, 2 feet 6 inches (75 centimeters) wide. This trench was divided into a series of working areas (2 feet/60 centimeters long, marked out by vertical red lines down the side of the trench), which would have allowed at least fifty laborers to work on

100

A "PIOUS FRAUD": THE SEHEL FAMINE STELE

On the island of Sehel, immediately south of Aswan, is a rock-carved inscription known as the "Famine Stele." This purports to be a decree of King Djoser (2630–2611 B.C.) of the third dynasty recording his concern over a seven-year famine supposed to have been ended by the ram god Khnum, who controlled the rising of the waters. In fact, the text dates to Ptolemaic times, and it probably had a less altruistic purpose. It may simply have been designed to reinforce the claims of the priests in the temple of Khnum on Elephantine to tax local produce, although some scholars believe that it is a copy of an authentic document.

That famines took place during the Old Kingdom is not in doubt. The surviving visual evidence includes several fragments of relief from the walls of the fifth-dynasty causeway of the pyramid complex of Unas (2356–2323 B.C.) at Saqqara. These reliefs depict numerous emaciated figures, their ribcages clearly visible, seated on the ground and evidently weak from hunger. It has been argued by some scholars, partly on the basis of these reliefs, that the Old Kingdom (2575–2134 B.C.) ended largely because of prolonged drought and increasing desertification. However, such arguments have been undermined both by the fact that the Old Kingdom continued to flourish for another two centuries after Unas, and by the fact that another set of causeway reliefs found recently at Abusir seems to indicate that the emaciated figures are simply stereotyped images of Bedouin people.

The Ptolemaic Famine Stele on the island of Sehel.

each side of the obelisk. The surviving marks on quarry faces at Aswan show that overseers periodically assessed the depth of the trench—and therefore the work rates of different work gangs—by lowering a cubit rod into it and marking the top of the rod with a triangle. When the workmen had quarried down to the necessary depth, they slowly undercut the block, and it is evident that this process had only just begun in the case of the unfinished obelisk. In order to separate the obelisk finally from the surrounding rock, one end had to be totally quarried out, allowing the obelisk to be pulled out horizontally.

The Aswan granite quarries were worked from the Early Dynastic Period to the Roman Period, but most of the visible remains date to Ptolemaic and

Roman times. As well as the celebrated obelisk at the northern end of the quarrying region, there are also three unfinished colossal statues (probably of New Kingdom date) and seven Roman bathtubs in the southern part.

Further Reading

Jill Kamil's *Aswan and Abu Simbel: History and Guide* (Cairo, 1993) provides a good overview of the area as a whole. Elmar Edel has published a study of the Old Kingdom rock-tombs of Qubbet el-Hawa in his *Die Felsengräber der Qubbet el-Hawa bei Assuan* (Wiesbaden, 1967–). The unpublished battle scenes in the tomb of Setka are briefly summarized by Henry Fischer in "The Nubian Mercenaries of Gebelein" (*Kush* 9, 1961, pp. 44–80), and by Alan Schulman in "The Battle Scenes of the Middle Kingdom" (*Journal of the Society for the Study of Egyptian Antiquities* 12, 1982, pp. 165–183).

The Ptolemaic temple of Isis (on the east bank at Aswan, not far from the famous Old Cataract Hotel), currently being restored and excavated by the Egyptian Supreme Council for Antiquities, is described by Edda Bresciani and Sergio Pernigotti in *Assuan: Il tempio tolemaico di Isi, i blocchi decorati e iscritti* (Pisa, 1978). Regular reports on the German excavations of the town and temples on Elephantine have been published since 1970 in the journal *Mitteilungen des Deutschen Archäologischen Instituts, Abteilung Kairo*. Nilometers are discussed by P. Heilporn in "Les nilomètres d'Elephantine et la date de la crue," *Chronique d'Egypte* 64.127–8 (1989), pp. 283–285.

There are several publications dealing with the Aramaic papyri documenting the Jewish garrison on Elephantine; probably the three best English-language accounts are Emil Kraeling's *The Brooklyn Museum Aramaic Papyri* (New Haven, 1953; with a fairly detailed discussion of the archaeology of their discovery), Bezalel Porten's *Archives from Elephantine* (Berkeley, 1968), and a volume of papers by several scholars, *The Elephantine Papyri in English* (Leiden, 1996), edited by Porten.

Reginald Engelbach's *The Problem of the Obelisks* (New York, 1923) was an early pioneering attempt to understand the whole process of quarrying and erecting Egyptian obelisks, including detailed analysis of the unfinished obelisk. More recently, Dieter Arnold has discussed the likely methods used by Egyptian stone-workers and masons in *Building in Egypt: Pharaonic Stone Masonry* (Oxford, 1991). Marshall Jon Fisher and David E. Fisher's *Mysteries of Lost Empires* (London, 2000) includes accounts of several experimental modern attempts to transport and erect granite obelisks.

Further Viewing

Many objects excavated at Aswan, Elephantine, and other sites farther to the south can be seen in the Nubia Museum at Aswan, which opened in 1999, including some exceptional Old and Middle Kingdom funerary statues. As well as the Elephantine Nilometer, a number of examples have survived else-where, including those associated with the Ptolemaic and Roman temples at Philae, Edfu, Esna, Kom Ombo, and Dendera. At Geziret el-Rhoda in Cairo there is an Islamic Nilometer, dating to 705–715 A.D., which was pos-sibly built on the site of an earlier pharaonic example; it worked on the same principles as its ancient counterparts, except for the use of an octagonal pil-lar (rather than steps) as the measure.

Granite obelisks similar to the unfinished monument at Aswan have been transported and re-erected at a number of capitals outside Egypt: Rome con-tains thirteen examples (including the tallest known), while London, Paris, New York and Istanbul have one each.

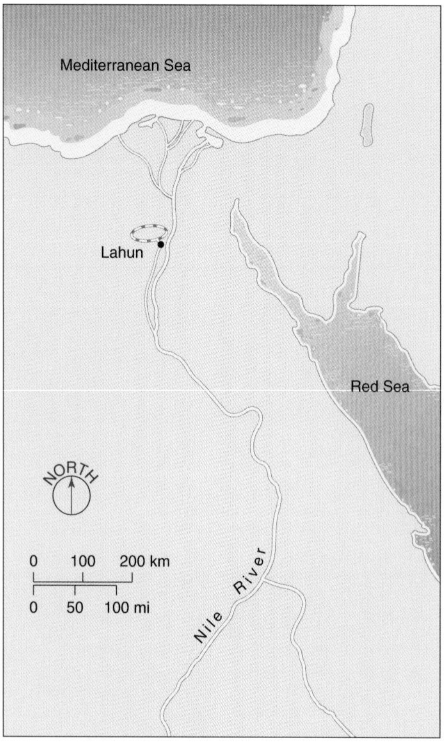

Mediterranean Sea

Lahun

Red Sea

NORTH

0   100   200 km

0   50   100 mi

Nile River

Lahun

c. 1880–1650 B.C.

A Middle Kingdom pyramid and

town in the Faiyum

In the Egyptian Western Desert about 40 miles (64 kilometers) southwest of Cairo lies a fertile depression covering an area of about 8,000 square miles (20,720 square kilometers). Before the Palaeolithic period, this region, now known as the Faiyum, had a huge saltwater lake at its center. The lake eventually became linked to the Nile River by the Bahr Yusef canal and was thus transformed into fresh water Lake Moeris, now known as the Birket el-Qarun, which forms the central point of a vast area of farm land.

In the mid-1920s, two British women, the Egyptologist Gertrude Caton-Thompson and the geologist Elinor Gardner, undertook an intrepid survey of the northern Faiyum region in Lower Egypt, including the pioneering use of aerial photography. They identified a number of prehistoric sites, which they divided into two distinct cultures, Faiyum A and B. Because of the unusual geology of the Faiyum basin, they initially assigned the Faiyum B material (rich in microlithic tools and low in ceramics) to the late Neolithic, but radiocarbon dating eventually demonstrated that they had placed the two phases in the wrong chronological order: the Faiyum B (or Qarunian) culture was actually an earlier "Epipalaeolithic" phase preceding the Faiyum A Neolithic.

In the early twelfth dynasty, the agricultural potential of the Faiyum (then known as Ta-she, "the lake") began to be seriously developed, and in connection with this some of the marshes were probably

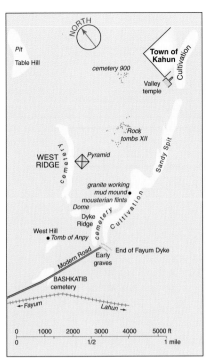

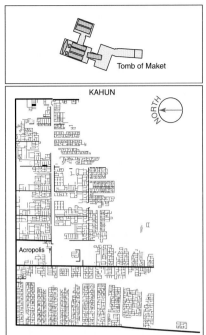

The Lahun pyramid-workers' town (right: plan showing the town of Kahun).

drained. From the mid-fifth century B.C. on, Classical writers such as Herodotus perpetuated a mistaken connection between the term "Moeris" (probably derived from *mi-wer* "great lake") and Nimaatra, one of the five names of Amenemhat III (1855–1808 B.C.). It was suggested that this ruler was responsible for the development of the Faiyum, but in fact, the process was probably already under way by the time of Amenemhat I (1985–1965 B.C.). The first ruler to build his pyramid complex in the Faiyum, however, was Senusret II (1897–1878 B.C.), whose pyramid complex was excavated by Flinders Petrie in 1888–1889 at the site of Lahun on the eastern edge of the region.

Senusret II's strong connections with the overall revival of the Faiyum are indicated by the religious monuments that he erected at the edge of the region. Around this time, a dike was built and canals were dug to connect the Faiyum with the waterway now known as the Bahr Yusef. These canals siphoned off some of the water that would otherwise have flowed into Lake Moeris, resulting in gradual evaporation around the edges of the lake as the canals extended the amount of new land; this reclaimed land was then farmed. The use of various sites in the Faiyum for temples and royal pyramid complexes from Senusret II's time on (such as the temple of Medinet Maadi and the Hawara pyramid) perhaps indicates the importance of the irrigation scheme, since it is usually assumed that the royal palaces of each ruler were built close to their funerary monuments.

Flinders Petrie and the Pyramid of Senusret II

It was in the Faiyum region that the young British archaeologist Flinders Petrie undertook some of his earliest and most important excavations. In November 1888, when he was excavating the pyramid complex of Amenemhat III at Hawara, he was informed that Kruger, a German antiquities dealer, was planning to dig at Lahun, the site of the pyramid of Senusret II. Petrie therefore sent a small group of workmen to excavate unsupervised both at Lahun and the nearby New Kingdom harim-town of Gurob, in order to stake a claim to the area. By February 1889, he had finished at Hawara and was directing the simultaneous excavations at Gurob and Lahun.

Petrie experienced great problems in his attempts to find the entrance passage of the Lahun pyramid. The reason for his difficulties lay in the fact that the entrance passages of most pyramids before Senusret II are located on the north side, whereas it eventually became apparent that the Lahun pyramid was entered via a vertical shaft at the east end of the south side. The reason for this change may have lain in the desire of the architects to safeguard the security of the tomb, even at the expense of its ritual alignment with the circumpolar stars. Alternatively, it is possible that some now unknown ritual alignment or astronomical orientation was being sought.

Petrie eventually found a pit near the southeast corner of the enclosure wall surrounding the pyramid, which he thought might be worth investigating further. However, he had to leave the site to work elsewhere, so he left his assistant George Wiloughby Fraser, a British civil engineer, to supervise the clearance of the shaft down to about 40 feet (12 m). At this depth, Fraser found a horizontal corridor leading both southward to another entrance shaft

The pyramid of Senusret II at Lahun. Once the limestone outer casing had been robbed away, probably in the Middle Ages, the pyramid took on the appearance of a vast heap of mud bricks.

and northward, via a vaulted hall, toward the pyramid. The vaulted hall had a deep well shaft at its eastern end; neither Petrie nor any subsequent explorers of the pyramid were able to find out what—if anything—lay at the bottom of this well shaft because it descends deep below the water table. Petrie recorded a tragic incident in which a local Bedouin boy fell down the well and died. Fraser and his digging team then gradually cleared the horizontal passage, which rose slowly as it approached the southeastern section of the pyramid. The passage reached an antechamber and turned sharply to the left.

Eventually, Fraser and Petrie—who had now rejoined the operation—were able to clamber through a corridor leading between the antechamber and burial chamber. On the south side of this corridor, they entered a passageway first heading south and then looping almost all the way around the burial chamber, eventually entering it through its northern wall. The German Egyptologist Rainer Stadelmann recently suggested that the final part of this "looping passage" might have provided a means for the king's spirit to head northward through the pyramid and reach the entrance chapel beyond, thus allowing him to reach the circumpolar stars by an unusual route. It is also possible, however, that the corridor surrounding the burial chamber was part of the cult of the god of the dead, Osiris, one of the central elements of which was the creation of a subterranean "island" (as in the Osireion at Abydos, described in chapter 2).

The burial chamber, lined with granite blocks and covered by a gabled roof, is situated about 60 feet (18.6 meters) southeast of the center of the pyramid. It contained a red granite sarcophagus, a travertine offering table, and a solid gold and lapis-lazuli uraeus (a representation of a cobra, frequently attached to royal crowns and headdresses) inlaid with faience, feldspar, cornelian, and garnet.

Although the original entrance shaft had been very difficult to locate, it seems that the actual process of reaching the Lahun burial chamber was ultimately fairly straightforward—unlike the pyramid of Amenemhat III at Hawara, where Petrie had been obliged to crawl over mud on his stomach, wriggle through narrow openings, and wade through chest-deep water. The typically understated account of his Indiana Jones-style exploration of the internal passages of the Hawara pyramid occupies a substantial section of Petrie's published report on the site.

The Lahun pyramid complex was also innovative in the composition of its superstructure, which was to influence the design of the pyramids of Senusret III and Amenemhat III at Dahshur. Whereas Old Kingdom pyramids were built entirely of stone, the inner core of Senusret II's pyramid was made largely of mud brick. It consisted of a 40-foot-high (12-meter) knoll of rock on which a checker-board network of limestone walls was constructed, with the large gaps filled by a dense matrix of mud-brick walling. The outer parts of the brickwork were intersected by numerous corridors and rooms, no doubt designed to confuse tomb-robbers.

At the foot of the pyramid's limestone outer casing blocks (the lowest courses of which were sunk into the bedrock), a shallow trench was dug, and alongside it a thick mud-brick wall was constructed. When filled with sand, the trench was probably intended to soak up rainwater flowing off the face of the pyramid, preventing the surrounding marl (soft limestone) from turning into mud on the rare occasions that the complex experienced heavy rain. Beyond the trench and wall, a line of trees was planted in soil-filled pits. These seem to have served a ritualistic purpose, because twelve were planted along the western side of the pyramid, and forty-two along the eastern and southern sides, respectively (the latter perhaps corresponded to the traditional forty-two provinces of ancient Egypt).

As in many other Old and Middle kingdom pyramid complexes, there is a small "queen's pyramid" beside the main pyramid at Lahun. Petrie was unsuccessful in his search for the burial chamber under the queen's pyramid; he excavated a network of tunnels and a deep shaft directly beneath it without ever finding any sign of the queen's burial place.

The Town at Lahun

In February 1889, Petrie was working at the eastern end of Lahun next to the valley temple, which had been destroyed in the pharaonic period and reused for a cemetery in the Christian period. There he discovered an area of about 24 acres (9.5 hectares) scattered with Middle Kingdom potsherds. His survey of the area revealed the outlines of a large town consisting of numerous mud-brick houses.

In the pages of his journal covering the period from 24 February to 2 March 1889, Petrie wrote:

> The town beyond the temple (called Medinet Kahun I hear) I now suspect to be of the age of the temple, 12th Dynasty, and to be almost untouched since then. If so, it will be a prize to work for historical interest of dated objects. I cannot be certain yet as to its age, but the pottery is quite unlike any I yet know, except some chips of the 12th Dynasty that I got at Hawara.

As this extract indicates, Petrie called the town "Kahun," to distinguish the settlement site from the pyramid site, but it appears from the same journal that only one local villager used this name (probably mistakenly) to describe the site. Many modern archaeologists, therefore, have begun to call the town site "Lahun" too, since it is essentially part of the same site as the pyramid. An alternative way of distinguishing between the two sites is to use the ancient toponyms Hetep-Senusret (probably the town) and Sekhem-Senusret (the pyramid complex or mortuary temple), both of which are often mentioned on papyri from Lahun, although there is some debate as to whether these place names can be definitely interpreted in this way.

Several "pyramid towns" have been found in the vicinity of Old and Middle Kingdom pyramids, but the settlement at Lahun is by far the largest and best-preserved example. A rectangular, planned town, measuring about 1,245 by 1,088 feet (384 by 335 meters), it is thought originally to have been built to house the workmen who constructed the pyramid. Later it accommodated the officials responsible for Senusret's royal mortuary cult. Finally, by the late Middle Kingdom, it had probably grown into a provincial town in its own right, judging from the papyri indicating that it had acquired its own mayor (*haty-a*).

Unlike the sprawling Middle Kingdom cities of Thebes or Memphis, the Lahun town was very much a planned entity, divided into two unequal halves by a thick wall. On the western side of the town there were more than two hundred small rectangular buildings, each covering an area as large as 1,800 square feet (170 square meters) and consisting of three to seven rooms. On the eastern side there was a group of about a dozen considerably larger houses, each including as many as 70 rooms and ranging between 11,000 and 27,000 square feet (1000–2400 square meters) in total area. It has been suggested that the funerary models depicting parts of the households and estates of Middle Kingdom officials such as Meketra (see chapter 10 on Deir el-Bahari) might usefully be compared with the ground plans of the large houses at Lahun in order to speculate on the kinds of fittings, furniture, and activities that filled the various rooms. It would be unwise to attempt to estimate the distribution of wealth in the Middle Kingdom from the pattern of housing at a single, probably untypical settlement, but it is nevertheless tempting to see the sharp residential contrast between the large and small houses at Lahun as confirmation that the resources of Egypt at this date were concentrated primarily in the hands of a small elite, a situation already suggested by the funerary evidence.

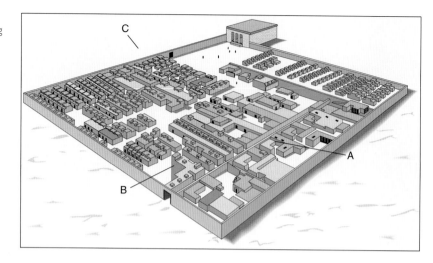

An artist's reconstruction of the town of Lahun showing (A) workers' houses, (B) palace, and (C) villas.

The Lahun Papyri

The "Lahun papyri," three archives of hieratic documents dating to the late Middle Kingdom (the earliest dates to the fifth year of the reign of Senusret III), were discovered in the pyramid town and valley temple of Lahun in the last decade of the nineteenth century. Some, consisting mainly of administrative records from the town, were excavated by Flinders Petrie in 1889–1890. Others were found in the pyramid complex in 1899; the first examples appeared illicitly on the Cairo antiquities market, and later papyri were scientifically excavated by the German archaeologist Ludwig Borchardt. Many of these which are now in the Berlin Museum, comprise a more homogeneous group of documents, largely concerned with temple administration and belonging to a temple official called Horemsaf.

One papyrus, discovered still folded and sealed, is inscribed with the will of a priest called Wah, bequeathing his property to his wife and family:

> I am creating a transfer deed for my wife . . . she herself shall
> pass it on to any of the children that she shall bear me, as she
> chooses. I give to her the three Asiatic (slaves) that were given to
> me by my brother, Ankhreni, the trusted sealbearer of the Chief
> of Works. She herself can give them to any of her children that
> she wishes. With regard to my tomb, I and my wife will be
> buried in it, without anyone being allowed to interfere with it.

Documents of this kind can provide all kinds of incidental information concerning the social and economic systems of Middle Kingdom Egypt. Thus, we know from Wah's will not only that women could inherit and own property in their own right, but also that they could pass it on to their

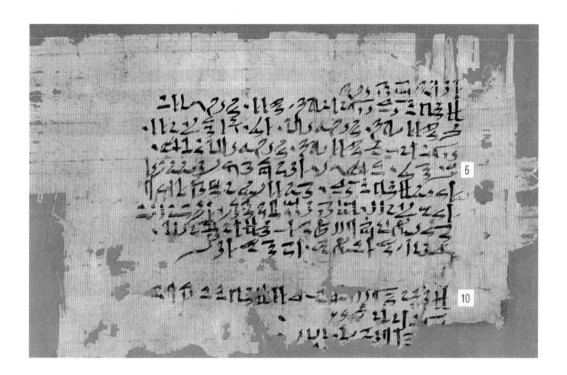

children. In addition, we learn that captured (or perhaps purchased) Asiatic women were treated as personal possessions who could be transferred to other members of the family. Finally, although there are very few indications of Egyptian military forays into Western Asia during the Middle Kingdom, the presence of three Asiatic women in one household emphasizes that there was extensive contact and commerce between Egypt and the Levant throughout this period.

Another of the Lahun papyri, a letter dated to a specific day in the reign of the twelfth-dynasty ruler Senusret III, is significant purely because of its date, which has turned out to be a crucial piece of evidence helping Egyptologists to construct the traditional framework of Egyptian chronology. Like Papyrus Ebers (an eighteenth-dynasty Theban medical papyrus), it includes a record of the so-called heliacal rising, an astronomical event in which the Dog Star, Sirius, appeared at sunrise on the first day of the inundation season. By assigning dates to each of these documents on the basis of the astronomical phenomena described, Egyptologists have been able to extrapolate a set of absolute dates for the whole of the pharaonic period, using the surviving records of the lengths of reign of the other kings of the Middle and New Kingdoms.

One of the Lahun papyri: The will of Meryintef son of Intef.

Food, Granaries, and Rations

In the 1888/1889 and 1889/1890 seasons, Petrie found a large quantity of plant remains in the town. Although some of these may derive from the New Kingdom and Roman phases of the site, when it was used as a cemetery and a "quarry," respectively, the majority probably date to the Middle Kingdom and therefore provide evidence about the diet of the twelfth- and thirteenth-dynasty inhabitants of the Lahun settlement. Immediately after their discovery, the 1888–1889 remains were studied by Percy Newberry, who had also examined the plant remains from the necropolis of Amenemhat III at Hawara, but their current location is unknown. The botanical specimens from the 1889–1990 season were not studied by Newberry and have survived in the collection of Liverpool Museum, where they have been studied by the German botanist Renate Germer. The only grain identified among the remains by Newberry and Germer is barley, although the Lahun papyri mention both it (barley) and bedet (emmer wheat). The granaries and store-rooms at the Lahun town are estimated to have contained enough grain to support a population of 5,000 on maximum rations, and 9,000 on minimum rations.

Fruits and seeds from Kahun. Middle Kingdom. Clockwise from top: Dum palm (*Hyphaene thebaica*); fruits of date palm (*Phoenix dactylifera*); barley (*Hordeum vulgare*); melon (*Citrullus vulgaris*); peas (*Pisum sativum*); beans (*Vicia faba*); and grape (*Vitris vinifera*).

Alternatively, if each of the smaller houses at Lahun contained an average of six persons, as some archaeologists have suggested, the population might have been as low as 3,000.

The remains of fruits excavated at Lahun included sycomore figs, Christ's thorn fruits, carob, juniper berries, and dum-palm and argun-palm nuts, but dates (ancient Egyptian *bener*) were evidently not found, despite the fact that they are mentioned in the papyri from the site. Carob fruits and juniper berries have survived only rarely from the Middle Kingdom and were probably imported from Palestine. The nuts of the argun palm (now extinct in Egypt) were sometimes used as handles or knobs on the wooden furniture found in the town. The remains identified by Newberry and Germer also included pulses (legumes) such as horsebeans and peas. The presence of black cumin seeds and safflower fruits (both also found in the tomb of Tutankhamun) suggests that these were already being used in cooking during the late Middle Kingdom. Before Germer's studies of the Lahun material, it had been assumed that cumin and safflower were not imported from Palestine until the eighteenth dynasty. This ties in with the fact that recent analyses of Middle Kingdom linen suggest that safflower was being used as a red dye. The botanists found traces of vegetables such as radishes and cucumbers, although these types have otherwise been attested no earlier than the Roman period, suggesting that some of the botanical remains may have come from post-Middle Kingdom deposits at Lahun.

The pottery excavated by Petrie can also provide information on the diet of the people of Lahun. The finds included long handmade bread molds, distinctive "hole-mouth" cooking bowls blackened by the smoke of fires, bottles for the storage of wine, water, or beer, water jars, and drinking cups. The potsherds from these distinctive Middle Kingdom pottery cups have survived in particularly large quantities, suggesting that they were a fragile type of vessel, frequently replaced and manufactured from local clay, rather than being imported from the vicinity of the capital in the north, as many other types appear to have been.

The Jewelery of Princess Sithathoriunet

In February 1914, Petrie and his assistant Guy Brunton discovered the mouth of a shaft-tomb, about 40 feet (12 meters) southeast of the entrance shaft to the main pyramid. After five days of digging, they reached an antechamber leading to a plundered burial chamber. This turned out be the final resting place of a princess called Sithathoriunet, a daughter of Senusret II and aunt of Amenemhat III. Inside her burial chamber were the broken-up remains of her body, a red granite sarcophagus, and a limestone chest in which her travertine canopic jars had been placed (the latter contained not the actual viscera but symbolic bundles of linen, resin, and mud). In addition, a small fragment of black granite, perhaps from a statue, was found to be inscribed

This silver mirror from the tomb of Sithathoriunet at Lahun has an exquisite handle in the form of the head of the cow goddess Hathor, made from gold, obsidian, and inlays of faience and electrum.

LAHUN

At the site of Qasr el-Sagha, in the desert cliffs at the northeastern corner of the Faiyum 50 miles (75 kilometers) southwest of Cairo, is a large stone building, clearly some kind of temple, that has been dated approximately to Senusret II's reign on the basis of architecture and associated pottery. Like many other buildings of this king's reign, which was perhaps only a few years long, the temple was left undecorated, uninscribed, and incomplete. Measuring 33 by 16 feet (10 by 5 meters), the building consists of seven shrines and a long offering room.

Just a short distance from the temple is a rectangular, planned settlement measuring about 374 by 260 feet (115 by 80 meters), with a nearby cemetery. To the northeast of the main settlement is a slightly larger but more amorphous area of mud-brick housing. Both settlements have been dated to the twelfth dynasty on the basis of their pottery. Like the roughly contemporary pyramid-town at Lahun, the rectangular village apparently housed a specialized community under direct state control. In the vicinity, there are also a number of smaller, much earlier settlements dated by radiocarbon to the Neolithic period (c. 5000 B.C.).

The site of Qasr el-Sagha appears to be linked by an ancient paved road with the basalt quarries of Gebel Qatrani, about 6 miles (10 kilometers) to the north. The obvious assumption is that the settlements and temple relate directly to the quarries' exploitation, but it has been pointed out by a number of scholars that basalt was mainly used in the Old Kingdom and Late Period, and indeed the pottery associated with the quarry road itself is primarily Old Kingdom in date. It is therefore something of a mystery as to why the major features of archaeological remains at Qasr el-Sagha should date to the twelfth dynasty, when very little basalt was being used. Perhaps Qasr el-Sagha originated as a very small quarry-workers' settlement. There are as yet no traces of Old Kingdom activity at the site, but by the Middle Kingdom it had evidently developed into a different kind of community with some as yet unknown function, perhaps connected with the empty, unfinished temple.

Although the unfinished Middle Kingdom temple at Qasr el-Sagha bears no inscriptions, its architectural style and the nature of the pottery found in the immediate vicinity suggest that it dates to the end of the twelfth dynasty.

with part of a text identifying the princess. It initially appeared that none of her other grave goods had survived, but the excavators soon came upon a recess in the west wall of the antechamber that had been plastered over, presumably to conceal its contents from robbers. Inside were five boxes (two made from inlaid ebony) holding the princess's wigs, toiletry equipment, and jewelry, including bracelets, necklaces, rings, pectorals, and a gold diadem incorporating a uraeus (similar to the one found in the king's burial chamber), as well as a silver mirror, the obsidian handle of which was decorated with gold and inlaid gemstones. Once the mud-caked items had been laboriously cleaned, it was found that much of the jewelry bore the cartouches of Senusret II and Amenemhat III.

Petrie and Brunton discovered three other shaft tombs on the south side of the pyramid, each containing the burials of members of Senusret II's family, but none of these contained funerary equipment comparable with that of Sithathoriunet. Similar caches of Middle Kingdom jewelry had been found by Jacques de Morgan in the tombs of six royal women at Dahshur (in 1894–1895), and in 1994 the jewelry and sarcophagus of the unforgettably named Queen Khnemetneferhedjetweret were discovered by Dieter Arnold in a small shrine-like room under mastaba-tomb 9, south of the pyramid of Senusret III at Dahshur. The twelve pieces of jewelry found by Arnold comprised more than 6,500 beads of gold, carnelian, lapis lazuli, and turquoise, as well as two matching amethyst scarabs inscribed with the names of Amenemhat II. Fortuitously, one of the Lahun papyri mentions Queen Khnemetneferhedjetweret, indicating that she died early in the reign of Senusret III.

Further Reading

The best sources on the pyramid complex and town of Senusret II at Lahun are still the reports published by Flinders Petrie: *Kahun, Gurob and Hawara* (London, 1890); *Ilahun, Kahun and Gurob* (London, 1891); and *Lahun II* (London 1923). However, Rosalie David's *The Pyramid Builders of Ancient Egypt* (2d ed., London, 1996) is a good popular account of the town site. The "treasure" of Princess Sithathoriunet was published by Guy Brunton as *Lahun I: The Treasure* (London, 1920). Stephen Quirke's edited volume, *Lahun Studies* (New Malden, 1998), provides an excellent overview of the site (particularly the history of its excavation), with fascinating insights into the links between the archaeological finds and the specialized vocabulary used in the Lahun papyri.

The papyri have not yet been fully published. Most of those now at Berlin have been published by Ullrich Luft in *Das Archiv von Illahun (Hieratische Papyri)* (Berlin, 1992). A preliminary report on the examples now in London was compiled by F. Ll. Griffith as *The Petrie Papyri: Hieratic Papyri from Kahun and Ghurob* (London, 1898), and a more detailed catalog is being prepared by Stephen Quirke and Mark Collier. Translations and discussions of some papyri from Lahun are included in Richard Parkinson's *Voices from Ancient Egypt: An Anthology of Middle Kingdom Writings* (London, 1991, pp. 78–79, 88–93, 108–112).

The enigmatic temple at Qasr el-Sagha was published by Dieter and Dorothea Arnold in *Der Tempel Qasr el-Sagha* (Mainz, 1979), while the Middle Kingdom settlements were excavated by a Polish expedition headed by

Boleslaw Ginter and published as *Qasr el-Sagha 1980: Contributions to the Holocene Geology, the Predynastic and Dynastic Settlements in the Northern Faiyum Desert* (Warsaw and Krakow, 1983).

Further Viewing

The other important Middle Kingdom sites that can be visited in the Faiyum region are the pyramids of Amenemhat I and Senusret I at Lisht and that of Amenemhat III at Hawara. Part of the jewelry of Princess Sithathoriunet is on display in the Egyptian Museum, Cairo, and the rest can be seen in the Metropolitan Museum, New York. Similar items of jewelry were also found in the tombs of the female relatives (Khnumet, Ita, Sithathor, Merit, and Weret) of Amenemhat II and Senusret III at Dahshur, and these objects can also be seen in the Egyptian Museum, Cairo. Some of the Lahun papyri are at the Berlin Museum, and the rest are at the British Museum and the Petrie Museum (University College, London).

Beni Hasan

c. 2125–1795 B.C.

The rock-tombs of the Oryx Nome

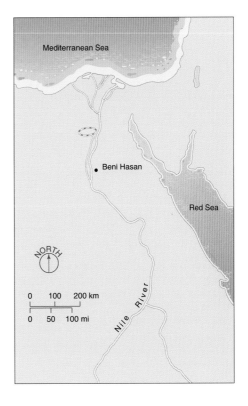

Beni Hasan is the site of a necropolis cut into the cliffs on the east bank of the Nile about 15 miles (24 kilometers) north of el-Minya. As the river passes through Middle Egypt it slowly meanders, creating strips of bright green fertile land on either side, usually considerably wider on one side than on the other. At Beni Hasan, the widest strip is on the west bank, and the fields stretch off toward the main Cairo-Aswan road in the far distance. On the east bank, a vivid strip of cultivated land separates the river from the cliffs, which are pitted near the top with the highly visible entrances of tomb-chambers.

The tombs at Beni Hasan date principally to the eleventh and twelfth dynasties, although there are also some small tombs dating back to the sixth dynasty. There are thirty-nine rock-cut tombs in a neat row, several belonging to the eleventh- and twelfth-dynasty nomarchs (provincial governors) of the sixteenth province of Upper Egypt (the "Oryx Nome"). Thirteen of these rock-cut tombs are decorated with wall-paintings of funerary rituals and daily life, including some intriguing depictions of Asiatic traders, as well as battle-scenes and rows of wrestlers. Scattered over the lower parts of the cliffs are almost a thousand Middle Kingdom shaft-tombs that were excavated by the Liverpool University archaeologist John Garstang in the early 1900s. The equipment from these undecorated tombs, including painted coffins and models, forms an important range of evidence concerning the funerary beliefs and practices of provincial

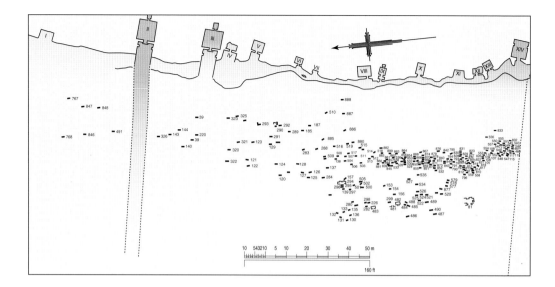

Plan of the main part of the necropolis, showing both decorated rock-tombs (I–XIV) and some of the hundreds of shaft-tombs scattered across the slopes below.

officials during the Middle Kingdom. At the very base of the cliffs are several chamber-tombs and pit-tombs dating to the latter part of the Old Kingdom, many of which were reused for Middle Kingdom burials.

The Rock-Cut Tombs of the "Oryx" Nomarchs

In the nineteenth century, Beni Hasan was visited and described by various pioneering Egyptologists, including Nestor l'Hôte, Joseph Bonomi, Luc de Saint-Ferriol, Ippolito Rosellini, and Jean-François Champollion, but it was not until 1890 that the rock-cut tombs were first properly investigated and recorded, by a team from the Egypt Exploration Society. This work was directed and published by Percy Newberry and George Fraser. The group of epigraphers also included Howard Carter, then eighteen years old and working on his first expedition to Egypt.

The "biographical" inscriptions on the walls of at least ten of the rock-cut tombs at Beni Hasan provide us with details of the names, titles, and careers of a large group of nomarchs, many of whom also held the post of "overseer of the Eastern Desert": Amenemhat (tomb BH2), Khnumhotep I (BH14), Khnumhotep II (BH3), Baket I (BH29), Baket II (BH33), Baket III (BH15), Khety (BH17), Nakht (BH21), Netjernakht (BH23), and Remushenta (BH27). One uninscribed tomb (BH18) is sufficiently similar to the rest to suggest that it too was intended for a nomarch.

There are three architectural types of elite rock-cut tombs at Beni Hasan. The first and earliest type comprises decorated and inscribed chapels, such as those belonging to Baket I, Baket II, and Remushenta, which are at the southern end of the row (BH29, 33, and 27). All these are similar in size and decoration, each consisting of a single chamber with a gabled ceiling and no

columns, wide smooth façades, and no forecourt or causeway. Tombs of the second type also consist of only one chamber, but this incorporates one or more rows of lotus columns, as well as a causeway and forecourt leading up to the entrance façade. There are two tombs of this kind, belonging to Baket III and Khety (BH15 and 17). Finally, there are three tombs having a much smaller single chamber with one or more rows of plain columns, but no causeway or forecourt; these belonged to Khnumhotep I, Nakht, and Netjernakht (BH14, 21, and 23).

Very few of the tombs contain any definite indications of their precise date, although some of the later twelfth-dynasty examples have distinctive pairs of proto-doric (sixteen-sided polygonal) columns in front of their façades. Thus, when Newberry and Fraser published the epigraphic work of the 1890s, they worked on the assumption that the tombs belonged to a long sequence of officials covering the whole span of the eleventh and twelfth dynasties. In 1992, however, the Austrian Egyptologist Christian Hölzl demonstrated that most of the tombs were built during a fairly short period during the twelfth dynasty. He argued that the three simple tombs of the first type described above did indeed form a small sequence and were evidently earlier than those of the second and third types, but that the two latter groups were probably roughly contemporaneous, simply belonging to individuals at different levels in the local hierarchy. Hölzl therefore proposed that the owners of the smaller tombs (Khnumhotep I, Nakht, and Netjernakht), although techni-

Several of the Middle Kingdom rock-tombs at Beni Hasan have elaborate portico-style façades, including this one with "proto-doric" columns (BH3), which belonged to Khnumhotep II, a governor of the "oryx province" during the reign of Amenemhat II.

cally holding the title "nomarch," must actually have been less powerful contemporaries of Baket III and Khety.

If Hölzl's theory is correct, then we have to find a reason why the "Oryx" nomarchs appear to have abandoned the Beni Hasan cemetery from the mid-twelfth dynasty on. The answer seems to lie in a gradual process of change in the relationship between the Egyptian king and his provincial representatives during the Middle Kingdom. After the time of the nomarch Khnumhotep II, whose tomb contains an inscription specifically dated to the sixth year of the reign of King Senusret II, the Beni Hasan elite started to build their tombs near those of the twelfth and thirteenth-dynasty kings in the vicinity of Itj-tawy, the Middle Kingdom capital. The powers of the provincial governors at places like Beni Hasan in Middle Egypt became severely reduced starting around the reign of Senusret III. Khnumhotep III, a nomarch of about the time of Amenemhat III, probably had two funerary monuments: an unfinished rock-tomb at Beni Hasan, and a mastaba-tomb at Dahshur, near the "Residence" (a term used during the Middle Kingdom to refer not only to the royal palace but also, by extension, to Itj-tawy, the capital city where it was located).

The Dutch Egyptologist Harco Willems has suggested that the continued building of a few large nomarchs' tombs at other Middle Egyptian sites until very late in the twelfth dynasty indicates, first, that the process of deliberately reducing Middle Egyptian nomarchs' power was not a single act but a gradual process, and second, that this process probably occurred at different speeds in different regions.

One of the scenes in the tomb of Khnumhotep II (BH3) shows a group of Asiatics (probably Bedouin of the Eastern Desert) bringing a consignment of lead sulfide (galena, used for eye-paint) from mines on the Red Sea coast into the nomarch's presence. Since Khnumhotep's titles, as provincial governor of the Oryx Nome, also included "overseer of the Eastern Desert," we are given a strong indication that the local governors controlled and exploited not only the agricultural resources of the Nile Valley but also the mineral

Part of the decoration in the tomb of Khnumhotep II shows the arrival of a group of bedouin bringing galena (lead-based eye-paint) introduced by a chief huntsman called Khety and a scribe called Neferhotep (holding a papyrus sheet, far right).

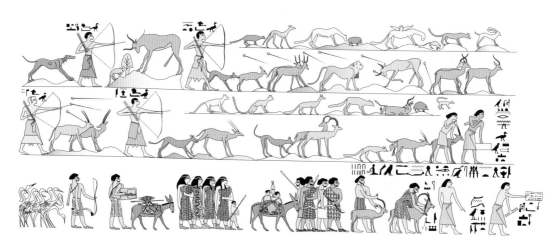

resources of the adjacent desert regions. It is not apparent, however, whether such provincial administrators were generally obtaining metals or stones for their own use and enrichment, or whether they were always acting as representatives of the kings, who would presumably have regarded all mineral resources as their own property.

Early Battle Scenes

The eleventh-dynasty tombs of Khety and Bakt III (BH17 and BH15) and the twelfth-dynasty tombs of Khnumhotep and Amenemhat (BH14 and BH2) all contain painted scenes of battles. Such warlike images seem to have formed an integral part of the tombs' decorative schemes, and in all four cases they are located at the bottom of the eastern wall of the main chamber. Along with the depictions of funerary offerings and such activities as dancing, hunting, fishing, or agriculture, they were intended both to encapsulate the many aspects of the life of the deceased and to justify his continued existence in the afterlife.

Given the tendency of Egyptian art to draw on a reservoir of general motifs appropriate to particular circumstances, there must be some doubt as to the historicity of any battle scene on the wall of any particular tomb: the battle depicted may have been a combination of smaller skirmishes or may never have taken place, just as the deceased may never actually have speared fish from a papyrus skiff, even though he is regularly portrayed in this act. It has been pointed out that the battle scenes at Beni Hasan—all depictions of the sieges of fortified towns—resemble one another closely enough to suggest that none necessarily depicts a unique historical event (or perhaps

Scenes of wrestling and military conflict in the tomb of Amenemhat (BH2).

only the earliest do). The fortifications are shown as high walls, crenellated at the top and strengthened with a slight batter at the base. Sixty eleventh-dynasty soldiers buried in a mass grave near the mortuary temple and tomb of King Nebhepetra Mentuhotep II at Deir el-Bahari had numerous head wounds, probably indicating the fatal consequences of attempting to storm such battlements.

There are only three surviving Old Kingdom depictions of battles and all of these appear to show conflicts between Asiatics and Egyptians, forming part of the evidence for the Egyptians' attempts to establish an economic and political sphere of influence in Palestine during the twelfth dynasty. In contrast, the Middle Kingdom scenes at Beni Hasan appear to document civil war between rival factions of Egyptians. This suggests that the content of funerary art was responding, to some extent, to historical events rather than endlessly repeating the same generalized motifs. The Beni Hasan scenes have roughly contemporary royal counterparts in the fragments of relief surviving from the temple of Mentuhotep II at Deir el-Bahari (see chapter 12) and the funerary causeways of the twelfth-dynasty rulers Senusret I and III, at Lisht and Dahshur, respectively. The onset of civil war in the First Intermediate Period, combined with the gradual move toward professionalization of the army, would have helped to raise the profile of military activities in the lives of some provincial governors, leading them to include depictions of battles on the walls of their tombs alongside their more peaceful activities.

It has been suggested by some scholars that the early Middle Kingdom battle scenes all show individual episodes from a historical narrative concerning the eleventh-dynasty assault by Theban armies on the city of Herakleopolis, which represented the climax of Mentuhotep II's reign and the crucial campaign that effectively brought an end to the First Intermediate Period. However, the reliefs from the temple of Mentuhotep II (and also the paintings in the tomb of his general, Intef) all appear to show the siege of an Asiatic town. It therefore seems more likely that the image of the siege of Herakleopolis became a kind of archetypal way of portraying any siege, even of an Asiatic town.

Garstang's Excavation of the Shaft-Tombs

The extensive cemetery of around a thousand Middle Kingdom shaft-tombs at Beni Hasan was excavated by John Garstang in the early 1900s. The equipment from these undecorated tombs, belonging to middle-ranking local officials and including painted coffins and models, forms an important source for the funerary beliefs of the Middle Kingdom. In his publication of the site, Garstang provided detailed descriptions of four intact shaft-tomb burials: those of the courtier Intef (no. 1), the physician Nefery (no. 116), the treasury superintendent Nefwa (no. 186), and a pair of individuals called Khnemnakht and Netjernakht (no. 585).

An unusual form of female figurine that appeared in Middle Kingdom cemeteries was the wooden "paddle doll."

Garstang's excavations uncovered about a hundred intact coffins and many fragments of others, which are now spread throughout various museum collections, making up the most important single-site corpus of Middle Kingdom coffins. These have been analyzed by Harco Willems to produce a new seriation (dated sequence) of Beni Hasan coffins, helping to date the shaft-tombs more accurately. As with Hölzl's dating of the elite rock-cut tombs at the top of the terrace, Willems's dating of the individual shaft-tombs shows that the cemetery grew roughly from south to north. Thus, the earliest coffins (Willems's "type A") are from shaft-tombs directly in front of the nomarch's tombs, which Hölzl dates to the earliest Middle Kingdom phase at Beni Hasan (BH 14–29, which date from the eleventh dynasty to the first reign of the twelfth), while his "type B" coffins derive from tombs in front of the nomarchs' tombs at the northern end of the necropolis.

Funerary Practices of Ordinary People in the Middle Kingdom

During the Old Kingdom, the afterlife had been the prerogative of the king, who in death was identified with Osiris and transformed into a god. For this reason, Old Kingdom courtiers sought burial close to the king, hoping for inclusion in his funerary cult so that they too might be granted some form of afterlife—although the best they could hope for was a continuation of their earthly status. With the collapse of the Old Kingdom came greater self-reliance, and with it a process that is sometimes described by

John Garstang and Percy Newberry recording finds in one of the rock-tombs at Beni Hasan that had been converted into a temporary dig-house.

Egyptologists as the "democratization of the afterlife." This meant that everyone could have access to the afterlife, without being associated directly with the royal cult. These new aspirations of the deceased are set out in the collections of spells painted in cursive hieroglyphs inside wooden coffins of the Middle Kingdom.

Many of the coffins excavated at Beni Hasan are decorated with selections from a group of more than a thousand spells known as the Coffin Texts. These spells were often inscribed on coffins during the eleventh and twelfth dynasties (2040–1783 B.C.). They derived partly from the Pyramid Texts, a sequence of often obscure utterances carved on the internal walls of the Old Kingdom pyramids (see chapter 3).

The Coffin Texts were intended to guarantee survival in the afterworld, and some of them are the ancestors of spells found in the New Kingdom *Book of the Dead*. They have titles such as the self-explanatory "Not to rot and not to do work in the kingdom of the dead," and "Spell for not dying a second death," which was designed to prevent the dead man or woman from being judged unfit to enter the kingdom of Osiris and so condemned to oblivion. Although most coffins bore fewer than two hundred spells, a total of 1,185 have been recorded. The Coffin Texts also incorporated a new set of "utterances" that could be grouped to form a kind of guidebook to the afterworld, not only outlining its character but also giving the correct phrases to gain admission to its various sectors. The best known of these guidebooks, the Book of Two Ways, has been found in Middle Kingdom tombs at Deir el-Bersha, another Middle Kingdom elite rock-cut cemetery a few miles south of Beni Hasan.

Many Middle Kingdom coffins were inscribed with extracts from the so-called Coffin Texts; the floor of the outer coffin of a twelfth-dynasty physician buried at Deir el-Bersha (a few kilometres to the south of Beni Hasan) was decorated with the *Book of Two Ways*, which provided details of the necessary route to the hereafter.

SPEOS ARTEMIDOS

In a *wadi* (ravine) at the southern end of Beni Hasan, about 2 miles (3 kilometers) east of the Middle Kingdom necropolis, is a New Kingdom rock-cut temple known from Ptolemaic times on as the Speos Artemidos (Greek, "cave of Artemis") and nowadays called Istabl Antar ("stable of Antar"). This shrine—dedicated to the local lion goddess Pakhet, whose name translates as "she who scratches"—was constructed in the reigns of Hatshepsut and Thutmose III (1479–1425 B.C.). Pakhet is known from the Coffin Texts as a nocturnal huntress, so it is not surprising that the Greeks identified her with their own hunting goddess, Artemis. There is, however, no evidence for any cult of Pakhet in the area of Beni Hasan before the New Kingdom.

The Speos consists of a vestibule supported by eight Hathor-headed columns, connected by a short corridor with an inner chamber where the cult image would once have stood, although only the niche survives. An inscription on the architrave above the vestibule describes the ravages of the Hyksos rulers (a group of Asiatics who gained control of Lower Egypt during the Second Intermediate Period), and the work of Hatshepsut in restoring the damage they had caused. It is usually assumed that this text simply uses the Hyksos as convenient personifications of disorder, since their expulsion had taken place more than seventy-five years earlier under the reign of Hatshepsut's great-grandfather, Ahmose (1550–1525 B.C.). Ironically, the queen's own name was hacked out by Sety I (1306–1290 B.C.), who inserted his own cartouches instead. The temple is surrounded by the much-plundered burials of sacred cats, most of which date to the Late Period (712–332 B.C.).

Both the Pyramid Texts and the Coffin Texts present more than one version of the destination of the deceased: it was possible to travel the sky with the sun god Ra, or, alternatively, to pass down into the underworld of Osiris. The latter view became increasingly common from the time of the Coffin Texts on, setting the scene for the funerary beliefs of the New Kingdom.

Further Reading

The decorated rock-cut tombs at Beni Hasan were published by Percy Newberry in *Beni Hassan* (4 vols., London, 1893–1900). The architecture and dating of the tombs are discussed in Christian Hölzl "The Rock-Tombs of Beni Hassan: Architecture and Sequence" in *Attidi VI Congresso di Egittologia*, vol. 1 (Turin, 1992), pp. 279–83. John Garstang published much of the material excavated from Middle Kingdom shaft-tombs at Beni Hasan in *The Burial Customs of Ancient Egypt* (London, 1907). Janine Bourriau's *Pharaohs and Mortals* (Cambridge, 1988), the catalog of an exhibition of Middle Kingdom objects, includes several entries on items from Beni Hasan. Both Raymond Faulkner's *The Ancient Egyptian Coffin Texts* (3 vols., London, 1972–1978) and Harco Willems's *Chests of Life* (Leiden, 1988) provide detailed information on Middle Kingdom coffins and their decoration.

Ahmed Fakhry published the first description of the Speos Artemidos in the *Annales du Service des Antiquités d'Egypte*, vol. 39 (1939). Hatshepsut's inscription was translated by Alan Gardiner in the *Journal of Egyptian Archaeology*, vol. 32 (1946). More recent epigraphic work at the site was published by Suzanne Bickel and Jean-Luc Chappaz in "Missions épigraphiques du fonds de l'Égyptologie de Genève au Speos Artemidos," *Bulletin de la Société de l'Egyptologie de Genève*, vol. 12 (1988), pp. 9–24.

Further Viewing

The coffins and funerary equipment from the shaft-tombs excavated by Garstang are divided mainly among the Egyptian Museum in Cairo, the Liverpool Museum, and the collection of the School of Archaeology, Classics and Oriental Studies, University of Liverpool.

CHAPTER

NINE

———

South Sinai

c. 2680–1069 B.C.

Turquoise and copper mines

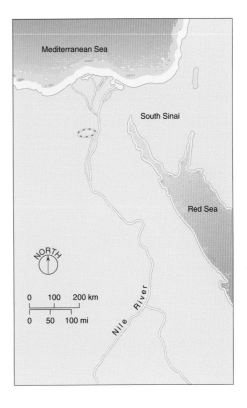

One of the earliest surviving examples of Egyptian royal jewelry is a set of four bracelets found wrapped around a linen-bandaged arm from the tomb of Djer at Abydos, perhaps one of the limbs of the king himself. These bracelets were fashioned from four of the most precious materials available at the time: gold, lapis lazuli, amethyst, and turquoise. The lapis lazuli was brought by trade from distant Afghanistan, but the other three materials were obtained from the deserts of Egypt itself. Perhaps the most quintessentially Egyptian of these was the beautiful blue-green turquoise. The two main ancient Egyptian sources of turquoise were in the Sinai Peninsula at Wadi Maghara, which was exploited from the Early Dynastic Period to the Middle Kingdom, and Serabit el-Khadim, worked from the Middle Kingdom until at least the Late Period.

Such outlying Egyptian quarrying and mining sites, less elaborate than longer-lived pharaonic sites in the Nile Valley such as Abydos or Thebes, nevertheless provide valuable information on the fundamental factors influencing Egyptian settlements. Their archaeological remains also incorporate such features as wells and dams and evidence of religious activity and the use of a variety of tools, reflecting the level of technology, the nature of the material extracted, and the availability of local materials from which different tools could be made. The subtle differences between structural remains at the

Plan of the temple at Serabit
el-Khadim. Below, map of Sinai
peninsula, showing locations of
Serabit, Wadi Maghara, and Heliopolis.

comparatively rudimentary and ephemeral accommodation associated with quarrying and mining sites express the Egyptians' ability to adapt their settlement strategies to changing contexts and circumstances. Like the string of functionally and topographically varied Middle Kingdom fortresses and garrisons in Nubia, they suggest a high degree of flexibility and spontaneity in Egyptian civilization.

The mines at Wadi Maghara, situated about 140 miles (224 kilometers) southeast of Cairo, were exploited particularly during the Old and Middle Kingdoms. When Flinders Petrie examined the site in 1904–1905, he found the mining adits (entrance tunnels), accompanied by impressive rock-carved reliefs and inscriptions, on one side of the wadi, and a hilltop miners' settlement on the other side. The latter was occupied primarily during the Old Kingdom and consisted of about 125 stone-built structures. There were also two unfortified groups of slightly larger and more regular Old Kingdom structures: one next to the remains of an enigmatic wall or dam built across the northern end of the wadi, and the other built on a rocky shoal at the southwestern end of the wadi (now largely destroyed by flash floods and modern quarrying activity). Petrie's excavations at Wadi Maghara revealed numerous artifacts, including evidence of copper-smelting in situ. The three components of the site—hilltop settlement, wadi-floor settlement, and wall/dam—reflect the isolation and vulnerability of the miners, housed in a tightly clustered, defensive main settlement combined with unprotected accommodation in reasonable proximity to the mines.

The later mines at Serabit el-Khadim, about 11 miles (18 kilometers) north of Wadi Maghara, are often accompanied by rock-carved stelae. Close by is an extremely unusual temple complex dating to the Middle and New Kingdoms (c.2040–1070 B.C.). In the temple precincts and the surrounding area, many rock-cut and free-standing stelae were dedicated by mining ex-

Many of the rock-carvings at Wadi Maghara depict the Egyptian king triumphing over foreigners. Presumably these served as symbols of Egyptian political control of the Sinai peninsula. In this example, the third-dynasty pharaoh Sanakht is smiting an Asiatic.

peditions to the goddess Hathor in her aspect of Nebet Mefkat ("Lady of Turquoise") and the god Soped, "Guardian of the Desert Ways."

Among the results of Israeli work at Serabit el-Khadim between 1967 and 1982 was the discovery that one of the mines contained equipment used in the processing of copper. This find has added to the controversy regarding the ancient Egyptians' precise aims in the Sinai. Many of the inscriptions at Wadi Maghara and Serabit el-Khadim refer to the procurement of a substance called *mefkat*, which was once translated as "malachite" and has more recently been taken to mean "turquoise." It is possible that the main aim of

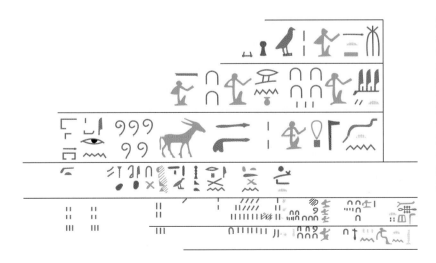

Some of the rock-carved stelae at the Serabit el-Khadim turquoise mines provide detailed descriptions of the personnel involved in specific mining expeditions. This inscription not only lists the various elements of the human labor force but also mentions 500 donkeys, presumably carrying provisions.

Egyptian operations at these two sites was to procure both copper and malachite, with turquoise perhaps only a convenient by-product of this mining. In this context, it is interesting to note that the surviving examples of turquoise as a gemstone form quite a small percentage of Egyptian jewelry; if these mines had been used primarily for its extraction, the numerous adits, shafts, and stelae at Wadi Maghara and Serabit el-Khadim would imply that vast quantities were obtained.

The Middle Kingdom Temple at Serabit el-Khadim

The temple of Hathor at Serabit el-Khadim is one of the most unexpected and dramatic of Egyptian sites. Visitors to the site generally climb up a moderately gentle slope, reaching the Rod el-Air cliffs about 3 miles (5 kilometers) west of Serabit. These cliffs are decorated with some of the most exquisite rock-carvings found anywhere in Egypt. Classic Egyptian motifs, including elegant battle-axes and the elaborate shapes of Nile skiffs, were carefully pecked out of the local sandstone, presumably by workmen who were en route to or from the mines.

Visitors tend to arrive on the undulating natural plateau of Serabit el-Khadim from the west, walking initially between about a dozen rough dry-

The original sanctuary of Hathor at Serabit el-Khadim is based around two simple shrines cut into a rock outcrop between the reigns of Senusret I and Amenemhat III. The Israeli archaeologist, Raphael Giveon, has argued that the northernmost shrine was at first intended to be a tomb-chapel with funerary-style inscriptions.

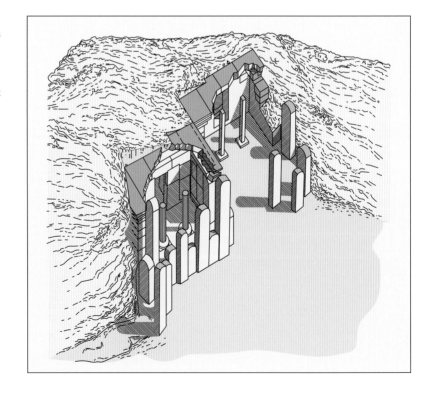

130

stone huts. Before long, the temple becomes visible on the horizon in the form of a cluster of monoliths, more reminiscent of a Neolithic stone circle in northern Europe than of an Egyptian religious monument. As a piece of architecture, the Serabit temple is perfectly adapted to its environment; the numerous stelae make up a dense, jagged avenue leading to the inner sanctum. As the deep stele-shaped excavations and half-quarried, unfinished slabs to the north of the temple clearly attest, the stelae were hewn entirely from local stone. The homogeneity of landscape and monument therefore creates the effect of a cluster of megaliths erupting out of the hilltop itself, ideally viewed as a spectacular silhouette against the rising or setting sun.

The rock-cut shrine at the eastern end of the temple, approached through the dense avenue of stelae, appears to have been founded in the reign of Senusret I, which would presumably have coincided with the first large-scale mining there. The Serabit mining site is one of many key archaeological sites first excavated by Petrie at the end of the nineteenth century. With its ancient turquoise workings, rock-cut inscriptions, and unusual stele-strewn temple, it has been awaiting proper scientific reassessment for many years. From 1968 to 1978, it was surveyed and excavated by an Israeli team led by Raphael Giveon, but so far this work has only been partially published. In the 1990s, the neglect was finally remedied by several seasons of excavation

The overall appearance of the temple at Serabit el-Khadim is virtually unique in Egyptian religion, but the use of round-topped commemorative stelae can be traced back to the first dynasty at Abydos. The dates on the stelae at Serabit suggest that one, and one alone, was set up by each expedition sent to the site.

131
—

In 1904, Flinders Petrie found a small sandstone sphinx at Serabit el-Khadim; it was decorated both with hieroglyphic signs (spelling out "beloved of Hathor, mistress of turquoise") and with a set of unfamiliar symbols that came to be known as Proto-Sinaitic. These texts, closely resembling the Proto-Canaanite inscriptions found at various sites in Palestine, were subsequently found at a number of sites in Sinai, including ten other inscriptions at Serabit el-Khadim.

The script consists of at least 23 signs, about half of which appear to derive from Egyptian hieroglyphs. The texts probably date mainly to the late Middle Kingdom (c. 1800–1640 B.C.) or Second Intermediate Period (1640–1532 B.C.), but they have still not been properly deciphered.

In 1916, Alan Gardiner demonstrated fairly convincingly that part of the Proto-Sinaitic text on Petrie's sphinx could be translated as "Balat," the name of a Syro-Palestinian goddess. He went on to argue that Proto-Sinaitic represented a kind of crucial "missing link" between the Egyptian hieroglyphic script and the early Western alphabet. Although this hypothesis was initially well received, the increasing discoveries of Proto-Canaanite inscriptions tended to indicate that the true genesis of the modern alphabet took place in Syria-Palestine rather than in Egypt. The most recent studies of Proto-Sinaitic suggest that, although there are undoubtedly strong links between this script and the Canaanite and Phoenician alphabets, it is more of an "economical syllabary" in which each sign is equivalent to a consonant plus a vowel, rather than an actual alphabet.

Intriguingly, the recent discovery of two lines of Proto-Sinaitic texts in Egypt's Western Desert have shed new light on the situation. Two American archaeologists, John and Deborah Darnell, made this find in 1999 while investigating an ancient pathway through the Wadi el-Hol, northwest of Luxor. The new inscriptions are interesting for two reasons: because they were found so far away from Sinai, and because they date to around 1900 B.C., much earlier in the Middle Kingdom than other known Proto-Sinaitic texts. John Darnell has proposed that the texts were inscribed by Semitic people serving as mercenaries in the Egyptian army, raising the possibility that some form of early Semitic alphabet had already begun to emerge directly out of the Egyptian hieroglyphic system by the beginning of the Middle Kingdom. In particular, these new finds may indicate that the origins of the alphabet lie in Egypt itself after all, rather than Syria-Palestine.

The American philologist William Albright compiled a table comparing proto-Sinaitic signs with Egyptian hieroglyphs, which formed part of his groundbreaking work, *The Proto-Sinaitic Inscriptions and Their Decipherment*.

and restoration directed by Dominique Valbelle and Charles Bonnet. Like the Umm el-Qa'ab late Predynastic and Early Dynastic cemetery at Abydos (reexcavated by Kaiser and Dreyer throughout the 1980s and 1990s) and the city of Amarna (resurveyed and partially reexcavated by Kemp since 1978), Serabit el-Khadim has now been subjected to a full archaeological reexamination and can at last be studied freshly, rather than continuing to be seen primarily through the eyes of early twentieth-century archaeologists.

Why Were Certain Deities Particularly Associated with Mining Expeditions?

Some of the gods and goddesses worshipped at Serabit el-Khadim were connected with the places in the Nile Valley from which the miners came—for instance, Ptah from Memphis and Atum from Heliopolis. However, the majority of the deities, such as Hathor, Soped, and Thoth, were associated with mining areas in general. They were regarded as manifestations of divine good will in foreign lands, sometimes effectively constituting Egyptian versions of foreign gods or goddesses; thus, Hathor, Lady of Byblos, was actually the local goddess Baalath Gebal.

In the Middle Kingdom, Hathor, Lady of Nekhent, was the patroness of the Gebel el-Asr gneiss quarries in the desert west of Tushka; Hathor, Lady of Mefkat, presided over the acquisition of copper, turquoise, and malachite in the Sinai; and the twelfth-dynasty fortresses at Buhen, Aniba, and Qubban were the cult centers of Hathor, Lady of Iken, Hathor, Lady of Abshek, and Horus, Lord of Meha, respectively. In the New Kingdom, a temple dedicated to a local form of Hathor was established in the vicinity of the copper mines at Timna in the Wadi Araba. It has been suggested that Hathor's popularity with miners might have derived, at least in part, from her association with the acacia tree, because the presence of those trees can indicate the presence of copper and lead ores, perhaps helping the ancient prospectors to identify new sources of copper, malachite, or turquoise. Acacia wood was also used for pit props in some Egyptian gold mines, and it is possible that this tree species was deliberately chosen because of its comforting religious associations.

The desert was regarded by the ancient Egyptians as a place where strange events might occur, particularly in connection with the provision of water or the quality of the materials being mined. In a turquoise-mining inscription of the sixth regnal year of the twelfth-dynasty ruler Amenemhat IIII (1849 B.C.), the "god's seal-bearer" Horurre describes how, although he arrived at Serabit el-Khadim in the summer, "when it was not the proper season for coming to this mining region," he was nevertheless rewarded with reserves of good-quality turquoise through the "power of the king" and the benevolence of the goddess Hathor.

In view of the close association between Hathor and mining, it is perhaps not surprising that our most detailed information concerning the Egyptians' cosmological views on mining have been found on the walls of the Ptolemaic and Roman temple of Hathor at Dendera (see chapter 17). In several of the rooms of this temple, rulers are shown presenting precious metals and stones to the goddess; the bases of the walls of the "silver-room" (or side-room XI) are decorated with a series of kneeling figures, each representing regions that produced particular metals or precious stones. The accompanying hieroglyphic texts show that the import of this depiction was not simply that precious gifts were being offered to the goddess, but that the entire mineral universe—gold, turquoise, emeralds, jasper, calcite, q^c mineral (black schist?), copper, carnelian, green feldspar, galena, lapis lazuli, silver—was being reassembled in microcosm to enable the temple to function as a reflection of the cosmos.

The significance of this situation in the context of Egyptian mining was the perception that the procurement of minerals was not merely an act of economic or political exploitation, but also—perhaps most importantly—an act of religious devotion through which the ruler was able to fulfil his obligation to maintain the harmony of the universe and to attempt to reenact the process of creation itself.

Further Reading

The first two substantial archaeological publications on Sinai were Raymond Weill's *Receuil des inscriptions égyptiennes du Sinai* (Paris, 1904) and Flinders Petrie and George Currelly's *Researches in Sinai* (London, 1906). An up-to-date and well-illustrated account of the current state of knowledge concerning the temple of Hathor at Serabit el-Khadim is Dominique Valbelle and Charles Bonnet's *Le sanctuaire d'Hathor, ma tresse de la turquoise. Sérabit el-Khadim au Moyen Empire* (Paris, 1996). The most recent survey of the Wadi Maghara turquoise mines is discussed in Maryvonne Chartier-Raymond, "Notes sur Maghara (Sinai)" in *Cahiers de Recherche de l'Institut de Papyrologie et Egyptologie de Lille*, volume 10 (1988), pp. 13-22.

Sinai: Pharaohs, Miners, Pilgrims and Soldiers (New York, 1979), edited by Beno Rothenberg, is an interesting collection of papers dealing with different aspects of the archaeology and history of the Sinai Peninsula. *Le Sinai durant l'antiquité et le Moyen Age: 4000 ans d'histoire pour un désert* (Paris, 1998), edited by Dominique Valbelle and Charles Bonnet, presents the results of a conference on the archaeology of Sinai from prehistory through to the Islamic period. The best discussion of the Proto-Sinaitic script is William Albright's *The Proto-Sinaitic Inscriptions and Their Decipherment* (Cambridge, Mass., and London, 1966), although his translations of the many crudely executed texts have not been universally accepted.

Further Viewing

A few of the royal rock carvings and inscriptions from Wadi Maghara are now in the Egyptian Museum, Cairo, including a magnificent depiction of the fourth-dynasty ruler Sneferu (deified by the Middle Kingdom miners at the Serabit el-Khadim temple) in the act of smiting a captive Asiatic. Petrie's "Proto-Sinaitic" sphinx statuette from Serabit el-Khadim is on display at the British Museum.

Deir el-Bahari

c. 2055–1425 B.C.

The cult temple of Queen Hatshepsut

In the history of Egypt during the dynastic period (c. 3000 to 332 B.C.), there were only two or three women who managed to to rule as pharaohs, rather than simply wielding power as the "great wife" of a male king. Probably the best-known member of this select group was Hatshepsut, one of the daughters of Thutmose I, who was evidently not content to fulfil the traditional roles of royal consort and mother but instead seized the opportunity to inherit the crown from her brother, Thutmose II, instead of allowing it to pass directly to her nephew and stepson, Thutmose III. She ruled for about fifteen years.

Hatshepsut's name is particularly associated with the huge temple complex on the west bank of the Nile opposite modern Luxor, which comprises temples and tombs dating from the early Middle Kingdom to the Ptolemaic Period. The site consists of a deep bay in the Theban cliffs containing her well-preserved cult temple, together with the remains of the funerary complex of the eleventh-dynasty ruler Nebhepetra Mentuhotep II (2061–2010 B.C.) and a temple built by Thutmose III (1479–1425 B.C.), as well as nonroyal tombs contemporary with each of these pharaohs. Hatshepsut's grandfather, Amenhotep I, built a mud-brick shrine at the northern end of the Deir el-Bahari bay, and it was presumably this building that inspired Hatshepsut to establish her cult temple there (dismantling Amenhotep I's shrine in the process).

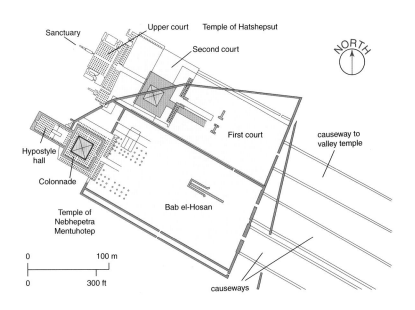

Sanctuary

Upper court   Temple of Hatshepsut

Second court

NORTH

First court

causeway to
valley temple

Hypostyle
hall

Colonnade

Temple of
Nebhepetra
Mentuhotep

Bab el-Hosan

0   100 m

0   300 ft

causeways

Plan of the Deir el-Bahari
temples of Hatshepsut,
Mentuhotep II, and
Thutmose III.

The Cult Temple of Hatshepsut

The temple of Hatshepsut, known to the Egyptians as *djeser-djeseru* ("the most sacred of sacred places"), is the best-preserved of three ancient temple complexes at Deir el-Bahari. Its three colonnaded terraces imitate the architectural style of Mentuhotep II's much earlier complex immediately to the south.

The temple was visited by Western travelers at least as early as the eighteenth century, and by the nineteenth century it was well known to local villagers as a lucrative source of antiquities such as coffins and mummies. The Prussian Egyptologist Carl Richard Lepsius was the first to identify Hatshepsut as the founder of the temple, but the first large-scale excavations at the site were undertaken by Auguste Mariette in the mid-nineteenth century. The architectural style of the temple is unlike any other in Egypt (apart from the eleventh-dynasty structure immediately next door to it), and Mariette described it as "an exception and an accident in the architectural life of Egypt." Even though more than half of the site was still engulfed in sand, by Mariette's time Deir el-Bahari was widely recognized as the most unusual and distinctive New Kingdom cult temple on the west bank at Thebes. In his first season, Mariette uncovered much of the southern part of the temple, including a chapel of the goddess Hathor and the section of the middle colonnade decorated with painted reliefs depicting an expedition to the exotic land of Punt (see below).

In 1892, the Egypt Exploration Fund (EEF) decided to embark on a major series of excavations at Deir el-Bahari in order to reveal the entire temple of Hatshepsut. The directors appointed Edouard Naville as their field director, thus instigating a new flashpoint in a long-running feud between Naville

The modern site of Deir
el-Bahari is dominated by the
three terraces of Hatshepsut's
mortuary temple at the
northern end of this semicircular bay in the Theban
cliffs, but the ruins of the
much earlier temple of
Mentuhotep II are also clearly
visible beside it.

138

and Flinders Petrie, both of whom had begun to work for the EEF in the
1880s. Petrie was convinced that Naville would neglect vital information by
concentrating only on the temple's columns and reliefs rather than on the
artifacts that could document its precise date and function. By his own admission, Naville was concerned more with monumental architecture than
with "small objects," and Petrie eventually managed to persuade the EEF to
send Naville to work at Karnak instead, where "he can do a minimum of
harm." But by the time this message was conveyed to Naville, already out
in Egypt, he had gained permission to work at Deir el-Bahari; he began
work there in February 1893, essentially ignoring the EEF's letter.

The name Deir el-Bahari means "northern monastery," and when Naville
began work, the site was still dominated by the mud-brick remains of the
Coptic monastery of Saint Phoebamon, which had been constructed on top
of the temple, transforming the ancient "southern hall of offerings" into a
church. Assisted by John Newberry as architect and Howard Carter as epigrapher, recording the painted reliefs and inscriptions as they were revealed,
Naville began to remove one of several deep mounds at the northern end
of the temple. Like many other early twentieth century excavators in Egypt,
he used the so-called Decauville carriages running on about 1,500 feet of
temporary railway tracks to speed up the removal of this upper layer of debris, employing a team of about 200 workmen to dig and to fill and empty
the carriages. The work proceeded at a rapid pace, primarily because—just
as Petrie had predicted—Naville was not spending much time on recording
the remains. (Indeed, ironically, his spoil heaps were steadily covering up a
part of the site where Herbert Winlock of the Metropolitan Museum, over
thirty years later, would find a tomb belonging to Hatshepsut's right-hand

man, Senenmut.) Naville uncovered the entire northern part of the upper terrace of the temple in a matter of weeks. The finds in this first season included a "northern hall of offerings," a chapel of Thutmose I, and the so-called altar court, in the center of which was a large limestone platform measuring 15 by 12 feet (4.9 by 4 meters) in area, intended for offerings to the sun god Ra-Horakhty.

In the second season (1893–1894), Naville uncovered the northern part of the middle terrace. To do so, he had to clear a diverse mixture of Mariette's spoil: Coptic remains, and a cemetery including burials from the Third Intermediate Period through to the Roman Period. This process might have taken the meticulous Petrie several seasons, but Naville claimed to have cleared an area of some 69,000 square feet (6,410 square meters) in about five months, removing some 78,500 cubic yards (60,000 cubic meters) of material, including a large number of coffins and mummies destined for the museums and private collectors who had sponsored the excavation (but, unsurprisingly, very few "small objects," or at least very few that were recorded). By early 1894, he had uncovered the reliefs along the northern portico of the middle terrace and had found a shrine dedicated to Anubis that paralleled the shrine of Hathor found by Mariette at the southern end of the portico. About halfway through this season, the EEF sent out yet another archaeologist, David George Hogarth, supposedly to assist Naville but actually to act as a spy, reporting on the standard of his work. As it turned out, Hogarth reported—no doubt to Petrie's great annoyance—that Naville's techniques were "satisfactory and appropriate to a site with such complex stratigraphy."

In his final season of excavation (1894–1895), Naville concentrated on the lowest terrace, finding a portico with reliefs showing the queen as a sphinx triumphing over her enemies and a fascinating set of scenes describing the quarrying and transportation of two granite obelisks from the quarries at Aswan (see chapter 6). This turned out to be the section of the temple that had been most severely damaged by the reuse of stone for the monastery, leading Naville to turn his attention to dismantling the remaining parts of the monastery itself; as a result, many sections of the temple were able to be restored, including some of the missing parts of the reliefs depicting the expedition to Punt.

The final stage of the EEF work at Hatshepsut's temple was the longest and most laborious of all: the process of epigraphic work and architectural restoration, which was undertaken by Carter and various assistants over the course of six seasons (1893–1898). To accomplish this, Carter pioneered an epigraphic method involving tracings made directly from the reliefs that were then reduced to a size suitable for publication by the use of a grid superimposed over the tracing.

Carter also made a significant contribution to the archaeological work with his discovery of the remains of a destroyed building on the edge of the cultivation, at the end of a long causeway running eastward from Hatshepsut's temple. He excavated "foundation deposits" (pits containing sacred objects, which were placed beneath the foundations of temples) and several blocks of stone bearing painted decoration. These were evidently all that remained of the valley temple of Hatshepsut's complex. Underneath some of the blocks there were ink graffiti identifying the architect of the building as a man called Puyemra.

How Did Hatshepsut Legitimize Her Rule As a Female Pharaoh?

One of the most intriguing reliefs discovered by Naville in the portico of the second terrace of Hatshepsut's temple at Deir el-Bahari was a scene showing the conception and birth of the queen as a result of sexual union between her mother, Ahmose, and the god Amun, alongside images of the creator god Khnum fashioning both the queen and her *ka* (a kind of spiritual double) on a potter's wheel. Finally, the queen is shown being purified by the gods Ra-Horakhty and Amun and crowned by Horus and Seth in the presence of her father, Thutmose I. Naville would have recognized immediately that this set of reliefs was comparable with those depicted in the so-called Birth Room at Luxor temple, showing the divine birth of the king.

Is it significant that the temple of Hatshepsut at Deir el-Bahari and Amenhotep III's section of the Luxor temple both include scenes showing the divine births of these rulers? There are at least three different points of

Scene at Deir el-Bahari showing the conception and birth of the queen as a result of sexual union between her mother Ahmose and the god Amun, alongside images of the creator-god Khnum fashioning both the queen and her *ka* (a kind of spiritual double) on a potter's wheel.

view on this question. One popular interpretation is that the queen, as a female ruler, was obliged to go to much greater lengths than her male counterparts to emphasize that she was indeed the legitimate ruler. There are, however, a number of flaws in this solution. First, we would need to explain why Amenhotep III had similar scenes carved in the Luxor temple, when he was a male ruler with no more apparent need to bolster his claims to the throne than any other eighteenth-dynasty rulers had. Second, several major temples from the Late Period on, such as Dendera and Edfu, include a building known as a *mammisi* ("birth house"), which was used to celebrate the divine birth of the king, and the reliefs in these structures have enough in common with the birth scenes of Hatshepsut to suggest that the former might be a later version of the latter; if this is the case, then the Hatshepsut instance seems even less like a unique solution invented by a female ruler.

Statue of Hatshepsut from her temple at Deir el-Bahari.

This "*mammisi* factor" leads neatly to another point of view: some scholars point out that it is sheer chance that complete versions of these scenes have survived only in temples belonging to these two rulers, and that some surviving fragments show the same event for other rulers' lives. Such scenes might simply not have been preserved for the rest of the New Kingdom, leaving an accidental gap in our archaeological knowledge until the appearance of the first known *mammisi*s in the Late Period.

A third point of view, first suggested by Colin Campbell in 1912, is that the motivation for the birth scenes of Hatshepsut and Amenhotep III was essentially religious rather than political, concerned with the replacement of the cult of the sun god Ra in the kingship by that of the ram god Amun. In other words, the primary aim of the scenes of the divine birth of Hatshepsut and Amenhotep III might have been not so much to legitimize the claim of that particular ruler but to make the more general point that all Egyptian kings were the sons of *Amun* rather than of Ra. A possible counterargument against this theory, however, is that Amun was already being described as the king's father as early as the reign of Ahmose.

Egypt and Punt: Long-Distance Trade in the Pharaonic Period

The middle terrace of Hatshepsut's temple includes an unusual group of painted reliefs showing a trading expedition to Punt, a region of East Africa to which Egyptian missions were sent from at least the fifth dynasty (2465–2323 B.C.) on. There is still some debate regarding the precise location of Punt. Although it was once identified with the region of modern Somalia, a strong argument has now been made for its location in southern Sudan or the Eritrean region of Ethiopia, where the flora and fauna correspond best with those depicted in Egyptian reliefs.

The Deir el-Bahari scenes of the Puntites' village show conical reed-built huts built on poles above the ground, entered via ladders. The surrounding

vegetation includes palms and myrrh trees, some in the process of being hacked apart in order to extract the myrrh. The ruler of Punt is distinguished from the Egyptians primarily by his beard and unusual costume, and his wife is depicted as an extremely obese woman—a detail that was evidently so striking that an ancient artist working in the Valley of the Kings later copied it in a rough caricature sketched on a fragment of limestone. The scenes also show living myrrh trees being loaded onto ships so that the Egyptians could produce their own aromatics from them. There are some traces of tree-pits in front of the lowest terrace at Deir el-Bahari, and so it seems likely that the trees depicted in these reliefs were replanted nearby in the temple.

Apart from myrrh, the Egyptians brought back many exotic animals, raw materials, and other products from Punt, including gold, resins, ebony, African blackwood, ivory, slaves, and wild animals, including monkeys and the sacred *Cynocephalus* baboons. The Egyptians also appear to have brought pygmies from Punt, judging from the funerary inscription of Harkhuf, an expedition leader at the time of the reign of Pepy II (2246–2152 B.C.), about seven centuries before Hatshepsut (see chapter 6). Some trading missions evidently traveled overland to Punt, but the more common route was by sea, usually departing from the ports of Quseir or Mersa Gawasis on the western shore of the Red Sea. A number of literary works and love poems (such as the *Tale of the Shipwrecked Sailor*) include references to Punt, which the Egyptians seem to have regarded as such a far-off and exotic land that it must have been almost the equivalent of Atlantis in the modern world.

Polish Excavations and Reconstructions

In 1962, a group of archaeologists from the Polish Center of Mediterranean Archaeology in Cairo discovered the temple of Thutmose III at Deir el-Bahari. They had begun work the previous year, primarily with the intention of pursuing a long-term program of reconstruction, so that the original appearance of each of the terraces of Hatshepsut's temple could be re-created as faithfully as possible.

While the team was attempting to clear a pile of rubble at the southern end of Hatshepsut's temple, they came upon the remains of *djeser-akhet* ("the sacred horizon"), a temple built by Thutmose III and dedicated to the god Amun as well as the cult of the king himself and his royal ancestors. Thutmose's temple was squeezed in between the temples of Mentuhotep and Hatshsepsut. The main section of the temple was eventually excavated in the cliffs, a little higher than Hatshepsut's uppermost terrace; there, about sixty years earlier, Naville had found a shrine from a chapel dedicated to the goddess Hathor, which was originally attached to Thutmose III's temple. Since the temple had been largely destroyed in ancient times, the Polish work has consisted mainly of the painstaking piecing together of many thousands of fragments of the painted reliefs that decorated its walls. However, sufficient columns and other pieces of architecture have survived *in situ* that it is now possible to discern the basic plan of the temple from aerial photographs.

Gaston Maspero and the Royal Mummies

In 1871, an eleventh-dynasty shaft-tomb (DB320) at the southern end of Deir el-Bahari was discovered and gradually robbed by a local family, the infamous Abd el-Rassuls. Over a period of almost ten years, items of funerary

Aerial photograph of the temple of Thutmose III, which was squeezed into the space between the monuments of Hatshepsut and Mentuhotep II.

equipment were stolen from the tomb, which contained a cache of about forty royal mummies from the Valley of the Kings. It was only when it began to be noticed that unusually high numbers of royal funerary items were appearing on the art market that investigations were conducted to try to find out the source of the material. Eventually, Abd el-Rassul Ahmed, the head of the family, admitted the existence of the tomb to the authorities, claiming the reward that was on offer for such information.

In 1881, the tomb was finally officially excavated by Émile Brugsch, the assistant of Gaston Maspero, then head of the Egyptian Antiquities Service. He later described the moments of the discovery itself:

> A cluster of mummy cases came into view in such number as to
> stagger me. Collecting my senses, I made the best examination of
> them I could by the light of my torch, and at once saw that they
> contained the mummies of royal personages of both sexes; and
> yet that was not all. Plunging on ahead of my guide . . . I found
> even a greater number of mummy-cases of stupendous size and
> weight. Their gold coverings and their polished surfaces so
> plainly reflected my own excited visage that it seemed as though
> I was looking into the faces of my own ancestors.

Terrified that the local villagers might be prepared to murder him for the contents of the tomb, Brugsch emptied it very rapidly. Within a few days, the mummies and funerary equipment were being shipped up the Nile to the main museum at Bulaq, near Cairo. The combination of the Abd el-Rassuls' ten years of robbing and the great haste of Brugsch's excavations means that the archaeological context of the royal mummies is now very confused.

The kings whose bodies lay in the "Deir el-Bahari cache" were Seqenenra Tao II, Ahmose I, Amenhotep I, Thutmose I, II and III, Sety I, Ramesses II, III, and IX, and Pinudjem I and II. On the basis of ink inscriptions in the hieratic script written on mummy bandages and wooden dockets attached to the coffins and mummies, it became apparent that they had been deliberately reinterred at Deir el-Bahari by twenty-first-dynasty priests, presumably to safeguard them at a time when robbery was rife in the Valley of the Kings. Maspero noticed that there were two sets of mummies: one group dated to the Second Intermediate Period and New Kingdom, and the other to the Third Intermediate Period. What was puzzling, from an archaeological point of view, was the fact that the more recent mummies were evidently found in the inner part of the tomb and the earlier ones nearer the entrance, exactly the reverse of what would logically be expected.

For a long time, this problem of the date and positions of the mummies proved intractable, but recent reexaminations of the tomb and study of the dockets and bandages have helped to clarify matters. The most likely scenario now seems to be that the earlier mummies of the kings and various family members were initially moved from their resting places in the Valley of the Kings to the tomb of Queen Ahmose-Inhapy, perhaps the tomb now known as WNA, which is situated high in the cliffs about 820 yards (750 meters) southwest of DB320. They were subsequently moved again, during the twenty-second dynasty, to DB320, which appears to have been the family tomb of the chief priest Pinudjem II (hence the positioning of these Third Intermediate Period mummies in the inner part of the tomb).

A second "mummy cache" consisting of 153 reburied mummies of twenty-first-dynasty priests was found in a tomb at Deir el-Bahari in 1891. Seven years later, another cache of royal mummies was found in the tomb of Amenhotep II in the Valley of the Kings (KV35) by the French Egyptologist Victor Loret (see chapter 13).

The Tombs of Meketra and Senenmut

Three other highly significant tombs were excavated at Deir el-Bahari: one belonging to Meketra, and two made for Senenmut. The careers of these two important officials were separated by more than five centuries. All three tombs were excavated by teams from the Metropolitan Museum, New York.

The tomb of Meketra (TT 280), chancellor in the time of Mentuhotep II and III (c. 2055–1992 B.C.), consisted of a large courtyard and a portico of octagonal columns, but the decorated reliefs inside have survived only patchily. The tomb itself and its equipment have been redated to the reign of Amenemhat I (c. 1985–1965 B.C.). The burial chamber contained more

Excavator's photo of the interior of the tomb of Meketra.

Detail of a wooden boat
model from the tomb of
Meketra (late eleventh/early
twelfth dynasty).

146

than 1,200 model tools and weapons, as well as Meketra's coffin, and in
1919–1920, Herbert Winlock discovered twenty-five models of his estate
under the floor. The tomb of Wah, the inspector of Meketra's storehouses,
was located in the courtyard of Meketra's tomb; it was discovered intact in
the 1920s, the entrance having been blocked by chips of rock and a brick
wall. The small, undecorated burial chamber contained Wah's complete coffin and mummy wrapped in 9,100 square feet (845 square meters) of linen,
including a gilt stucco mask with a beard and moustache, as well as scarabs
and necklaces. The only other equipment in the tomb was a meal of bread,
beer, and meat placed beside his coffin.

Senenmut, the influential and powerful "chief steward" of Hatshepsut,
built two tombs for himself. The first (TT71) is high on the hillside at Sheikh
Abd el-Qurna and still preserves a rock-cut block-statue portraying him in
his role as royal tutor, with Hatshepsut's daughter Neferura seated on his
lap. This is one of six surviving block statues of Senenmut and Neferura,
although the rest are free-standing rather than rock-cut. About 150 ostraca
were found in this tomb, including sketch-plans of the tomb itself and various literary texts.

Senenmut later began a second and grander tomb (TT353) to the east of
the first court of the temple of Hatshepsut at Deir el-Bahari. This is sometimes described as the "secret tomb" and was one found by Winlock buried
underneath some of Naville's spoil heaps. Its walls are decorated with scenes
from the *Book of the Dead*, and its roof is the earliest known "astronomical
ceiling." The tomb was never completed, and, like the images of Senenmut

at Deir el-Bahari and elsewhere, it was defaced in antiquity. This defacement probably resulted from some fall from grace, since there is no further
record of Senenmut from late in the reign of Hatshepsut.

Senenmut's duties included overseeing the royal building works at Thebes,
a duty mentioned on one of his many surviving statues. It was probably as
a result of his influence in construction projects that he was able to have
himself portrayed in the temple at Deir el-Bahari, although his figures stand
behind shrine doors in the sun court at the north of the temple, where they
were not readily visible. He is also credited with organizing the transport
and erection of the two great obelisks of Hatshepsut in the temple of Amun
at Karnak, as depicted on the lower terrace of the Deir el-Bahari temple.

Senenmut's numerous titles included the roles of steward of Amun and
tutor to Hatshepsut's only daughter Neferura. There is no evidence that
Senenmut ever married, and he is usually depicted only with his parents or
with Neferura. This has led some scholars to speculate that he may even
have been Hatshepsut's lover, although evidence for this theory is distinctly
flimsy. Neferura died in Hatshepsut's eleventh regnal year, and it has been
theorized that Senenmut may then have attempted to ally himself with
Thutmose III (1479–1425 B.C.), with whom Hatshepsut was supposedly co-
regent. The American Egyptologist Peter Dorman has suggested that
Senenmut may have outlived Hatshepsut and continued as an unrecorded
official during the sole reign of Thutmose III.

Several modern histories of ancient Egypt have claimed that Senenmut
must have enjoyed unusual influence during the queen's reign because of
her need to rely on at least one male courtier to bolster her tenuous claims
to the throne. In 1961, for instance, Alan Gardiner argued:

> It is not to be imagined . . . that even a woman of the most vir-
> ile character could have attained such a pinnacle of power with-
> out masculine support. The Theban necropolis still displays many
> splendid tombs of her officials, all speaking of her with cringing
> deference. But among them one man stands out preeminent.

In 1967, the Canadian Egyptologist Donald Redford went so far as to
write that "her steward Senenmut, a man of low origin . . . throughout
most of her reign appears to have been something of a power behind the
throne . . . She had a circle of favorites, a motley collection of individuals
with no common background and little reason to share political goals."

However, the French Egyptologist Suzanne Ratié strikes a much more
objective note on the careers of both Senenmut and his queen:

> The personality of Senenmut was . . . rich and complex.
> Certain aspects of his career are impenetrable. It seems that his
> influence is visible in all the great achievements of the reign at
> least until year 16. It is difficult to differentiate the role played by

A "block" statue of Neferura,
the only child of Hatshepsut
and Tuthmosis II, and her
tutor Senenmut. Senenmut
held many high official positions during the reign of
Hatshepsut. He was the
queen's chief architect and
was in charge of the construction of her great temple at
Deir el-Bahari.

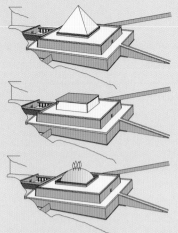

Three reconstruction drawings of the mortuary temple of Mentuhotep II.

148

In 1897, while Naville was still engaged on the study of Hatshepsut's temple, he had already dug a sondage (test pit) to the south of the queen's enclosure wall, uncovering an intriguing group of eleventh-dynasty tombs. Six years later, he finally managed to persuade the Egypt Exploration Fund to provide the extra funds to allow him to excavate this part of the site. This time, however, he was given a co-director: H.R.H. Hall, an employee of the British Museum, whose greater interest in antiquities, as opposed to architecture, seems to have ensured that a much higher proportion of objects were recorded and published, compared with the work on the Hatshepsut temple.

Statue of Mentuhotep II from his cenotaph at Deir el-Bahari.

Beneath piles of debris comparable with those that had already been moved from the northern part of the site, Naville and Hall gradually uncovered an unusual terraced funerary complex, the reconstruction of which is still a matter of debate among Egyptologists. Naville believed that the major structure against the cliffs at the western end of the complex had been a pyramid, but this is now considered unlikely. The temple as a whole appears to have been an ingenious combination of elements of the local Theban *saff*-tomb, the Old Kingdom *mastaba*-tomb, and the symbolism of the Primeval Mound. Within a month after commencing the work, sandstone columns bearing a king's name had been excavated. These showed that the complex belonged to Mentuhotep II Nebhepetra, the eleventh-dynasty founder of the Middle Kingdom. The complex incorporated a cenotaph containing a seated statue of the king, as well as the tombs of six of his queens, including a magnificent set of limestone sarcophagi. More than 500 years later, the plan of his temple was copied and elaborated by Hatshepsut in the design of her own temple next door.

the queen and her "advisor" in various decisions and activities. We use the term "advisor" to describe Senenmut, but we deliberately avoid the use of the term "favorite," for this aspect of the lives of Hatshepsut and Senenmut is completely out of our reach and does not rest on any objective evidence.

Further Reading

The earliest significant archaeological report on the temple of Hatshepsut at Deir el-Bahari is Edouard Naville's seven-volume publication, *The Temple of Deir el-Bahari* (London, 1894–1908). Joyce Tildesley's *Hatchepsut: The Female Pharaoh* (Harmondsworth, 1998) includes discussion of a range of current views on the nature and symbolism of her cult temple. The most recent Polish work at Deir el-Bahari is described in a three-volume work edited by Z. Wysocki, *The Temple of Queen Hatshepsut* (Warsaw, 1980–1985).

The temple of Thutmose III is described by the Polish Egyptologist Jadwiga Lipinska in *Deir el-Bahari* II: *The Temple of Tuthmosis III* (Warsaw, 1974). Peter Dorman has written two detailed discussions of the career and monuments of Senenmut: *The Monuments of Senenmut: Problems in Historical Methodology* (London, 1988), and *The Tombs of Senenmut* (New York, 1991).

The temple of Mentuhotep II was first published by Naville as *The Eleventh Dynasty Temple at Deir el Bahari* (London, 1907–1913), but the most up-to-date report is that of Dieter Arnold in *The Temple of Mentuhotep at Deir el-Bahari* (New York, 1979). Herbert Winlock's discovery of the tomb of Meketra was published as *Excavations at Deir el-Bahari, 1911–31* (New York, 1942). The royal mummies from tomb DB320 were first published in Gaston Maspero's *Les momies royales de Deir el-Bahari* (Cairo, 1889). More recent discussion and analysis are provided by Nicholas Reeves in *Valley of the Kings: The Decline of a Royal Necropolis* (London, 1990).

Further Viewing

Painted blocks from Hatshepsut's valley temple, an early statue of the queen (already represented as king), and the burial equipment of Meketra can all be seen in the Metropolitan Museum, New York. The chapel of the cow goddess Hathor from Thutmose III's temple is on display in the Egyptian Museum, Cairo, complete with a full-scale statue of a cow wearing sun-disk and feathers, with a figure of the king standing in front. The items displayed in the recently opened Museum of Mummification at Luxor include the twenty-first-dynasty mummy and coffin of the chief priest Masaharta, son of Pinudjem I, and the coffin of Padiamun, all of which derive from the cache of mummies and coffins found in tomb DB320 at Deir el-Bahari.

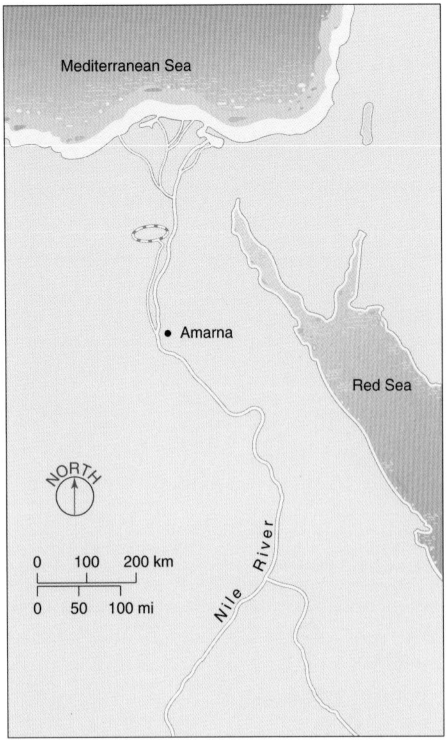

The map contains labels: Mediterranean Sea, Amarna, Red Sea, NORTH, Nile River, 0 100 200 km, 0 50 100 mi

Amarna

c. 1360–1330 B.C.

City of the Heretic King

A few miles south of the modern town of Mallawi, the high cliffs on the east bank of the Nile open out to form a large semicircular expanse of desert approximately 6 miles (10 kilometers) long and a maximum of 3 miles (5 kilometers) wide, with a thin strip of cultivation along its western edge, beside the river. At 11 miles (17 kilometers), this is probably the widest section of the floodplain in Egypt, and in recent years improved irrigation techniques have been employed by the inhabitants of the villages of et-Till and Hagg Qandil at the northern and southern ends of the site. Thus, the area of cultivated land has expanded farther into the desert, gradually eating away at the edges of the remarkably well-preserved archaeological remains of Amarna.

The origins and history of the New Kingdom settlement at Amarna are inextricably linked with the reign of Akhenaten (1352–1336 B.C.), the infamous "heretic" pharaoh. Born in the early fourteenth century B.C., he was the son of Amenhotep III (1390–1352 B.C.) and probably came to the throne some years before the death of his father (although there is considerable debate as to whether there was any "co-regency" between the two). In his fifth regnal year, he made two crucial and iconoclastic decisions: he changed his name from Amenhotep ("Amun is content") to Akhenaten ("glory of the sun-disk"); and he began to construct a new capital city called Akhetaten ("horizon

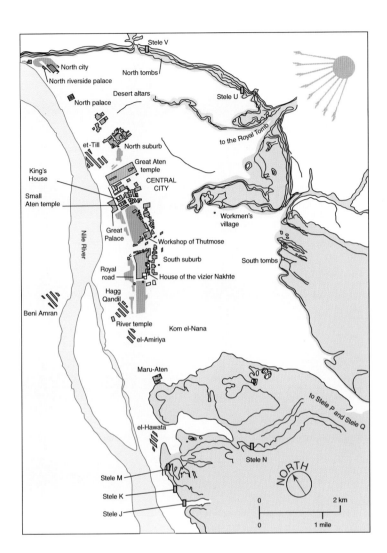

Map of "greater Akhetaten," showing the locations of the boundary stelae marking out the edges of the city on the Nile (after Kemp, 1989).

to the Aten") at the site now known as Amarna in Middle Egypt. This newly founded settlement was evidently intended to replace both Memphis and Thebes as the religious and administrative center of the country. The site has given its name to the brief phase in Egyptian history (about twenty years) consisting of Akhenaten's reign and that of his ephemeral successor, Smenkhkara: the Amarna Period.

There are, therefore, many aspects of the site of Amarna that are unusual and surprising, but one of the most important aspects of the site, from the point of view of archaeologists, is the fact that the city was largely abandoned as little as fifteen years after it had been founded. The majority of the site was occupied only for a single generation in the mid-fourteenth century B.C. The first excavators at the site called it Tell el-Amarna (because of the presence of the village of et-Till), but it is not a tell-site in the true sense of the

Many of the surviving reliefs from Amarna, like this one (now in the Egyptian Museum, Berlin), show the king, queen, and princesses making offerings to the Aten.

word. Such mounds usually consist of many interleaved and superimposed layers of occupation, but the settlement remains at Amarna are virtually all of one period, and the walls of the houses often stand to a height of several feet, never having been leveled by succeeding inhabitants.

Akhenaten and the Foundation of the City of Akhetaten

Few city sites in the history of the world can have been so closely linked to the personality and activities of one individual. The figure of Akhenaten, the tenth ruler of the eighteenth dynasty, completely dominates the city of Akhetaten ("horizon of the Aten"), which he founded in about 1350 B.C. as both a new Egyptian capital and a cult center for the Aten, a deity whose name simply means "disk," the sun-disk being the most obvious physical manifestation of the sun god. When Akhenaten first appeared on the scene, he was still linked, both by name and monuments, with the "state-god" Amun, but by the second year of his reign he had begun to construct new temples dedicated to the Aten, particularly at East Karnak. He also instituted a process of religious change in which Amun was reviled and his name removed from monuments. Whereas all other Egyptian kings (even Hatshepsut, one of the few female rulers) portrayed themselves in an idealistic manner as paragons of masculinity, Akhenaten deliberately chose to have himself depicted as a grotesque amalgam of male and female characteristics, perhaps in an attempt to symbolize the fertility of the sun cult. As his ideology hardened, the worship of the entire Egyptian pantheon was proscribed, apart from the Aten and a few other deities closely associated with the sun cult. A tantalizing inscription on a block from one of the temples to the Aten at Karnak appears to spell out the way in which Akhenaten dealt with the other gods, but the surviving text is too brief and fragmented to provide more than a vague idea.

By the fifth year of his reign, the king had changed his name to Akhenaten ("glory/spirit of the Aten") and had founded Akhetaten, a new royal city at the virgin site of Amarna, untarnished by the cult centers of any other gods, thus abandoning the traditional administrative centers of Thebes and Memphis. Akhetaten is the most complete major pharaonic city to have survived, and its value for the study of Egyptian town-life is almost incalculable. Fragmentary areas of towns have survived at sites such as Elephantine and Tell el-Dab'a, but so far it is only at Amarna that a comprehensive range of official and residential buildings is visible, showing in its plan the essential elements of an Egyptian royal city in the mid-fourteenth century B.C.

The City

The city of Akhetaten extends for about 4.5 miles (7 kilometers) from the North City and North Palace down to the Maru Aten in the south. An unknown proportion of the settlement (including, at the very least, the main residence of the king, and presumably also harbors and quays), has now vanished under the cultivation at the western edge of the site. However, a huge number of buildings have been preserved in the desert to the east, along with the wells, grain silos, bakeries, and refuse dumps that were the fundamental framework of production and consumption throughout the community.

The borders of the city were marked out by a set of at least fourteen rock-cut "boundary stelae," carved in Akhenaten's fifth, sixth, and eighth regnal years; these bear reliefs and inscriptions describing the proposed nature of the new city. Some of the stelae are located to the west of the Nile, evidently outlining the extent of the farmland on which the population of Akhetaten must have relied for basic supplies of grain. The inscriptions nar-

The edges of the city at Amarna were marked out by a series of so-called boundary stelae, several of which were flanked by statues of the king and his family. Their prime purpose seems to have been to indicate that the enclosed area of land, in which the city of Akhetaten was founded, was dedicated to the Aten, the god of the sun-disk.

rate the king's arrival at the site and his decision to found the city. They also give numerous details concerning the ceremonial buildings and tombs that were to be constructed. The kernel of the city, the basic components of which are described in the inscriptions on the boundary stelae, was the central cluster of official buildings called the "Island of Aten distinguished in jubilees." This consisted of two temples to the Aten (the larger at the northern end of the central city and the smaller at the southern end), a palace of Akhenaten connected by a bridge to a mud-brick royal residence (the so-called King's House), a series of magazines, barracks, and offices, the residence of a chief priest, and a set of houses comprising a "central village," which were probably the dwellings or workplaces of the lowlier bureaucrats employed in the public buildings.

To the north and south of the central city extended the houses of Akhenaten's subjects, ranging from ramshackle mud huts to the cool and spacious villas inhabited by his wealthiest courtiers. The total population is estimated to have been somewhere between 20,000 and 50,000, and probably about three-quarters of them were housed in the area usually called the South Suburb, which stretched from the smaller Aten temple down at least as far south as the site of the temple known as the Maru Aten. Whereas most of the major public buildings throughout the city were clearly aligned with one another according to the original plan, the arrangement of the residential areas was much more complicated.

The earliest houses in the South Suburb were evidently the largest villas, built on plots of land probably assigned to favored individuals from the outset. These buildings and their surrounding estates are roughly aligned with the main ceremonial road, the Sikkat es-Sultan, which runs through the entire city from north to south. This road (still used today by the increasingly frequent motor traffic) undoubtedly formed the major route for the royal party as they processed in chariots between the principal temples and palaces. The rest of the houses, which gradually filled in the gaps between the great villas, were arranged much more haphazardly, roughly organized into neighborhoods through the presence of a few major streets leading eastward or westward from the main north-south artery. The heterogeneity of the residential buildings suggests that the population included a wide range of levels of wealth, and in many cases the excavated objects provide clues that the inhabitants practiced such trades as carpenter or metalworker. It seems likely that individuals throughout the city were exchanging goods and services among themselves, but this evidence for private enterprise is counterbalanced to some extent by the location of most of the grain stores and wells in the grounds of the largest houses, and the presence of vast temple bakeries in the central city, all of which suggest that the most basic aspects of the economy—the provision of bread, beer, and water—were strongly centralized.

Although the mud-brick elements of the temples and palaces at the site have survived very well, the vast majority of the temple masonry was re-

In this aerial view of the southern part of the center of the city at Amarna (taken in the 1930s) it is possible to see the clear outline of several of the main public buildings erected by Akhenaten. In the foreground is the so-called Mansion of the Aten, the smaller of the two main temples at Amarna, which may have served as Akhenaten's mortuary temple.

moved by Akhenaten's successors, who regarded him as a heretic and used the blocks from his constructions simply as rubble to fill the interiors of walls and gateways at cities such as Hermopolis Magna, on the other side of the Nile about 12 miles (20 kilometers) to the northwest. Fortunately, however, the basic ground plans of the stone buildings at Amarna have survived to some extent in the form of painted lines and masons' marks laid out on the original plaster over which the foundation blocks were laid.

We can also gain some idea of the original appearance of these temples from the painted decoration in the rock-cut tombs of Akhenaten's high officials, which were cut into the cliffs at the northern and southern ends of the site. These depictions suggest that the religious architecture of the Aten was quite different from that of traditional Egyptian deities; whereas the conventional Egyptian temple comprised a succession of colonnaded courts and hypostyle halls leading to a dark sanctuary containing the cult statue, the two principal temples in the center of the city at Amarna largely consisted of wide courts open to the sky, entered through mud-brick pylon gateways and filled with offering tables and altars. Having replaced the old gods with a single abstract sun-disk, Akhenaten's temples were evidently geared simply toward the repeated dedication of offerings to the Aten by the royal family, instead of the time-honored sequence of rituals and festivals based primarily on the maintenance and movement of cult statues.

Akhetaten and the Archaeologists

The site of Amarna had undoubtedly been the target of a great deal of unsystematic collection and excavation even before Sir John Gardner Wilkinson surveyed it (calling it the city of "Alabastron") in 1824. The exposure of large amounts of brickwork, which ensured that a great deal of the "central city" could be mapped by the Prussian archaeologist Richard Lepsius without resort to excavation, is an indication of the extent to which the site had already been sporadically cleared by the 1840s. Lepsius's team also copied the scenes depicted in several of the tombs and on some of the boundary stelae, providing the main sources of information on the Amarna Period for about fifty years, until Flinders Petrie's work revealed fresh evidence in the main city. By the end of the nineteenth century, the surface of the site had already been disturbed through a combination of *sebakhin* (the Arabic word for those who remove for agricultural purposes the fertile soil, or *sebakh,* of which most ancient mud-brick remains are composed), casual local surface collection, and organized "treasure-hunting." Nevertheless, large areas of the site remain unexcavated today, despite the fact that in the course of nearly fifty seasons of excavation over a period of more than a century, the site has been dug by several generations of archaeologists using a variety of methods and strategies. To list the individuals who have worked at Amarna is to recite a roll-call of prominent

The depictions of the royal family at Amarna often incorporate Akhenaten's many daughters. This painting, delicately removed by Petrie from the wall of one of the rooms of the so-called King's House, shows two of the younger princesses at the feet of their parents and elder sisters during a feast.

archaeologists of the past hundred years, from Petrie and Howard Carter to Ludwig Borchardt and Sir Leonard Woolley.

The excavations of Petrie, assisted by Carter, between November 1891 and May 1892, uncovered a variety of structures in the central city and South Suburb. They studied the two largest buildings in the central city—the Great Palace and the Great Temple—as well as a dozen of the houses in the residential parts of the city. Petrie was particularly successful in his discovery and removal of sections of painted plaster from the floors and walls of the public buildings, including a mural depiction of two of Akhenaten's youngest daughters seated at the feet of their elders during a lavish feast (now in the Ashmolean Museum, Oxford). He also uncovered a large, exquisitely painted section of floor in the harem quarters of the Great Palace, but this was subjected to modern vandalism. Having roofed it over to form a kind of on-site museum, Petrie had left it in the care of a group of locals, but it was soon ripped up in an act of malice apparently prompted by a village feud. Although Petrie's work provided an excellent basis for later excavations at the site, the remains at Amarna are extremely diverse, and his characteristically industrious season could really do no more than scratch the surface.

There was no more archaeological work in the city for about fifteen years, but in 1901, the British epigrapher Norman de Garis Davies embarked on the formidable task of copying the scenes and inscriptions from the many rock-tombs and boundary stelae in the cliffs surrounding Amarna. He worked for about two months every year until 1907, publishing the results of his labors in the six volumes of *Rock Tombs of El Amarna,* which also include invaluable photographs of the interiors. The scenes recorded by Davies are virtually the only surviving insights into the historical events that took place at Amarna, such as Akhenaten's ceremonial reception of tribute from foreigners in the twelfth year of his reign, and the apparent arrival of his mother Queen Tiy as a resident in the city at some unknown date.

The elegant painted head of Nefertiti, found in a sculptor's studio that probably belonged to a chief craftsman called Thutmose, is probably the most famous artifact from Amarna. Excavated by the German archaeologist Ludwig Borchard, this bust is now in the Egyptian Museum in Berlin, where it has achieved cult status among Berliners.

It was the general surveying work of the German archaeologist Paul Timme in 1911 that provided the first real sense of the site in its full topographical and geographical setting. Timme's survey, which was not actually published until 1917, formed part of the same project as the large-scale clearances of the classically trained German excavator Ludwig Borchardt from 1907 to 1914. Borchardt's work concentrated almost exclusively on uncovering large areas of housing in the South Suburb. It was during this period that the famous painted head of Nefertiti was discovered in the house of the chief sculptor Thutmose, where many other items of unfinished stone and plaster statuary were unearthed. The Nefertiti head, now one of the prize exhibits in the Berlin Museum, has become the supreme icon of the Amarna Period. With the onset of World War I, however, Borchardt lost the concession. When excavations finally resumed in the spring of 1921, it was Eric Peet, assisted by Leonard (later Sir Leonard) Woolley, who directed work on behalf of the Egypt Exploration Society.

Over the next two seasons, Peet and Woolley concentrated on continuing the German work in the South Suburb as well as the excavation of three more peripheral areas: the Workmen's Village, the Maru-Aten, and the so-called River Temple. The Workmen's Village (described in detail below) proved to be a small, relatively self-contained community that serves in some respects as a microcosm of the city as a whole. The Maru-Aten was initially interpreted as some kind of pleasure palace, but it is now widely regarded as a garden-style sanctuary for the worship of the Aten. The River Temple, considered by both Borchardt and Woolley to be an important ceremonial building dating to the post-Amarna period, has now been fairly conclusively identified as a group of houses typical of the Third Intermediate Period (1069–747 B.C.), when a small later town seems to have grown up at the south end of the site. The subsequent British work, directed by Francis Newton, F. Ll. Griffith, Henri Frankfort, and John Pendlebury, covered many different areas of the site, from the comfortable, almost middle-class dwellings of the North Suburb to a group of houses probably belonging to the very highest officials at the northern tip of the site (the North City) as well as the major public buildings in both the central city and the surrounding desert.

One of the most impressive discoveries made during the British work in the 1920s was the North Palace, an isolated structure situated about a mile north of the central city and east of the main north-south route. This extremely well preserved royal palace included not only the expected reception halls and domestic chambers but also a small sun temple, numerous gardens, and a series of rooms in which animals and birds had been kept. Fragments of inscribed blocks from the complex often repeat the name of Meretaten, Akhenaten's eldest daughter, for whom it was probably constructed as a personal residence, independent of the North Riverside Palace (probably the main home of the king and the rest of the royal family), the thick eastern wall of which is preserved less than half a mile to the north.

British work continued at the site until 1936, when the approach of World War II led to the premature cessation of the excavations. John Pendlebury, who had been the director during the last few seasons of the 1930s, died tragically on Crete during the war, and there was no attempt to resume work until 1977, when Barry Kemp undertook a new long-term examination of the site on behalf of the Egypt Exploration Society. This most recent work has combined a broad survey of the area (integrating and reassessing the previous work) with reexcavation of parts of the Central City and detailed and painstaking analysis of two outlying areas: the Workmen's Village, which still contained large unexcavated sections; and the previously neglected site of Kom el-Nana at the southeastern edge of Akhetaten, which has proved to be another temple site, perhaps to be identified with the so-called "sunshade of Queen Nefertiti," one of the buildings mentioned on the earliest boundary stelae.

The Workmen's Village: A Community in the Desert

To the east of the long strip of land occupied by the main city there are two residential areas close to the cliffs: the Workmen's Village and the Stone Village. The latter, still unexcavated, was not discovered until Kemp's 1977 survey of the site. It consists of a group of rough stone houses without any surrounding enclosure wall, covering an area of about an acre (0.4 hectare) and situated about two-thirds of a mile (1 kilometer) east of the Workmen's Village. It may have served a purpose similar to that of the stone huts on the col between the Theban workmen's village at Deir el-Medina and the Valley of the Kings, which seems to have provided temporary accommodation for those tomb-workers who were undertaking their eight-day work shift at the Valley.

The Workmen's Village itself is a much more substantial site, about three-quarters of a mile (1.2 kilometers) east of the main city. It is often compared with the tomb-workers' village at Deir el-Medina (see chapter 13) because both are planned, walled, roughly rectangular settlements located close to elite and royal cemeteries. The Amarna village was excavated by Peet and Woolley in 1921–1922 and by Kemp between 1979 and 1986. It consists of about seventy mud-brick houses arranged in six rows and surrounded by a thick square enclosure wall, with extramural remains of a quarry, animal pens, small garden plots, and chapels. Presumably because of the brief period of occupation, the Amarna village—unlike Deir el-Medina—has no rock-cut tomb chapels, which might otherwise have shed some light on the individuals who occupied the village.

Above all, however, there have been very few written documents found at the Amarna village, whereas the Deir el-Medina equivalent yielded a vast number of ostraca and papyri, forming an invaluable source of information on the history and purpose of the community. Without such texts, and despite more intensive excavation than in any other part of Amarna, the function of the Workmen's Village remains somewhat uncertain. Although it still seems likely that the occupants were employed for at least part of the time as semiskilled laborers on the cutting and decoration of the royal tombs and the tombs of the nobles, there is evidence for animal husbandry (including pig-farming) as well as the possibility of involvement in the policing of the desert to the east of the city, which may have been alternative activities for some of the villagers.

What Happened to the Corpses of Akhenaten and His Courtiers?

Akhenaten stated explicitly in his inscriptions on the boundary stelae that, wherever he died, he should be brought back for burial at Akhetaten, the sacred city of his "father" the Aten. He therefore made provision for building tombs for himself and the rest of his family down a rocky gorge now known as the Wadi Abu Hasah el-Bahari (often called the "royal wadi"), and it has also been suggested that the smaller Aten temple in the central city may have served as a funerary chapel connected with his burial, especially since it is aligned fairly closely with the location of the royal tombs, 7 miles (11 kilometers) to the east.

None of the tombs in the royal wadi was completed, but work was well advanced on one of them, which contains sufficient surviving decoration to indicate that plans were made to bury at least the king and one of the princesses there. This tomb, located in a side wadi, consists of one sequence of descending corridors and steps leading to a small antechamber followed by a large, square, pillared burial chamber. There are also two annexes leading off from the right-hand wall of the descending corridor, the smaller of which comprises a set of three rooms probably intended for the burial of a princess (since scenes from the funeral of at least one of them are depicted in one of the rooms). The larger annex consists of three continuous passages, and it has been suggested that it was intended for Queen Nefertiti. It certainly resembles some Theban tombs of New Kingdom royal women, but the rough, unfinished walls bear no reliefs or inscriptions, and so there is no actual textual evidence to corroborate such a connection.

Apart from a few fragments of two sarcophagi in the main burial chamber of the royal tomb, there is no indication of the whereabouts of the bodies of the king and his family. Given the violent reaction to the king and his cult in the aftermath of the Amarna Period, it is possible that the bodies of Akhenaten, Nefertiti, and Smenkhkara (the ephemeral king who ruled for a very brief period after Akhenaten) were actually destroyed or thrown into the river. There is one other piece of enigmatic evidence relating to the fate of the royal family's bodies: tomb KV55 in the Valley of the Kings, which is discussed in chapter 13.

160

CHAPTER ELEVEN

The high officials of Akhetaten built more than forty rock tombs in two main groups at the northern and southern ends of the site, respectively. Only about half of the tombs were at all close to completion when the site was abandoned, and only one appears to have been used to bury the intended occupant (that of the scribe Any, which contains a set of funerary stelae). Those in the southern group seem to have belonged mainly to courtiers involved in the secular aspects of life at Akhetaten, such as the chief of police Mahu, the royal scribe and steward Ipy, and the royal chamberlain Tutu, perhaps in charge of foreign correspondence. Those in the north were constructed mainly for religious officials such as the priests Meryra and Panehsy. One of the officials who built a tomb for himself in the southern group was an influential figure called Ay, who was probably related to Akhenaten's mother, Queen Tiy. His tomb contains the longest surviving version of the so-called *Hymn to the Aten*. Ay outlived Tiy, Akhenaten, Nefertiti, and even the young king Tutankhamun, and it was he who rose to the throne as the penultimate king of the eighteenth dynasty. By the time that Ay was buried in the Valley of the Kings at Thebes, the city of Akhetaten had already been abandoned, and his successor, Horemheb, commenced the demolition of its stone temples and palaces.

The Amarna Letters

Despite all the religious and political factors that make Amarna such an unusual and important site for Egyptologists, it is for yet another reason that the site is well known to historians of the ancient Near East. Around 1887, a local village woman discovered a cache of cuneiform tablets that were initially regarded as forgeries by local dealers, so unlikely did it seem that an Egyptian site should yield such a hoard of Asiatic-style documents. As a result of this illicit discovery, the 382 known tablets were sold through dealers and dispersed into a number of different collections, the majority ending up in the British Museum, the Bodemuseum in Berlin, the Louvre, and the Egyptian Museum in Cairo.

The tablets seem to derive principally from the "House of Correspondence of Pharaoh" in the central city at Amarna, but the handful of tablets that subsequently were legally excavated suggest that they were discarded documents buried under the floor, rather than being filed in an official archive or library. This impression is reinforced by the fact that they are mainly incoming letters, whose contents would presumably have been translated into the Egyptian language and transferred onto papyri, rendering the original clay tablet redundant. Their exact chronology is still debated, but they cover a period of fifteen to thirty years, beginning around year 30 of Amenhotep III and extending no later than the first year of Tutankhamun's reign, with the majority dating to the time of Akhenaten.

All but thirty-two of the documents in the archive are items of diplomatic correspondence between Egypt and the great powers in Western Asia,

The "House of Correspondence of Pharaoh" at Amarna was the find-spot of an archive of cuneiform tablets, most of which comprised correspondence between the Egyptian king and contemporary rulers in western Asia. This example, now in the British Museum, is inscribed with a letter written by King Tushratta of Mitanni to Amenhotep III.

Earlier Egyptian rulers showed proclivities for particular cults, but Amenhotep IV was the first to devote himself solely to one god, apparently rejecting even the all-powerful Theban god Amun. It is a mistake, however, to regard the religious milieu of the Amarna Period as a sudden dramatic act of "heresy." The study of New Kingdom religion indicates that Akhenaten did not so much invent the cult of the Aten as raise it to unprecedented prominence. The distinctive icon of the sun-disk with oustretched arms, for instance, was being depicted at least as early as the reign of Amenhotep II. During the eighteenth dynasty, the god Amun was gradually syncretized with the sun god Ra, and the funerary myths relating to the royal progress through the underworld/afterlife began to be centered not so much on Osiris, the god of the dead, as on the three forms of the sun god: Ra, Atum, and Khepri. Thus, Akhenaten's championing of the cult of the sun disk was to some extent a logical consequence of the increasing absorption of other cults into that of the sun.

A great deal of upheaval in the Amarna Period had presumably less to do with the championing of the Aten and more to do with the accompanying neglect of the traditional deities, including the outright persecution of the previously omnipotent Amun. If Akhenaten had simply shown a preference for Aten and a corresponding lack of interest in the rest of the pantheon, the impact on religious iconography would have been relatively restricted. Instead, his agents embarked on the systematic defacement of inscriptions incorporating the name of Amun; in many cases, the name of Amun's mother, the goddess Mut, was also removed, as well as the plural form of *netjer* ("gods"). Both Akhenaten and his subjects changed their personal names so that the names of such traditional gods as Amun and Horus were replaced by the name of the Aten. One of the more visible effects of the regime was the severe reduction of the role of Osiris in both royal and nonroyal funerary cults, so that the tomb chapels of the nobles at el-Amarna are dominated by depictions of the royal family and the cult of the Aten rather than by the traditional scenes of daily life and portrayals of the deceased seated before piles of offerings or making offerings to the gods.

The *Hymn to the Aten*, supposedly composed by the king, not only resembles earlier hymns to the sun god but also shows undoubted similarities to Psalm 104 in the Bible. Both the hymn and Akhenaten's repeated statements to the effect that the Aten was the one true god have been used by many scholars (including Sigmund Freud) to argue that the religion of the Amarna Period was a precursor of the Judaeo-Christian-Islamic tradition of monotheism. Careful analysis of the relevant texts, however, indicates that, unlike the God of the Old Testament, the Aten was an essentially isolated and amoral deity who could be approached only via the Egyptian king. The similarities between the *Hymn to the Aten* and Psalm 104 are perhaps better explained in terms of the common literary tradition of ancient Egypt and Israel.

such as Babylonia and Assyria, or the various vassal city-states of Syria-Palestine. Most are written in a dialect of the Akkadian language, which was effectively the lingua franca of the Near East at that time, although a few documents are also written in the languages of the Hittites, Hurrians, and Assyrians. They provide a revealing glimpse of the political and economic links between Egypt and the rest of the ancient Near East and Mediterranean during the Amarna Period. The references to royal gifts of glass, gold, lapis lazuli, and iron help to provide a documentary context for such finds as the Ulu Burun shipwreck (a seagoing boat that sank off the Turkish coast in the fourteenth century B.C. while carrying a load of trade items between the Mediterranean, the Levant, and Egypt).

The Amarna Letters present a picture of Egypt's loose hegemony over a group of Levantine states, apparently under repeated threat of invasion both by their neighbors and by the Mitannian and Hittite armies. For a long time, this was taken to be proof that Akhenaten's religious and artistic experiments, perhaps conducted in some isolation at Amarna, had led him to pursue a much more pacifist or "soft" foreign policy, neglecting the empire assiduously built up by such warrior kings as Thutmose III and Amenhotep II. This view, however, ignores the fact that we have very little comparable documentation for Egyptian imperial policy during other periods of the New Kingdom. We cannot therefore be sure whether the situation during the Amarna Period was anomalous, or whether the triumphalist reliefs and stelae of the eighteenth through twentieth dynasties were vastly oversimplifying an imperial policy that was actually beset by constant problems and reverses like those described in the Amarna Letters.

Further Reading

The nonroyal rock-tombs belonging to the elite officials at Amarna were documented at the turn of the century by Norman de Garies Davies in the six volumes of *The Rock Tombs of El Amarna* (London, 1903–1908). The royal tomb at Amarna, probably intended for the burials of Akhenaten, Nefertiti, and at least one of the princesses, has been most recently studied by Geoffrey Martin in the two-volume work *The Royal Tomb at El-Amarna* (London, 1974–1989).

The Egypt Exploration Society's expeditions to Amarna during the 1920s and 1930s were published by the various directors of the work, T. Eric Peet, C. Leonard Woolley, Henri Frankfort, and John Pendlebury, in the three volumes of *City of Akhenaten* (London, 1923–1951), as well as annual preliminary reports in the *Journal of Egyptian Archaeology*. The results of the excavations of the last three decades of the twentieth century, directed by Barry Kemp, have been published by him as the six volumes of *Amarna Reports* (London, 1984–1995) and as one chapter of Kemp's *Ancient Egypt: Anatomy of a Civilization* (London, 1989, pp. 261–317).

The most up-to-date translation of the cuneiform tablets found at Amarna is William Moran's *The Amarna Letters* (Baltimore, 1992). The most illuminating set of discussions of their significance is found in a conference publication, *Amarna Diplomacy: The Beginnings of International Diplomacy,* edited by Raymond Cohen and Raymond Westbrook (Baltimore, 2000).

Further Viewing

Many of the major sculptures of the Amarna period, including colossal statues of Akhenaten himself, are displayed in the Egyptian Museum in Cairo, the Berlin Museum, and the Louvre. Most of the Amarna cuneiform tablets are displayed at Cairo, Berlin, and the British Museum.

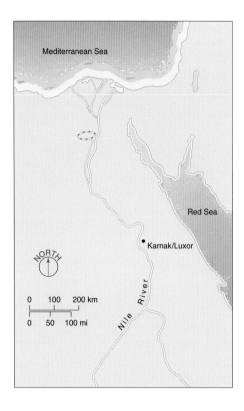

Mediterranean Sea

Red Sea

Karnak/Luxor

NORTH

0   100   200 km

0   50   100 mi

Nile River

CHAPTER

TWELVE

———

Karnak and Luxor

C. 2055 B.C.–395 A.D.

The Theban temples of Amun-Ra

The single most important archaeological site in Upper Egypt is undoubtedly ancient Thebes, the remains of which cover both sides of the Nile about 400 miles (600 kilometers) south of Cairo. When the Greeks called it "hundred-gated Thebes," this was partly to distinguish it from the Greek city of Thebes in Boeotia, but the fact that the latter was only "seven-gated" indicates how impressed they must have been by the successions of massive pylons in the temples of Egyptian Thebes. Comparatively little has survived of the ancient city itself, but the two religious complexes around which it clustered—the temples of Karnak and Luxor—are among the most magnificent surviving monuments of the New Kingdom and later periods.

Although Karnak has been subject to numerous excavations since the late nineteenth century, the vast majority of resources have been devoted to the conservation and re-erection of the standing monuments. It is the largest and best-preserved temple complex of the New Kingdom, and its reliefs and inscriptions incorporate valuable epigraphic data concerning the political and religious activities of imperial Egypt. So many important reliefs, inscriptions, and pieces of statuary have survived at Karnak and Luxor that it would almost be possible to write a history of the eighteenth to twentieth dynasties solely on the basis of material from these two temples.

Thebes, called Waset by the ancient Egyptians, began as a modest settlement founded on the east bank of the Nile early in the pharaonic period, although excavations east of Karnak have revealed an area of Old Kingdom housing covering an area of several thousand square feet. The city eventually rose to a position of enormous influence and prosperity as the home town of the Middle Kingdom pharaohs, and by the New Kingdom it must have rivaled the northern capital, Memphis, in size and opulence. By then, Thebes was sometimes simply called Niwet (literally, "the city").

The so-called White Chapel of Senusret I, the oldest surviving monument at Karnak, is inscribed with a list of places providing offerings or taxes to the king, including the city of Waset itself. The Theban city is also mentioned in a similar fiscal list in the Abydos temple of Rameses II and another inscribed by Ptolemy IV at Edfu. It is impossible to imagine how much of a shock it must have been to the people of Upper Egypt when, in 667 B.C., the Theban temples and town were sacked by the Assyrian ruler Ashurbanipal. From then on, the city center gradually moved southward to the area around Luxor temple, over a mile (1.6 kilometers) away. Much of the ancient Theban settlement, therefore, presumably lies underneath the modern city, rendering it largely inaccessible to archaeologists.

(Left) Map of Karnak Temple with (right) map of Thebes as a whole, to show relationships between Karnak and Luxor and between eastern and western Thebes.

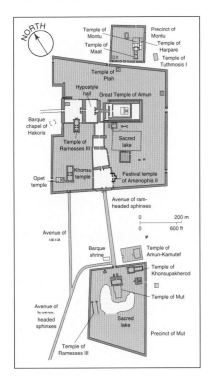

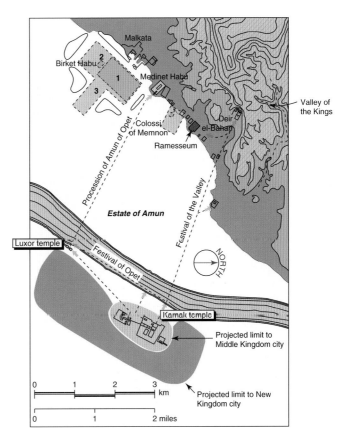

Just as the northern city of Memphis was accompanied, to the west, by the vast and sprawling city of the dead made up of pyramids and mastaba-tombs, stretching from Abu Rawash down to Meidum, so Thebes had its own vast necropolis on the west bank of the Nile, including the Valley of the Kings (see chapters 10, 13, and 14). By the New Kingdom, the symmetry of the Memphite region in the north and the so-called Thebaid in the south had been firmly established not only in governmental terms (each of the cities was the headquarters of one of the two viziers, the next most important official below the king) but also in the realm of religious symbolism; thus, Thebes was sometimes referred to as Iunu-resy, literally "the southern Heliopolis," the latter being the town just north of Memphis that was the principal cult-center of the sun god. There were also parallels between the two cities with regard to connections with the outside world: Memphis was the embarkation point for the military and commercial expeditions that forged Egypt's empire in Western Asia; Thebes, from the Middle Kingdom on, was the administrative center for the network of fortresses and colonies in Nubia. The whole region of Thebes and Lower Nubia was treated as one administrative entity known as "the Head of the South."

Karnak

The original god of the Theban region seems to have been Montu, a local warrior deity. Four eleventh-dynasty rulers known as Mentuhotep incorporated his name in theirs, but by the twelfth dynasty the most popular royal name was Amenemhat, reflecting the fact that Amun, first mentioned in the Old Kingdom Pyramid Texts as a kind of god of chaos, had become the preeminent universal deity both at Thebes and elsewhere. Amun (whose name means "the hidden one") was most often represented as a man wearing a headdress consisting of two long plumes, although he was sometimes shown as a man with a ram's head, or as a goose. Karnak temple at Thebes was the principal Egyptian temple devoted to his cult as well as to those of his consort, Mut, and his son, Khonsu; together, these three deities made up the so-called Theban Triad. From the Middle Kingdom on, Amun was combined with the sun-god into the universal deity Amun-Ra, a blend of the invisible divine power of Amun and the visible omnipotence of the sun-god, whose name and image are repeated endlessly across the walls of the Karnak complex.

Karnak is not just one temple, but a sprawling complex of religious buildings covering more than 250 acres (100 hectares) in the northeastern part of modern Luxor. There are essentially three major sacred precincts dedicated to the deities Amun-Ra, Mut, and Montu, each surrounded by trapezoidal mud-brick enclosure walls. These enclosures also encompass several smaller temples dedicated to Ptah, Ipet, and Khonsu, respectively. The main temples were continually extended and embellished by the rulers of Egypt from at least the Middle Kingdom (2040–1640 B.C.) until the Roman Period (30 B.C.–395 A.D.), although most of the surviving remains date to the New Kingdom (1550–1070 B.C.). This reflects the fact that, from the New Kingdom on, the Egyptian state's economic surplus poured increasingly into the construction, decoration, and maintenance of temples in the major cities, whereas in the Old and Middle Kingdoms it had been the pyramid complexes that were the principal focus of royal attention. The precinct of Amun at Karnak was one of the greatest architectural expressions of the king's maintenance of the gods' cults, which was the principal way in which he upheld the state of cosmic truth and harmony personified by the goddess Maat. In the colonnaded courts of Karnak, the king's activities on behalf of the gods were celebrated in reliefs and inscriptions.

The principal temple at Karnak was known as *ipet-sut* ("most select of places") and was dedicated to Amun-Ra. It was built along two axes (west-east and north-south), each comprising a succession of pylons and courtyards interspersed with obelisks, smaller temples, shrines, and altars. The earliest axis stretches from west to east, incorporating the Great Hypostyle Hall of Ramesses II (1290–1224 B.C.), which is greater than 12 acres (5 hectares) in area. The second axis extends the temple southward toward the nearby precinct of the goddess Mut.

As Egyptologists have studied the disposition and meanings of the painted reliefs on the temple walls at Karnak and elsewhere, it has become clear that the apparently repetitive motifs and scenes were not simply thrown together randomly but were placed in precise relationships with one another and arranged in such a way that they can be "decoded" to reflect the activities that took place within the temple. Even particular epithets given to the ruler can be interpreted as a reflection of cult activity: for instance, the route taken by king (or, in daily reality, the chief priest substituting for him) as he processed with offerings from the main temple of Amun to the small temple of Ptah to the north can be followed by tracking down those figures of the king captioned with the epithet "beloved of Ptah." Everything in the so-called grammar of the temple appears to have been deliberately designed and located in order to express and facilitate the purpose of the divine cults housed within the temple.

Southeast of the junction of the two axes of the precinct of Amun at Karnak is a vast, rectangular sacred lake. Many Egyptian temples included artificial expanses of water within their precincts. The lake in the Temple of Amun at Karnak is a rectangular, stone-lined reservoir filled by groundwater and entered via several stairways, which the Egyptians called a *she netjeri* ("divine pool"). The sacred lake fulfilled a number of different cultic purposes: it was a setting for the sailing of barks (sacred boats) containing images of the gods, the home of aquatic sacred animals such as geese or crocodiles, and a source of pure water for the daily ritual ablutions and libations of the temple. As well as this conventional rectangular type of lake, there were a number of other forms, such as the horseshoe-shaped pool (known as an *isheru*-water) that enclosed the main buildings in the Temple of Mut at Karnak.

The Great Hypostyle Hall

Most of the courts and halls at Karnak were no doubt intended to create a strong impression on the viewer, but by far the most awe-inspiring piece of architecture is the Great Hypostyle Hall. Most classic Egyptian temples included a large court crowded with pillars and lit only by clerestory windows just below the roof. The columns could be of various diameters and heights, but those lining the main axis route of the temple were usually the tallest and broadest. It was not uncommon for a single major temple to have two or even three hypostyle halls.

Hypostyle halls were designed to recreate, on a massive scale, the idea of a reed swamp growing on the fringes of the Primeval Mound, since each

The Hypostyle Hall of Karnak. Since the mid-nineteenth century archaeologists have restored the rows of huge columns to something approaching their original appearance.

temple was regarded as a microcosm of the process of creation. Beyond the hypostyle, the roof of the temple gradually descended, the floor grew higher, and the rooms grew smaller as the priest or worshipper gradually neared the dark sanctuary at the rear, which symbolized the original place of creation. At Karnak, this cosmogonic symbolism takes the form of a dense forest of 134 stone columns, the bases of which evoke the earth around the roots of papyrus plants. The twelve great columns along the main east–west axis stand 72 feet (22 meters) high, ending in massive open papyrus flowers; the other 122 columns are about 50 feet (15 meters) high and have closed papyrus-bud capitals. The interior walls of the hall are decorated with reliefs showing Sety I and his son Ramesses II engaged in various temple rituals and processions, while the external surface of the northern wall is carved with scenes from Sety I's military campaigns.

The Restoration Stele, the most important surviving document from Tutankhamun's reign, was found in 1905 in the Karnak Hypostyle Hall, near the Third Pylon; two years later, fragments of a copy were found in the nearby temple of Montu. The decree on this red granite stele was issued by Tutankhamun at the beginning of his reign in order to restore stability to domestic and foreign policy after the Amarna Period. The scene at the top of the stele originally showed Tutankhamun and his wife, Ankhesenamun (one of Akhenaten's daughters), making offerings to Amun and Mut, but the two figures of Ankhesenamun were deleted when Horemheb usurped the stele. The inscription describes the state of chaos in which Akhenaten's reforms were supposed to have left the country (see chapter 11), including temples

169

The northern exterior wall of the Great Hypostyle Hall at Karnak temple is decorated with reliefs depicting the military campaigns of Sety I.

left in ruins and the cults of many deities abolished. The decree claims that the gods had therefore abandoned Egypt and were no longer answering prayers.

East Karnak and the *talatat* blocks

During the reign of Akhenaten (1352–1336 B.C.), the "heretic" king, a temple complex dedicated to the Aten (the *per-Aten*) was built on the eastern perimeter of the temple of Amun at Karnak. This sprawling complex appears to have included at least four temples: *gem-pa-Aten* ("the Aten is found"), *rud-menu* ("sturdy are the monuments [of the Aten forever]"), *teni-menu* ("exalted is the monument [of the Aten forever]"), and *hut-benben* ("mansion of the benben-stone").

The buildings at East Karnak, like the palaces and temples at Amarna, were razed to the ground in the period after Akhenaten's death. They have survived, however, in the form of tens of thousands of so-called *talatat* blocks found reused as rubble in the second, ninth, and tenth pylons at Karnak, as well as below the pavement of the Great Hypostyle Hall. The term *talatat* may be the plural of the Arabic word for "three," referring to the characteristic length of the blocks (three hand's breadths), or it may be from the Italian word for "cut masonry," *tagliata*. The distinctive shape of these small sand-

In this reconstruction of a colonnade from one of the East Karnak temples we can see examples of the many depictions of Queen Nefertiti (here accompanied by her daughter, Meritaten). This section of the complex was reconstructed on the basis of fragments of pillars found by the French archaeologist Henri Chevrier in the center of the Second Pylon at Karnak, as well as pieces of architraves from the Ninth Pylon.

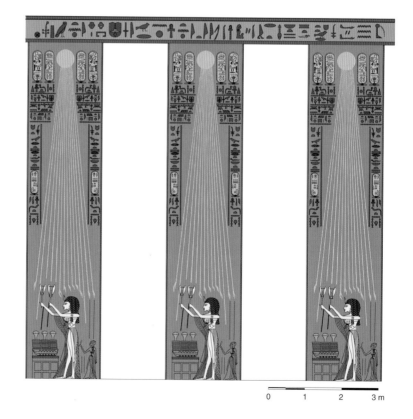

0 1 2 3 m

Detail from a scene of Akhenaten sacrificing a pin-tail duck, on a limestone *talatat* block.

stone relief blocks is thought to derive from the rapid construction techniques employed by Akhenaten in commissioning the temples of the Aten, which necessitated the provision of large quantities of smaller, more roughly carved blocks than those used in the temples constructed during the rest of the New Kingdom.

Talatat blocks have also been found reused in other post-Amarna constructions, such as the pylon of Ramesses II at Luxor. By 1965, a total of about 45,000 blocks had been recovered. Many of these have since been pieced together, and the excavations of the Canadian archaeologist Donald Redford have allowed much of the East Karnak complex to be "rebuilt" on paper.

The *gem-pa-Aten* seems to have been both the earliest and largest of the four buildings, consisting of a rectangular court covering an area of about 26,000 square meters and surrounded by a roofed colonnade punctuated by colossal statues of Amenhotep IV. The relief scenes between the statues were concerned largely with the celebration of the king's sed-festival (jubilee), despite the fact that this event was not usually supposed to take place until the king had reigned for thirty years. It is perhaps significant, in view of the increasing female influence on Amenhotep IV's reign, that the "great wife" Nefertiti was depicted approximately twice as often as the king himself at East Karnak; indeed, she alone was portrayed on the blocks from the *hut-benben*. However, as Donald Redford has pointed out, there is little more that can be deduced from this, other than the likelihood that Nefertiti had already achieved an unusual degree of religious and/or political importance in the first years of her husband's reign.

From Karnak to Luxor: The Ipet Festival and the Cult of the Royal Ka

At the heart of most Egyptian temples was some kind of shrine containing the cult images of one or more deities, but the rest of the temple is generally best understood as a kind of physical materialization of processions and festivals, particularly from the New Kingdom on. At various set times during the year, it was considered necessary for the cult images to be removed from the shrine, or naos, and paraded along in a sacred boat carried on the shoulders of as many as thirty priests.

The original center of the temple of Amun at Karnak, when it was founded in the Middle Kingdom or earlier, is marked now by a large open area between the Sixth Pylon and the Great Festival Hall of Thutmose III, although, in purely architectural terms, the area between the Third and Fourth Pylons is arguably the center point. If we set off from the Third Pylon and walk through the sequence of courts and stone gateways taking us to the southernmost edge of the temple and then through the nearby temple of Amun's consort, the goddess Mut, it is possible to follow the route of a sphinx-lined processional way stretching southward to Luxor temple about 1.5 miles (2.5 kilometers) away. Only a few of the sphinxes have survived, at either end of the processional way, the majority of the route having been covered by the asphalt, sidewalks, and buildings of the modern city. This was a well-trodden way along which the cult-statues of the divine triad

On the southern wall of the Hall of Appearances in Luxor Temple, Amenhotep III is depicted kneeling in front of his "father" the god Amun. It was in the Hall of Appearances that the king and his royal *ka* (spiritual essence) were deified during the annual celebration of the Ipet Festival.

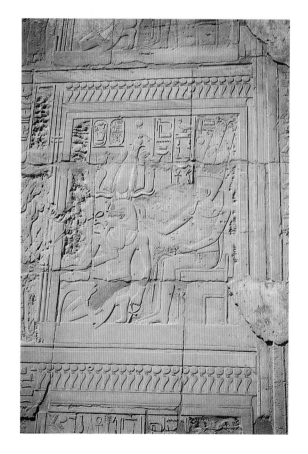

(Amun, Mut, and Khonsu) were brought in celebration of the Ipet Festival in the second month of the inundation season every year.

Luxor temple, like Karnak, was dedicated to the cult of Amun, but its ancient name—*ipet resyt*, "the southern private chambers"—shows that it was deliberately created as a destination for the Ipet Festival. It was at Luxor that the fertility of Amun Kamutef (literally, "bull of his mother"), Amun's creator aspect, was celebrated. Here, too, the divine birth of the king was celebrated, but above all, Luxor was connected with the cult of the royal *ka*. The Ipet Festival, which lasted for eleven days, provided an annual opportunity for the king to "merge" with his divine royal *ka* in the presence of Amun. Once his claim to the kingship had been reinforced in this way, the ruler would appear out of the inner sanctuary of the temple with both royal and divine essence revitalized, thus enabling the temple inscriptions to describe him as "foremost of all the living *ka*s" when he passed back out of the temple.

The visitor to Luxor temple approaches it from the direction of the river, soon arriving in front of the great pylon entrance, with several colossal statues of Ramesses II in front of it. There is also a single red granite obelisk in front of the eastern side of the gateway, which was once half of the only pair of temple obelisks still standing *in situ*, until its companion was removed by French engineers in 1831 to become the centerpiece of the Place de la Concorde in Paris. The surface of the pylon is carved with sunk relief decoration depicting scenes from the Battle of Qadesh, fought by Ramesses II against the Hittites and their allies (see chapter 14 below). Like most New Kingdom temples, the external walls of Luxor were decorated principally

173

Luxor temple.

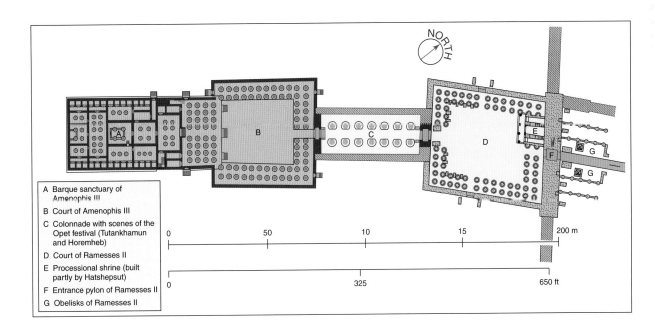

A Barque sanctuary of
  Amenophis III
B Court of Amenophis III
C Colonnade with scenes of the
  Opet festival (Tutankhamun
  and Horemheb)
D Court of Ramesses II
E Processional shrine (built
  partly by Hatshepsut)
F Entrance pylon of Ramesses II
G Obelisks of Ramesses II

0   50   10   15   200 m

0   325   650 ft

with scenes of warfare, conveying the sense that the king was constantly defending both the temple and the state from incursions by outsiders.

After passing through the center of the pylon, the visitor arrives in a peristyle court built by Ramesses II, which originally had colonnades along all four sides. The most obvious feature of the court, occupying the northeastern corner, is the medieval mosque of Yusuf Abu el-Haggag, which towers in slightly precarious fashion over both the pylon and the court. In a distant echo of the purpose of the temple on which it stands, the mosque (the earliest parts of which date to the late eleventh century A.D.) forms the focus for an annual traditional festival involving the dragging of a large boat in procession, and bearing more than a passing resemblance to the ancient Ipet Festival.

In the northwest corner of the First Court, built up against the inner side of the western part of the pylon, is the earliest part of the temple: a triple shrine dedicated to the Theban Triad. One of the walls of the central shrine, sacred to Amun, bears a scene of Thutmose III running toward the god, and it is this ruler who was reponsible for the construction of the triple shrine that eventually gave rise to the temple as a whole. On the western and southern walls of the court, the reliefs show a procession of seventeen of his sons toward a depiction of the temple pylon itself, complete with flags fluttering from tall wooden poles inset into the masonry in niches that are still visible in the real pylon. The two statues of Ramesses II that flank the southern entrance to the court have been identified as special seated images of the king known as *ka*-statues; these are representations of his divine essence, emphasizing the temple's role as a means of uniting the mortal king with his divine *ka*.

Beyond the southern entrance to the First Court is a huge colonnade consisting of seven pairs of columns with capitals in the form of open papyri, constructed by Amenhotep III. The colonnade stands in a long rectangular stone court, the walls of which were decorated during the reigns of Tutankhamun and Horemheb with scenes of the celebration of the Ipet Festival, including sacred boats carried by priests and a troop of soldiers carrying musical instruments and military standards. This colonnade leads to another peristyle court, roughly the same size as Ramesses II's but built and decorated in the time of Amenhotep III.

As the visitor passes through this court and enters a densely columned hypostyle hall, Luxor becomes a classic New Kingdom temple, with a succession of antechambers and annexes leading to the dark innermost sanctuary at the rear of the temple, originally containing the principal image of Amun Kamutef. However, there are now some intriguing features in these parts of the temple that emphasize its importance not only for the rulers of the pharaonic period but also for those of later periods. The first antechamber still has the remains of a painted apsidal recess dating to its conversion into a church in the fourth century A.D., when the reliefs of Amenhotep III were coated with a thick layer of gypsum and painted with incongruous ec-

The first court on the north-south axis at Karnak is known as "cachette court" because an impressive collection of thousands of pieces of statuary (mostly now in the Egyptian Museum, Cairo) was discovered here in 1902, buried under the temple floor. When a temple had once been established, the sacred spot usually continued as a temple through the centuries, with the original shrine gradually being covered up by new buildings. It seems that the sacred nature of the stone blocks and statuary meant that they often were reused as rubble, either within pylons or beneath floors, as the temple was gradually rebuilt and expanded.

In 1989, a smaller cachette of exquisitely carved and well-preserved stone statuary, similar to the Karnak cachette, was excavated from beneath the floor of the court of Amenhotep III at Luxor temple. The sixteen statues, mainly dating to the reigns of Amenhotep III, Tutankhamun, and Horemheb, may have been buried there by the priests in order to protect them from pillaging invaders. Alternatively, it is possible that, as with the Karnak cachette, the priests—reluctant simply to discard such sacred images—compromised by burying them under the temple pavement.

This granite statue of Amenhotep III, from the Luxor cachette (now in the Luxor Museum), is evidently intended to be a representation not of the king himself but of a *statue* of the king, since the sculpture incorporates the sledge on which it was mounted for transportation during a festival.

175

clesiastical images. More significantly, however, this chamber had previously been converted into a shrine to the cult of the deified Roman emperor, no doubt indicating a clear awareness on the part of the Romans—or their Egyptian advisors—that this building was specifically designed to imbue pharaohs with the divine spark of kingship. Evidently Alexander the Great had been equally well advised, for the so-called Sanctuary of the Sacred Boat, a little farther on, not only has reliefs of Amenhotep III around its walls but also a totally new chapel built inside it and decorated with scenes showing Alexander making offerings to Amun-Ra. It is possible to stand between the two sets of reliefs and touch each wall with the knowledge that over a thousand years of history separates them, and yet both were created to enable a king of Egypt to be united with his royal *ka*.

Further Reading

Most of the fundamental primary sources on the archaeology and architecture of Karnak and Luxor are written in French, since the vast majority of the work of restoration, conservation, and epigraphy at these two temples has been undertaken by French Egyptologists. An ongoing series dealing with the study of the Karnak complex is the *Cahiers de Karnak*, published by the Centre Franco-Égyptien d'Étude des Temples de Karnak since 1943. R. A. Schwaller de Lubicz's lavish publication *The Temples of Karnak* (London, 1999), is well worth consulting, primarily for its excellent black-and-white photographs of the reliefs and inscriptions.

Lanny Bell's fundamental discussion of the role played by the Luxor temple in the celebration of the cult of the royal *ka* was published as "Luxor Temple and the Cult of the Royal Ka" in volume 44 (1985) of the *Journal of Near Eastern Studies*, pp. 251–294. The cache of statuary found at Luxor temple is described by Mohammed el-Saghir in *The Discovery of the Statuary Cachette of Luxor Temple* (Mainz, 1991).

Further Viewing

The basement of the Luxor Museum is devoted to an excellent display of the cache of statuary found in the court of Amenhotep III at Luxor. Most of the principal items from the Karnak cachette (such as the travertine statue of King Sety I and the sandstone kneeling figure of Prince Khaemwaset) can be seen in the Egyptian Museum, Cairo.

The Valley of the Kings and the Theban Necropolis

c. 1504–1069 B.C.

Death and afterlife in the New Kingdom

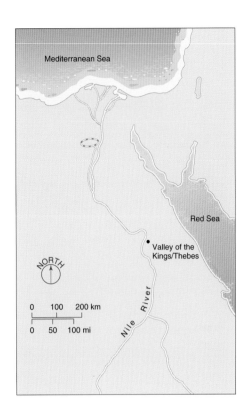

The cemetery of the New Kingdom pharaohs is situated on the west bank of the Nile about 3 miles (5 kilometers) west of modern Luxor. Even in its current state of decline, swarming with visitors and partially submerged under the heaps of debris left behind by centuries of pillaging and excavation, the Valley of the Kings is a breathtaking site, with its serpentine wadis and cliffs and the brooding presence of el-Qurn, a natural pyramidal knoll that probably originally drew the Egyptians to this secluded spot.

Exploring the Valley

Modern tourists approach the site by much the same route as the ancient kings must have done, following a winding wadi floor (now occupied by a paved road) from the flat expanse of the Theban river valley into the steeply sloping confines of the Theban cliffs. The "valley" actually consists of two separate wadis. The "eastern valley" is the main royal cemetery of the eighteenth through twentieth dynasties. The "western valley" (or "cemetery of the monkeys, or apes") contains only four tombs: those of Amenhotep III (c. 1353 B.C.; KV22) and Aye (c. 1319 B.C.; KV23), and two others that are uninscribed (KV24–5). There are more than sixty tombs in the Valley of the Kings as a whole. They range in design from the gently curving passages of the early eighteenth-dynasty tomb of Thutmose I

Map of the West Bank (top) at Thebes with map (bottom) of the Valley of the Kings.

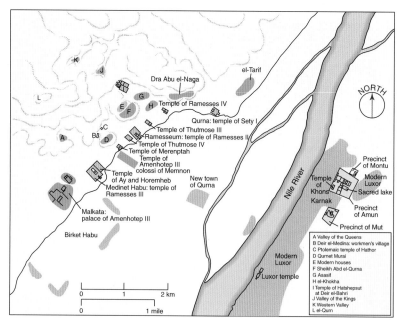

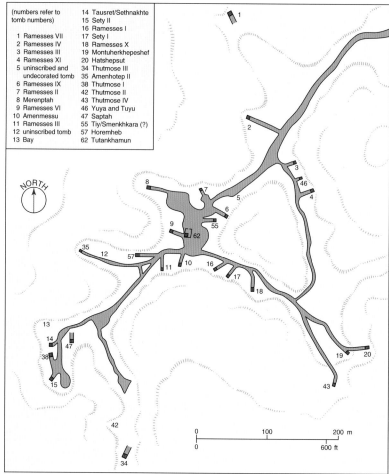

(c. 1500 B.C.) to the single monumental descending corridor that led to the burial chamber of Ramesses XI, the last ruler of the twentieth dynasty (c. 1070 B.C.). One of the major features of the tombs is their separation from the royal mortuary temples, which—for the first time since the Early Dynastic Period—were built some distance away from the kings' burials, at the edge of the cultivation.

In 1827, the trail-blazing British Egyptologist Sir John Gardner Wilkinson assigned each tomb a number in a sequence roughly corresponding to the dates of discovery. He wrote these numbers in red paint above the tombs' entrances, where many are still visible today. At that time, there were only about thirty known tombs, but Wilkinson's sequence has been extended by later archaeologists as new tombs have been discovered, so that the tomb numbers now run from KV1 (the tomb of Ramesses VII, which had been accessible since ancient times) to KV62 (the tomb of Tutankhamun). The painted and sculpted extracts from the various "books of the netherworld" adorning the walls and ceilings of the royal tombs are without parallel in the ancient world in their lavish use of color and vivid depictions of the perils besetting the king as he voyaged through the netherworld in the sun god's boat.

On reaching the narrow entrance to the main, eastern wadi, visitors first pass (on the right) two twentieth-dynasty tombs set back deep into the cliffs, belonging to Ramesses VII and Ramesses IV. The tombs of Ramesses II and his immediate successor, Merenptah, are the next features on the right, but before drawing parallel to them it is possible to see an inconspicuous opening on the left. This is the entrance to KV5, the largest tomb in the valley, which was partially described and surveyed by James Burton in 1825, then rediscovered in 1987 by the American Egyptologist Kent Weeks. The excavations undertaken by Weeks during the 1990s unexpectedly revealed a tomb with a unique and labyrinthine plan (so far comprising nearly a hundred rooms) that was evidently intended to contain the burials of many of Ramesses II's sons.

Each of the tombs in the Valley of the Kings consists of a long series of rock-cut corridors and chambers sloping downward into the cliffs. The earlier ones, from the time of Thutmose I to Amenophis III, consist of a bent-axis corridor leading down to a burial chamber, oval (or cartouche-shaped) in the earlier tombs and later square. The wall-decoration in these eighteenth-dynasty tombs represents scenes from the *Amduat* (literally, "what is in the underworld") executed in a simplified linear style, apparently imitating painted papyrus, with the background color changing from one tomb to another. During the course of the New Kingdom (1550–1070 B.C.), a large number of different "books" of the netherworld were painted or carved on the walls of the royal tombs, including the *Book of Caverns,* the *Book of Gates,* the *Book of the Heavens,* the *Book of the Earth,* and the *Book of Coming Forth by Day,* the set of spells now known as the *Book of the Dead.* The *Litany of Ra*—a funerary text stressing the king's identification with Ra—was first introduced on the pillars in the burial chamber of Thutmose III, but from Sety I on it decorated the entrance corridor of the tomb.

The theme of most of the royal books of the netherworld is the journey of the sun god through the realms of darkness during the twelve hours of the night, leading up to his triumphant rebirth with the dawn each morning. Many extracts from these books have been discovered, often with elaborate vignettes illustrating the text. During the New Kingdom, they were virtually confined to royal burials, but from the Third Intermediate Period (1070–712 B.C.) they began to appear in nonroyal tombs. Their placement in royal tombs is significant; for example, in the tomb of Ramesses VI (KV9; 1151–1143 B.C.), the *Book of Gates* is at the entrance to the upper level, the

Book of Caverns follows, and in the lower level, farthest from the entrance, is the *Book of Amduat.*

Favored locations for eighteenth-dynasty tombs are high in the sides of the cliffs, often within natural cracks in the rock. From Amenhotep III on, however, they tend to be constructed on the valley floor at the foot of the cliffs. Another difference between the earlier and later tombs is the greater concealment of the entrances of the eighteenth-dynasty tombs, compared with the much more elaborate and visible entrances to Ramessid tombs.

Probably the earliest tomb in the Valley is KV38, which is thought to have been the burial place of Thutmose I; it is possible, however, that the tantalizingly uninscribed (and still not fully excavated) KV39 may be older, if, as some scholars argue, it is the tomb of his predecessor, Amenhotep I. The entrance to KV39 lies at the foot of a sheer cliff on the southern periphery of the Valley, in a position that some scholars have claimed resembles the enigmatic description of the tomb's location given in Papyrus Abbott, a document recording an official inspection of various royal tombs in the sixteenth year of the reign of Ramesses IX. Other archaeologists, however, have argued that the best candidate for Amenhotep I's burial is tomb ANB, discovered by Howard Carter in 1913; it lies almost a mile to the east of the Valley, in the Dra Abu el-Naga region, and contained many fragments of stone vessels inscribed with the names of Amenhotep I and his parents, Ahmose and Ahmose Nefertari, as well as one intriguing example bearing the name of the Hyksos ruler Apepi, with whom Ahmose and Amenhotep are supposed to have been at war.

The only female ruler to be buried in the Valley of the Kings was Queen Hatshepsut. The tomb initially intended for her (KV20) was discovered by Carter in 1903, but there is no evidence that it was ever used for her actual burial. She may instead have been laid to rest in an earlier tomb, the "south tomb" in the Wadi Sikket Taqa el-Zeid in the cliffs to the south of Deir el-Bahari, which had been constructed before her rise to the throne. KV34, the tomb of her nephew Thutmose III, is the real prototype for New Kingdom royal tombs, with the introduction of a deep shaft (either to protect the burial from flooding or to provide ritual access to the underworld) and a pillared antechamber.

The tomb of Amenhotep II (KV35) is significant for a number of reasons. His architects abandoned the cartouche-shaped burial chamber, providing instead a columned rectangular room with a sunken crypt at the far end (perhaps to provide extra space for the nest of golden shrines around the sarcophagus). The decoration of this tomb, although unfinished, included a complete version of the book of *Amduat.* When it was excavated by Victor Loret in 1898, it was found to contain not only Amenhotep II's mummy, still in his sarcophagus, but also a "mummy cache": the bodies of eight other pharaohs (Thutmose IV, Amenhotep III, Merenptah, Sety II, Siptah, and Ramesses IV–VI), three women (one of whom may be Amenhotep III's

This three-dimensional
reconstruction of the
tomb of Tutankhamun
shows how each of the
four rooms was crammed
full of funerary equipment,
since most other royal
tombs would have been
much larger than this one
(after Ian Bott, 1990).

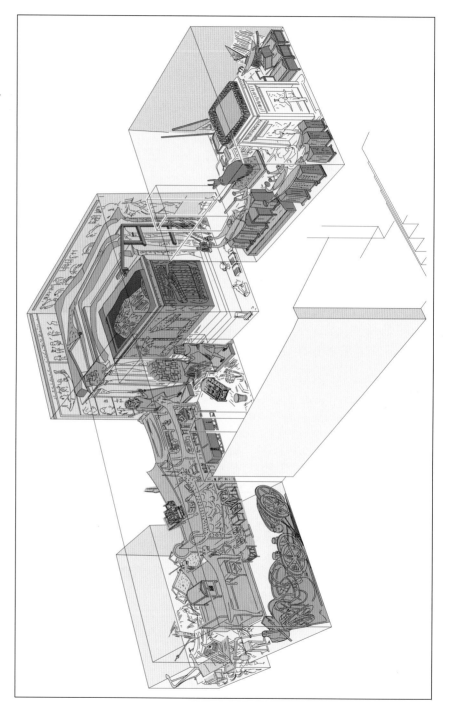

principal wife, Queen Tiy, or perhaps Queen Tawosret, who ruled in her own right in the late nineteenth dynasty), and a young boy (perhaps Sethnakht). The inscriptions on labels attached to some of these mummies indicate that they had all been brought to Amenhotep II's tomb in the twenty-first dynasty on the orders of the Chief Priest of Amun, Pinudjem.

The tomb of Amenhotep III (KV22) is one of a small group of burials located in the western wadi of the Valley of the Kings. It was decorated with scenes from the book of *Amduat,* and when excavated by Carter, it still contained about fifty small fragments of the red granite sarcophagus in the burial chamber (the lid having been usurped by Sety I, 1306–1290 B.C.), as well as various other small items of funerary equipment. When this tomb was re-excavated by a team of Japanese archaeologists in the 1990s, they found a large quantity of fragments of funerary equipment that had ended up on Carter's spoil heaps.

Amenhotep III's son, Akhenaten, built his tomb not at Thebes but beside his new capital city at Amarna in Middle Egypt, although there is an unfinished tomb in the western wadi of the Valley of the Kings that was perhaps originally intended for him (WV25). In the royal tomb at Amarna, the interior decoration consisted of carved reliefs rather than paintings, and the main axis of the tomb takes the form of a long continuous corridor rather than the typical eighteenth-Dynasty bent axis. Although Akhenaten was to be branded a heretic by his successors, certain aspects of the art and architecture of his reign had lasting effects on Egyptian culture of the late New Kingdom, including these two distinctive aspects of his Amarna tomb.

It seems likely that the original intention of Tutankhamun was to be buried in tomb WV23 in the western wadi, but this tomb was usurped by his successor, Ay, and Tutankhamun was buried instead in the much smaller KV62 in the main valley (see below). The shape and decoration of KV62 are much more reminiscent of a high official's tomb than of a royal one, and the few painted mural scenes include vignettes from the *Amduat,* the transport of the royal mummy to the tomb, and the performance of the Opening of the Mouth ceremony by Ay.

Just as Ay had usurped Tutankhamun's tomb, so Horemheb usurped Ay's mortuary temple in the vicinity of Medinet Habu in western Thebes. He also constructed a new royal tomb for himself in the Valley of the Kings, abandoning his virtually completed nonroyal tomb at Saqqara. His Theban tomb (KV57) is innovative both in its decoration (sunk relief scenes from the *Book of Gates*) and in its architectural style: it consists of a single almost straight corridor ("jogged axis") with side-chambers, rather than the bent-axis style of the previous eighteenth-dynasty royal tombs. In the burial chamber, his red granite sarcophagus remains *in situ,* but his body has not survived in either of the two royal mummy caches.

From Thutmose I to Ramesses III, the ceilings of the royal tombs were decorated with astronomical scenes depicting constellations and listing their

The burial chamber of Thutmose III is decorated with extracts from the *Amduat*, and still contains the king's yellow quartzite sarcophagus.

names. After Ramesses III, the astronomical ceilings began to incorporate scenes from the Books of the Heavens (the *Book of the Day, Book of the Night,* and *Book of Nut*). In the tombs of Ramesses VI, VII, and IX (KV9, KV1, and KV6 respectively), dating to the second half of the twelfth century B.C., a set of twenty-four seated figures representing stars were transected by grids of horizontal and vertical lines, allowing the passage of time to be measured via the transits of stars through the sky.

The most impressively decorated tomb in the Valley is undoubtedly that of Sety I (KV17), the walls of which bear exquisite painted reliefs illustrating parts of the *Litany of Ra,* the *Amduat,* the *Book of Gates,* and the *Book of the Divine Cow.* Discovered by the Italian adventurer Giovanni Belzoni in 1817, the tomb is the longest, deepest, and most complete in the Valley, exceeded in overall size only by the unusual tomb of Ramesses II's sons (KV5). Sety's tomb was the first to be decorated in its entirety. In the late twentieth century, these painted walls began to deteriorate quite significantly, and the tomb has therefore been closed to visitors since the 1980s in order to allow an expensive program of conservation to be undertaken (as in the case of the restoration of the tomb of Nefertari in the Valley of the Queens, which was eventually reopened to visitors in 1994).

Howard Carter and the Tomb of Tutankhamun

In the widest part of the eastern valley, the central feature is the entrance to the tomb of Tutankhamun, which is surrounded by a wall and approached down a flight of modern steps owing to its being at a somewhat deeper

level than the surrounding Ramessid tombs. The story of the tomb's discovery in 1922 has become almost the archetypal tale of the patient excavator and his benefactor who are eventually rewarded by an unprecedented find.

When Howard Carter and Lord Carnarvon first entered the tomb of Tutankhamun together, they walked down a short entrance stairway and corridor that lead to a group of four relatively small rooms that, at first glance, seemed to bear little relation to the classic design of an eighteenth-dynasty royal tomb. However, as Carter himself later pointed out, if the entire set of chambers were to be rotated through an angle of 90° relative to the entrance staircase and corridor, the plan would resemble the standard "bent-axis" design. Each of the four chambers could therefore be interpreted as the equivalent stage of a typical eighteenth-dynasty royal tomb: the annex, equivalent to one of the side-rooms off the burial chamber; the treasury, probably equivalent to the so-called crypt section of a standard tomb; the antechamber; and the burial chamber.

Carter's discovery of the tomb of Tutankhamun—almost exactly a century after Champollion's decipherment of hieroglyphs—opened the floodgates of public appreciation and exploitation of ancient Egypt. Archaeology as a whole attracts a level of popular interest not usually associated with more desk-bound disciplines, and the study of ancient Egypt has a particularly strong grip on the popular imagination. Even before the discovery of the tomb of Tutankhamun, nineteenth-century poets and novelists such as Percy Bysshe Shelley and H. Rider Haggard had presented a romanticized view of pharaonic Egypt that drew heavily on the new information provided by adventurers and archaeologists.

From a purely Egyptological point of view, it might be argued that Carter's discovery was something of a mixed blessing. Although his great predecessors, Flinders Petrie and George Reisner, had made sensational discoveries at certain points in their careers, their principal achievement had been to establish Egyptology as a rigorous scientific discipline concerned with the pursuit of knowledge rather than objets d'art. However, Carter's discovery of Tutankhamun in one fell swoop restored the popular view of Egypt as a treasure-hunters' paradise where sheer persistence might eventually be richly rewarded. After the initial days of euphoria, Carter was to spend the rest of his life cataloguing the funerary equipment he had discovered. Egyptologists have been dogged ever since by a public willing them to find something even more exciting than an intact royal tomb, and they have often found that their sober scientific agenda is at odds with the popular desire for buried treasure.

The Unsolved Mystery of Tomb KV55

The tomb of Tutankhamun may be the one find that has most excited the public, but the royal burial that has undoubtedly produced some of the most intense debate among scholars is KV55, a small, unfinished tomb just a few yards from that of Tutankhamun. It was discovered in January 1907 by Edward Ayrton, a British archaeologist working for Theodore Davis, the American enthusiast who financed most of the twentieth-century excava-

186
—
The enigmatic coffin and funerary equipment in tomb KV55, as they were first seen by Edward Ayrton in 1907. The royal cobra (uraeus) on the forehead of the coffin suggests that it contained either the re-buried body of Akhenaten himself or that of his short-lived coregent Smenkhkara.

tions in the Valley of the Kings. At first, it may not have appeared to be a particularly interesting find: an undecorated eighteenth-dynasty tomb containing a single body, accompanied by a small assortment of funerary equipment. One of the major finds in the burial chamber and corridor, however, was a large gilded-wood funerary shrine decorated with depictions of Queen Tiy and erased cartouches of her son Akhenaten, the "heretic pharaoh." Davis became convinced that they had found the burial of Tiy, wife of Amenhotep III, and in 1910 the finds were duly published as *The Tomb of Queen Tiyi*. In the meanwhile, however, Davis had chosen conveniently to ignore the fact that the body had been identified as that of a young man rather than an old woman. Apart from the male body, the tomb also contained four so-called magical bricks bearing the name of Akhenaten, and a coffin and canopic jars that appeared to have been made for the burial of Kiya, a secondary wife of Akhenaten.

Most Egyptologists now agree that this tomb contained a mixture of material from at least three Amarna-Period burials: Tiy, Kiya, and an unknown man. It is the identity of the man that has excited so much debate over the years, with two possibilities emerging as favorites. First, it has been suggested that the body was that of Smenkhkara, Akhenaten's co-regent and successor on the throne, who reigned for less than a year and probably died quite young. This theory is supported by the relative youth of the body (apparently confirmed by a recent reexamination by the bioanthropologist Joyce Filer), but it is contradicted by many Egyptologists' view that "Smenkhkara" might have been a pseudonym briefly adopted by Queen Nefertiti when she perhaps occupied the throne at the time of her husband's death. Second—and more exciting—it has been suggested that the body might be none other than Akhenaten himself, although its youthfulness is the major argument against this position. The tantalizing collection of clues in KV55 represents the classic archaeological scenario: just enough information to generate a really complicated set of arguments, but far too few certainties to resolve them fully.

The British Egyptologists Nicholas Reeves and Geoffrey Martin have argued recently that there may still be some hope of finding a second intact royal burial in the Valley. Their claim is based on two factors. First, the lack of surviving bodies or funerary equipment for several prominent members of the Amarna royal family, including Queen Nefertiti and King Smenkhkara (assuming that he was an actual male ruler rather than a pseudonym of the enthroned Nefertiti), suggests that there might at least be another cache of funerary material like that found in KV55. Second, the area between the tomb of Tutankhamun and KV55 appears never to have been fully cleared; if Carter had not made his amazing discovery, this would no doubt have been his target for excavation in 1923. Work currently being undertaken by Reeves and Martin in precisely this part of the Valley of the Kings may finally demonstrate whether the ancient wadi contains any further secrets.

The Tombs of the Nobles

The tombs of some of the pharaohs' high officials are scattered along the cliffs to the east of the Valley of the Kings, closer to the cultivation. Most of the earliest New Kingdom tombs of high officials have been found at Dra Abu el-Naga, north of Deir el-Bahari (currently being excavated by the German archaeologist Daniel Polz). The later burials, including some of the best-decorated and best-preserved rock-cut funerary chapels, are situated mainly in the cliffs of Sheikh Abd el-Qurna, south of Deir el-Bahari. The plans of these chapels were initially T-shaped in the early eighteenth dynasty, but they became more elaborate from the reign of Thutmose III on; for instance, the tomb of Kenamun (TT93), dating to the reign of Amenhotep II, consists of a double-T plan and also has a more complex substructure.

Whereas the pharaohs' tombs were largely decorated with mythological scenes, the tombs of high officials usually contained more personal details relating to their professions (often administrative), family life, and funerary arrangements. The tomb at Sheikh Abd el-Qurna (TT100) of Rekhmira, who was vizier during the reigns of Thutmose III and Amenhotep II, is unique among the nonroyal tombs in the Theban necropolis. Texts on its walls describe the process of installation of the vizier, a post of great importance, particularly at a time of imperial expansion. A further set of texts describes the duties of the vizier and the moral code within which his administration was intended to operate. It is stated that "there was nothing of which he [the vizier] was ignorant in heaven, in earth, or in any quarter of the underworld."

The painted decoration includes many scenes relating to agriculture and craftwork, providing information on such activities as jewelry-making and sculpting that has supplemented archaeological and experimental data. One

Detail of the painted decoration in the tomb of the vizier Rekhmira, showing craftsmen using scaffolding to work on royal statues.

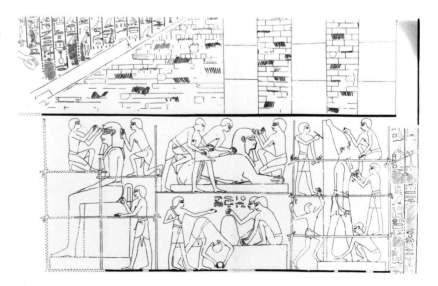

of the walls is decorated with scenes from the presentation of foreign tribute by Nubians, Syrians, Cretans, and representatives of other neighboring countries. These scenes include valuable information on trade and tribute, indicating the kinds of raw materials and artifacts that were acquired from particular geographical areas; this has also proved useful in dating surviving imported goods.

Episodes from Rekhmira's funeral are also represented in the tomb, including the Opening of the Mouth ceremony being performed on his mummy, following the funeral procession to the tomb. The chapel has no burial shaft below it, and it has been suggested that Rekhmira was actually buried in a shaft tomb in the Valley of the Kings, although this burial place—if it exists—has not yet been found.

The tomb of Ramose, vizier in the later eighteenth-dynasty reigns of Amenhotep III and Akhenaten (TT55), is of particular importance because it includes reliefs executed both in the distinctive "Amarna style" of Akhenaten and in the more traditional style of his father. The southern wall depicts the funerary processions of Ramose, while the west side preserves one of the earliest depictions of Akhenaten worshipping the Aten. Like many Theban tombs, it remained unfinished, and as with many who held office before Akhenaten's move to Amarna, the fate of its owner is unknown.

Who Built and Decorated the Royal Tombs?

No discussion of the Valley of the Kings is complete without some reference to the site of Deir el-Medina, where the royal tomb-workers were housed from the early eighteenth dynasty to the late Ramessid period (c.1550–1070 B.C.). Their walled village is situated in a bay in the cliffs midway between the Ramesseum and Medinet Habu. The site also incorporates the tombs of many of the workmen and a temple dedicated to various gods that was founded in the reign of Amenhotep III and almost completely rebuilt more than a thousand years later, in the reign of Ptolemy IV (221–205 B.C., see below). Deir el-Medina was excavated by Ernesto Schiaparelli from 1905 to 1909, and by Bernard Bruyère between 1917 and 1947. The superstructure of a typical Ramessid tomb at Deir el-Medina consists of an open courtyard and vaulted chapel surmounted by a brick pyramid with pyramidion, while the substructure comprises a shaft from the courtyard leading down to a vaulted burial chamber below the chapel. Usually the chapel was decorated and the burial chamber was not, but the tomb of Sennedjem is an exception to this rule.

The prime importance of this site to Egyptian archaeology as a whole lies in its unusual combination of extensive settlement remains with large numbers of ostraca that provide important evidence on the socioeconomic system of Egypt in the eighteenth to twentieth dynasties. Unfortunately, this

The tomb-workers' village at Deir el-Medina provides us with detailed evidence of the history of a single community during the Ramessid period.

unrivaled opportunity to synthesize contemporaneous textual and archaeological data from a single site has not been fully realized, primarily because of poor standards of the excavation.

The invaluable combination of archaeological and textual evidence at Deir el-Medina provides an astonishingly detailed picture of a small community of government workers engaged on the construction and decoration of royal tombs, from the time of Thutmose I (c. 1500 B.C.) until the end of the twentieth dynasty (c. 1100 B.C.). At its height (c. 1300–1100 B.C.), the village at Deir el-Medina consisted of about seventy houses arranged in rows. The number of workmen varied during the history of the village: in the reign of Ramesses II, there were at least forty-eight workers, but their number had dropped to about thirty-two by the end of this reign (presumably because the king's tomb was completed by then). It seems likely that new workmen were taken on at the beginning of each fresh reign. In the time of Ramesses III, there were forty men, and by the time work had begun on the tomb of his successor, Ramesses IV, the total had climbed steeply to 120. Six years later, the total had plummetted again to sixty; there were doubtless always far more men needed at the beginning of a reign, when work began on the excavation and decoration of a new tomb. The total village population, including the workmen's wives and children, probably peaked at about 500 in the late Ramessid Period.

In the twenty-first dynasty, when the royal necropolis had been moved north to Tanis, there was only a tiny skeleton staff of tomb-workers left. By then, they had been moved away from their ancestral village and into the precincts of the mortuary temple of Ramesses III at Medinet Habu, and their only task was to repair and maintain the existing tombs rather than to build new ones. The village at Deir el-Medina fell into disuse, although the area must have retained some significance even centuries after the demise of the community, since a temple of Hathor and Maat was built there by Ptolemy IV, and in the Coptic period it was converted into a monastery dedicated to Isidorus the Martyr. Apart from this later religious use of the site, there was no fresh activity until it was eventually plundered and excavated.

The community at the workmen's village of Deir el-Medina, in western Thebes, is strong proof of the existence of an Egyptian state-employed non military work force, evidently housed, fed, and equipped by a central authority. However, we do not know whether the existence of patronage and of "professional" craftsmen was a central and dominant feature of the Egyptian economy, or whether the majority of skilled craftsmen plied their trades as private individuals in their own houses. As the Danish Egyptologist Jac Janssen has pointed out in a textually based economic study of Deir el-Medina, "We seem to be in the following paradoxical situation: the only community about which our knowledge of its economy is at present sufficiently extensive to allow of reliable conclusions [i.e., Deir el-Medina]; cannot be regarded as representative of the situation in the rest of the country."

Who Robbed the Tombs?

A series of twelve so-called Tomb Robbery Papyri (seven of which are in the collection of the British Museum) has survived from the reigns of Ramesses IX, X, and XI. These records of the trials and punishments of individuals accused of tomb robbery are probably the most fascinating surviving set of legal documents from the entire pharaonic period. The bulk of them formed part of a remarkable collection of papyri acquired over a period of years by Anthony Charles Harris, a British diplomat based in Alexandria, and eventually sold to the British Museum by his daughter. Harris was simply told that the papyri were found behind the temple of Medinet Habu on the west bank at Luxor, but one of his contemporaries, the Egyptologist A. A. Eisenlohr, claimed that they came from a hole inside a tomb packed with mummies. Since there is no way of verifying (or even clarifying) this anecdote, the Tomb Robbery Papyri, like so many others found in the nineteenth and early twentieth centuries, effectively have no known archaeological context.

The texts of the papyri include lists of the stolen objects as well as the evidence given by the accused, who were beaten in order to make them confess their crimes. The tombs that they are accused of robbing include that of

During the New Kingdom, the burials of many nonroyal individuals included papyrus rolls bearing illustrated extracts from the so-called *Book of the Dead,* a collection of about 200 funerary spells known to the Egyptians as the *Book of Coming Forth by Day*. More than half of the spells were derived directly from either the Pyramid Texts or the Coffin Texts.

192

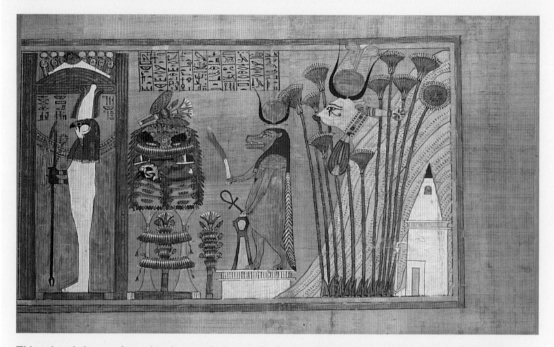

This painted vignette from the nineteenth-dynasty *Book of the Dead* papyrus of Any (now in the British Museum) includes a representation of Any's tomb-chapel, capped by a small pyramid (bottom right), and above it the cow-goddess Hathor emerging from the mountain face. In the center is the hippopotamus-goddess Ipet, and on the left is a shrine containing an image of the funerary god Sokar-Osiris.

the seventeenth-dynasty ruler Sobkemsaf II, that of his queen Nubkhas, and that of Isis, one of the wives of Ramesses III. There is also an account of a theft from the tomb of Ramesses VI (on Papyrus Mayer B); the date of this papyrus suggests that Ramesses VI's tomb was already being robbed before year 9 of Ramesses IX, only about thirty years after the former's death. The robber confessed:

> "The foreigner Nesiamun took us up and he showed us the
> tomb of King Nebmare Meriamun, life, prosperity, health, the
> great god . . . I spent four days breaking into the royal tomb,
> there being five of us there. We opened the tomb and we
> entered it."

The *Book of the Dead* included formulae, or spells, to receive offerings, to have power over the body, to control the elements of air, fire, and water, to assume forms appropriate to immortals, and to gain knowledge of the afterworld so as to pass through it unscathed. There were also declarations of purity for the moment of judgment, hymns to Ra and Osiris, and many vignettes elaborating and extending the meaning of the spells and hymns. The Coffin Texts of the Middle Kingdom had included occasional illustrations, but the *Book of the Dead* is centered on the use of vignettes. Chapter 125, the section of the *Book of the Dead* that is most commonly illustrated by a vignette, shows the last judgment of the deceased before Osiris and the forty-two "judges" representing aspects of Maat (divine order). The judgment took the form of weighing the heart of the deceased against the feather of Maat. An important element of the ritual was the calling of each judge by name while giving the relevant "negative confession":

Oh Far-strider who came forth from Heliopolis, I have done no falsehood.
Oh Fire-embracer who came forth from Kheraha, I have not robbed.
Oh Nosey who came forth from Hermopolis, I have not been rapacious.
Oh swallower of shades who came forth from the cavern, I have not stolen.
Oh Dangerous One who came forth from Rosetjau, I have not killed men.
Oh Double Lion who came forth from the sky, I have not destroyed food supplies.
Oh Fiery Eyes who came forth from Letopolis, I have done no crookedness.
Oh Flame which came forth backwards, I have not stolen the god's offerings.
Oh Bone Breaker who came forth from Herakleopolis, I have not told lies.

The desired outcome of these negative confessions was that the deceased was declared "true of voice" and introduced into the realm of the dead. Although vignettes always optimistically depict a successful outcome, the demon Ammut ("the devourer") was usually shown awaiting those who might fail the test.

The *Book of the Dead* was often simply placed in the coffin, but it could also be rolled up and inserted into a statuette of the funerary god Sokar-Osiris or even incorporated into the mummy bandaging. The texts could be written in the hieroglyphic, hieratic, or demotic script. Because most wealthy individuals were provided with copies of the *Book of the Dead*, numerous examples have survived.

The vignettes are not restricted to papyri; they can be found on the walls of both royal and nonroyal tombs, such as that of the twentieth-dynasty king Siptah, where the vignett for chapter 151 is depicted, showing Anubis embalming a mummy with Isis and Nephthys in attendance. Extracts could also be painted on coffins, such as the lid of the fourth-century coffin of Djedthutefankh from Hermopolis Magna (now in the Museo Egizio, Turin).

The papyrus goes on to list a number of items, mainly copper, that were stolen from the tomb. The mummy of Ramesses VI has survived, and it is obvious that it was very badly hacked up by the robbers, presumably while they were looking for precious amulets within the wrappings. The head and torso appear to have been chopped up with an axe but were later roughly reassembled and rewrapped by priests in the early Third Intermediate Period, when (along with the mummy of Ramesses V) Ramesses VI was moved to the "mummy cache" in tomb KV35. At the time that it was being moved, a woman's right hand and the right forearm and hand of Sety II were accidentally wrapped in with Ramesses VI's body.

It was once assumed, on the basis of the Tomb Robbery Papyri, that these thefts of precious materials from tombs were regarded as heinous crimes against the state, generally undertaken by the poorer members of Theban society. However, another piece of written evidence suggests that the situation may have been more complex. A letter from an important official at Thebes to Piankh, an extremely influential high priest and general at the end of the twentieth dynasty, confirms that the official has carried out Piankh's orders "to uncover a tomb among the tombs of the ancestors and maintain its seal until I return." One plausible interpretation of this letter is that the Theban elite at the end of the New Kingdom were deliberately reopening some—(perhaps all) of the royal tombs in order to recycle the gold and silver equipment stored inside. Certainly we know that high officials at this date were rewrapping and reinterring royal mummies, supposedly to protect them from the ravages of "tomb-robbers," but it now seems possible that this was simply a convenient pretext for the impoverished rulers of the Third Intermediate Period to gain access to the buried wealth of the past. It would have been all too easy for these rulers to imply that they were simply acting in the interests of their royal predecessors, "protecting" them (and, coincidentally, their rich burial equipment) from the depredations of criminals.

Further Reading

The Complete Valley of the Kings, by Nicholas Reeves and Richard H. Wilkinson, is the best currently available compendium of information on the history, architecture, decoration, and contents of the royal tombs at western Thebes. The history of exploration of the Valley is described in illuminating detail in John Romer's *Valley of the Kings* (London, 1981). Erik Hornung's *Valley of the Kings* is the only monograph to attempt seriously the unenviable task of analyzing and interpreting the iconography of the painted decoration on the walls of the royal tombs; the same author's collection of essays, *Idea into Image* (New York, 1992), discusses many of the themes and questions raised by the scenes depicted in the Valley. R. O. Faulkner produced an excellent translation of the *Book of the Dead* spells in *The Ancient Egyptian Book of the Dead,* edited by C. Andrews (London, 1986). The non-royal tombs of the Theban necropolis are eloquently described by Lise Manniche in *City of the Dead* (London, 1987), and by Nigel and Helen Strudwick in *Thebes in Egypt* (London, 1999).

The archaeological finds and texts from Deir el-Medina, the site of the tomb-workers' village, are discussed in a number of books, including John Romer's *Ancient Lives* (London, 1984), Morris Bierbrier's *The Tomb-builders of the Pharaohs* (London, 1982), Leonard Lesko's *Pharaoh's Workers: The Villagers of Deir el-Medina* (Ithaca and London, 1994), Lynn Meskell's *Archaeologies of Social Life* (Oxford, 1999), and Andrea McDowell's *Village Life in Ancient Egypt* (Oxford, 2000).

Further Viewing

The Luxor Museum contains a number of artifacts deriving from the Valley of the Kings and Valley of the Queens. The mummified bodies of most of the New Kingdom pharaohs are held in the Egyptian Museum, Cairo, along with many items of funerary equipment, including the stunning material from the tomb of Tutankhamun. Numerous museums in the United States and Europe also have objects deriving from the Valley of the Kings. The collection of the British Museum, for example, includes several resin-coated ritual wooden images of demons from the tomb of Horemheb, and two life-sized wooden "guardian statues" discovered by Belzoni in the tomb of Ramesses I. The contents of the tomb of the architect Kha, one of the royal tomb-workers at Deir el-Medina, are on display at the Museo Egizio, Turin. As far as the royal tombs themselves are concerned, there are considerable problems in balancing the demands of tourism and conservation; as a partial solution to the dilema, a replica of the tomb of Sety I is being created at a site near Cairo.

Abu Simbel

c. 1279–1213 B.C.

Colonial temple-building in Nubia

The Egyptians built many temples in Nubia, a country that often languished in their shadow, politically speaking. In the New Kingdom, most of this area immediately to south of Egypt proper had been securely absorbed into their vast empire. The high sandstone cliffs of northern Nubia seem to have provided a particularly suitable context for rock-cut temples. Ramesses II built five such temples in Lower Nubia. The four smaller examples are the sites of Derr, Wadi el-Sebua, Gerf Hussein, and Beit el-Wali. The most spectacular of Ramesses the Great's rock-cut monuments, however, is the Great Temple at Abu Simbel, which encapsulates in a single site the sheer hyperbole and grandiosity of Egyptian imperialism in the early Ramessid period, when Egypt was undoubtedly the dominant power in northeastern Africa.

Jean-Louis Burckhardt, a Swiss traveler from Lausanne who had studied at the universities of Leipzig, Göttingen, and Cambridge, was the first European to rediscover these two huge rock-cut temples on the west bank of the Nile, 174 miles (280 kilometers) south of Aswan. In 1813, when Burckhardt first arrived at the site, the monuments were mostly obscured by drifts of sand, and he was able to see only the Small Temple and the tops of the heads of the row of colossal statues in front of the Great Temple. In fact, he

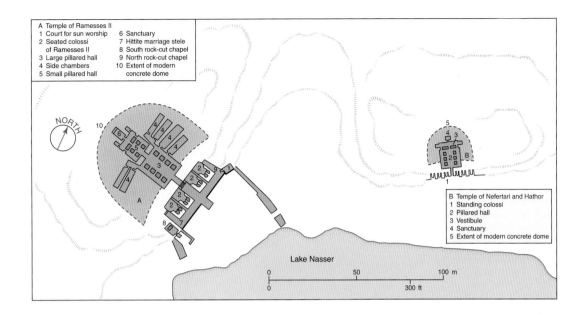

A Temple of Ramesses II
1 Court for sun worship
2 Seated colossi
   of Ramesses II
3 Large pillared hall
4 Side chambers
5 Small pillared hall
6 Sanctuary
7 Hittite marriage stele
8 South rock-cut chapel
9 North rock-cut chapel
10 Extent of modern
   concrete dome

NORTH

B Temple of Nefertari and Hathor
1 Standing colossi
2 Pillared hall
3 Vestibule
4 Sanctuary
5 Extent of modern concrete dome

Lake Nasser

0   50   100 m

0   300 ft

seems to have come perilously close to missing the main feature of the site al-together, according to his journal:

Plans of Great and Small Temples at Abu Simbel.

> Having, as I supposed, seen all of the antiquities of Ebsambal, I was about to ascend the sandy side of the mountain by the same way I had descended; when having luckily turned more to the southward, I fell in with what is yet visible of four immense colossal statues cut out of rock . . . they stand in a deep recess, excavated in the mountain, but it is greatly to be regretted that they are now almost entirely buried beneath the sands, which are blown down here in torrents.

Two years later, the Anglo-Italian adventurer and excavator Giovanni Belzoni arrived at Abu Simbel with the intention of clearing the entrance to the Great Temple. It is apparent from his published account that he had been deeply impressed by Burckhardt's descriptions of the site, but on this first visit he was evidently not prepared for the sheer amount of sand in-volved. As he approached the Great Temple by boat, accompanied by forty workmen, he observed:

> The sand from the north side . . . choked the entrance and buried two-thirds of it. On my approaching this temple, the hope I had formed of opening its entrance vanished at once; for the amazing accumulation of sand was such that it appeared an impossibility ever to reach the door.

On this occasion, Belzoni and his party were forced to admit defeat; but, undaunted, he returned with more workmen in 1816. He was eventually

The sanded up Great Temple
at Abu Simbel.

successful in removing the hundreds of tons of sand from both temples and
investigating the painted reliefs in their interiors. On this second expedition,
he was assisted by three British associates: Charles Irby and James Mangles,
both naval captains, and Henry Beechey, an artist who was secretary to Henry
Salt, the British consul-general in Egypt.

Belzoni was a barber's son from Padua whose early career had been spent
traveling through Europe as a circus strong man. He had arrived in Egypt
in 1814 and had turned to archaeology after he failed in his attempts to sell
a new type of water-wheel. Earlier in 1816, he had helped Henry Salt to
transport part of a colossal statue of Ramesses II from Luxor to London
(where it became one of the first Egyptian antiquities in the British Museum).
At this early date in the history of Egyptology, Belzoni was unquestionably
the right man for the forbidding task of uncovering the temples at Abu
Simbel. It was, however, this same sense of adventure and apparent invul-
nerability that led, seven years later, to his death from dysentery in Benin,
while he was attempting to find the source of the Niger.

Although Belzoni's methods were somewhat unorthodox and occasionally unnecessarily destructive, if judged by modern archaeological standards,
he was nevertheless an important pioneer in Egyptology. He did much to
encourage European enthusiasm for Egyptian antiquities, not only through
a famous exhibition at the Egyptian Hall in Piccadilly (London) in 1821, but
also through the published accounts of his discoveries. In the Great Temple,

he and James Mangles compiled a very accurate plan on which they marked the original positions of the various items of statuary.

The Great Temple

We know from inscriptions on stelae still *in situ* at Abu Simbel that the construction of the two temples there was supervised by three men: the viceroys Iuny and Hekanakht, and the first royal cup-bearer Ashahebsed. There seems to be no obvious reason why this particular spot was chosen for the most ambitious of Ramesses' monuments in Nubia, given that there are no traces of any ancient town in the vicinity. It appears that the two rocky hills into which the temples were originally cut were sacred to the local deities Horus of Maha (in the case of the Great Temple) and Hathor of Abshek (the Small Temple), but it is unclear whether these religious links actually pre-dated the monuments. They appear to have simultaneously symbolized Ramesses' triumph over Nubia and expressed his piety toward the gods.

The southern monument, now known as the Great Temple, was dedicated not only to three conventional deities—Amun-Ra, Ra-Horakhty, and Ptah—but also to a deified form of Ramesses II himself. In front of the temple was a forecourt circumscribed by mud-brick enclosure walls to north and south and by the Nile to the east. The rock-cut, pylon-style façade of the temple is dominated by four colossal seated figures of the king wearing the false beard, double crown, uraeus, and *nemes* headcloth, each 66 feet (20 meters) in height. Along the top of the façade, a row of twenty-two baboons are carved in worshipping posture, facing the sun. Beside the legs of the colossi are small statues (the term "small" here is only relative, as they are still larger than life-size) representing various members of the royal family, including Ramesses' wife Nefertari, his daughter Meritamun, and his sons Ramesses and Amonhirkhepeshef. Each colossal statue has an individual names inscribed on its shoulder: "sun of the rulers," "ruler of the two lands," "beloved of Amun," and "beloved of Atum." One of them also bears graffiti written many centuries later by Phoenician, Greek, and Carian mercenaries as they passed by the site on campaigns into Nubia, including soldiers sent by the twenty-sixth-dynasty ruler Ahmose II in 593 B.C.

An inscription on a statue of the viceroy Paser (found broken in two inside the Great Temple) tells us that the monument was severely damaged by an earthquake as early as the thirty-first year of the reign of Ramesses himself. Most of the damage was repaired by Paser's workmen (such as the cracking of some of the interior pillars and of the northern doorjamb of the entrance), but their best efforts were evidently insufficient to replace the upper half of the colossus to the south of the entrance, which still lies on the sand in front of the temple.

Between the two central colossi is an entrance leading to the interior, and on either side of the approach to the entrance are carved relief figures of the

"Nine Bows," the traditional enemies of Egypt. A more specific and realistic reference to international relations at this date has survived in the form of a large rock-cut stele at the southern end of the terrace that records Ramesses' marriage, in the thirty-fourth year of his reign, to a daughter of the Hittite king Hattusilis III—valuable evidence of diplomatic relations. Ironically, part of the relief decoration inside the temple is devoted to a massive depiction of Ramesses' supposed victory over the Hittites at Qadesh (see below).

Inside the temple, Belzoni and his colleagues found a conventional Egyptian temple layout consisting of two pillared halls followed by a vestibule and sanctuary, arranged one after the other along a single axis stretching 160 feet (50 meters) back into the cliff. The first pillared hall has seven storerooms carved with offering scenes leading off from it.

The first hall is the largest room in the temple, 60 feet (18.6 meters) long and 55 feet (17 meters) wide. Its roof is supported by eight columns, the front of each being carved in the form of the king holding the crook and flail, while the sides depict members of the royal family making offerings to the gods. The temple was decorated in the thirty-fourth year of Ramesses' reign, and there is a discernible decline in artistic standards compared with the decoration of the earlier temples of Ramesses and his father at Abydos. The vigorous reliefs on the walls of the temple still preserve much of their paint (primarily red, yellow, and black), and the content of the scenes is concerned mainly with the king's role as warrior. On the south wall appear highlights from Ramesses' campaigns against Nubians, Libyans, and Syrians; the entire north wall is dedicated to a portrayal of the Battle of Qadesh, a conflict with the Hittites that Ramesses seems to have regarded as a highly significant point in his Syro-Palestinian adventures. A small hieroglyphic graffito on the east wall of the first hall is worth noting: it was written by the sculptor Piay to show that he had executed the reliefs depicting princesses directly above the graffito—a rare instance of an artist's "signature" in ancient Egypt, where art was virtually always treated as anonymous craftsmanship rather than individual aesthetic expression.

Scenes of the king presenting prisoners to the gods flank the entrance to the rectangular second hall of the temple, which measures 25 feet (7.6 meters) long by 36 feet (11 meters) wide. Its roof is supported by four pillars. The walls are decorated with scenes focusing on the worship of the sacred barks of Amon-Ra and Ramesses. Three doorways at the western end of the second hall lead to a narrow vestibule, beyond which is the sanctuary.

The Sanctuary of the Great Temple: Archaeoastronomy in Action

Like a handful of other early monuments, such as Stonehenge in England and Newgrange in Ireland, the Great Temple at Abu Simbel was positioned so as to create an intriguing solar alignment. The sanctuary of the temple is

The four divine images at the rear of the sanctuary of the Great Temple at Abu Simbel, bathed in the sun's rays. From left to right, the statues represent Ptah, Amun-Ra, the deified Ramesses II, and Ra-Horakhty.

precisely located so that the rays of the rising sun penetrate to the inner sanctum on two days of the year, 22 February and 22 October, illuminating all four statues in the inner sanctum at the rearmost point of the temple. The statues represent the four main deities of the Great Temple: from right to left, Ra-Horakhty, the deified Ramesses II, Amun-Ra, and Ptah. A platform in front of the statues may have been used to support one of the sacred barks. Nowadays, it tends to be suggested that the two dates when all of the statues are illuminated corresponded to Ramesses' birthday and/or the date of his accession to the throne, but in reality the dates do not appear to tie in with any significant event in Ramesses' personal year. Because they equate roughly with the spring and fall equinoxes (the two times of the year when the sun crosses the equator and the length of the day is almost exactly equal to that of the night), they are probably linked with significant moments in the religious or agricultural calendar.

The Battle of Qadesh: Ancient Propaganda?

The Battle of Qadesh, a single military event in the fifth year of the reign of Ramesses II, was given enormous publicity. It was depicted on the walls of no fewer than five of his most important temples (Abu Simbel, Luxor, Karnak, Abydos, and the Ramesseum), and a literary account has also been preserved on three papyri. Qadesh is one of the most famous armed conflicts of antiquity, perhaps not so much because it was significantly different from earlier battles as because Ramesses, though unable to achieve his goals, presented it at home as a huge victory. He had it described publicly in lengthy compositions, which, in a propaganda campaign of unprecedented proportions, were carved on the walls of all the major temples.

The reliefs at Abu Simbel and the other four temples, supplemented by the literary account preserved on papyri, provide us with the basis for a very detailed account of the battle. In the lead-up to the conflict, Ramesses was engaged in a campaign in Syria–Palestine that aimed to restore Egyptian hegemony over the region, which had been severely disrupted by the expansion of the Hittite empire southward from Anatolia. Ramesses was wrongly led to believe that Mutawalli, the Hittite king, was in the far north at Tunip, too scared to confront the Egyptians; in reality, he was close by on the other side of the city of Qadesh, the stategic location of which had made it an important target for both Egyptians and Hittites in previous conflicts.

Ramesses made a quick advance to Qadesh with only one of his four divisions and then suddenly had to face the huge army the Hittite king had mustered against him. Muwatalli first destroyed the advancing second division, which was about to join the first, then turned around to crush Ramesses and his troops. In his later descriptions of the battle, Ramesses tells us that this was his true moment of glory, for when even his immediate attendants were ready to desert him, he called out to his father Amun to save him, then almost single-handedly managed to fight off the Hittite attackers. Amun heard his prayers and rescued the king by causing an Egyptian support force from the coast of Amurru to arrive in the nick of time. These forces now attacked the Hittites in the rear and, together with Ramesses' division, severely reduced the number of the enemy's chariots and sent the remainder fleeing, many of them ending up in the Orontes River.

With the arrival of the third division at the close of the combat, followed by the fourth at sunset, the Egyptians were able to reassemble their forces and were now ready to face their enemy the next morning. But even though the

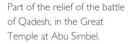

Part of the relief of the battle of Qadesh, in the Great Temple at Abu Simbel.

Egyptian chariotry now outnumbered their Hittite counterparts, Muwatalli's still formidable army was able to hold its ground, and the battle ended in stalemate. Ramesses declined a Hittite peace offer, but a truce was agreed. The Egyptians returned home with many prisoners of war and much booty, but without having achieved their goal. In subsequent years, the Egyptians conducted several other fairly successful confrontations in Syria-Palestine, but each time the conquered vassal states quickly returned to the Hittite fold once the Egyptian armies had gone home, and Egypt never regained Qadesh and Amurru.

The Abu Simbel reliefs depicting the Battle of Qadesh incorporate depictions of the interior of Ramesses II's main encampment near the River Orontes. The camp was surrounded by a rectangular stockade of shields, and the scenes include activities relating to the supply of food and maintenance of equipment. Among the details are ox-carts carrying supplies into the camp, a chariot being repaired, an archer restringing his bow, and a seated soldier whose leg wound is being tended. Ramesses' magnificent tent is shown surrounded by the smaller tents of his officers. There are also a number of dramatic tableaux, including depictions of the seated king discussing strategy with his generals and the interrogation and beating of Hittite spies.

Nearby, the relief shows the fortified city of Qadesh. The motif of a doomed fortress with its inhabitants peering over crenellated battlements is one of the most enduring images of Egyptian warfare. Initially—on Protodynastic palettes and in the tomb scenes of the late Old Kingdom— the fortress is portrayed in plan form, as if viewed from above, but from the First Intermediate Period onwards it is shown from the side. This side view, with the inhabitants either defending frantically or making pleas for mercy and elaborate gestures of surrender, is one of the principal aspects of continuity between the early Middle Kingdom portrayals of battle and the New Kingdom depictions of Ramessid campaigns in Syria-Palestine.

Although the scale of the commemoration of the battle implies that it was intended to be regarded as a high point in Ramesses' reign, the German Egyptologist Hans Goedicke has pointed out that, far from being a great victory over a foreign foe, it may actually never have developed into a full battle: "The only major outcome of the event was a number of Pharaonic soldiers killed, not by the enemy, but by Ramesses II as punishment for the cowardliness displayed at Qadesh." Goedicke therefore argues that the Qadesh reliefs may have been not so much a celebration of Egyptian military prowess as a warning to the military that cowardice would be severely punished.

However, it is also worth bearing in mind that the temple reliefs of the New Kingdom were inextricably linked with the religious cults observed within their walls. Just as the iconography of battle on Protodynastic votive objects was an idealization of the real situation, so it is likely that this process of simplification was carried over into the more elaborate arena of the pharaonic temple inscriptions and reliefs that purport to describe actual military events, such as the battles of Megiddo and Qadesh.

In 1959, when the construction of the Aswan High Dam was announced, it was obvious that, compared with the two previous rescue campaigns in Nubia, funding of a much greater order would be necessary to rescue the many threatened monuments. A UNESCO-supported appeal was therefore launched to encourage a multinational campaign. Because the new reservoir would result in the permanent submersion of many monuments, the campaign in the 1960s and 1970s had a much greater bias toward conservation than toward excavation.

About thirty-five major temples had to be moved, as well as a number of smaller monuments. Perhaps the most important temple to be rescued, apart from those at Abu Simbel, was the vast complex of buildings on the island of Philae, situated about 4 miles (7 kilometers) south of Aswan, midway between the High Dam and the earliest Aswan Dam on the edge of the First Cataract. Unlike the Abu Simbel temples, the buildings on Philae had been partially submerged since the construction of the first dam at the end of the nineteenth century, and by 1972 they were flooded year round up to about one-third of the columns' height.

The surviving elements of the sandstone Philae temple, dating from the thirtieth dynasty to the late Roman Period, were first protected from the rising waters by a huge steel coffer dam surrounding the entire site. Then, over two and a half years, the various structures were broken up into about 40,000 blocks (weighing about 27,000 tons altogether) and transferred to the nearby island of Agilqiyya, where they were cleaned, measured, and reconstructed.

Among the other temples moved during the campaign was that of Kalabsha (ancient Talmis), which was built in the Roman period and dedicated to the Nubian god Mandulis. In 1962–1963, West German engineers moved its 13,000 blocks of stone 32 miles (51 kilometers) to the north, relocating it almost in the shadow of the High Dam itself. In a distant echo of the Abu Simbel reliefs of the Battle of Qadesh, the Kalabsha temple includes a Greek inscription written by Silko, king of Nobatia, recording his battle against the nomadic Blemmyes in the fifth century A.D.

More than forty expeditions were launched in Lower Nubia in response to the UNESCO appeal. The archaeological work in Nubia between 1959 and 1970 exceeded that of all earlier periods together. There were many reasons for the success of the UNESCO campaign. First, it encompassed the archaeology of a whole region rather than just of isolated sites. Second, it was intended to be comprehensive in chronological and cultural terms, like the First Nubian Survey,

The temple reliefs were intended to illustrate basic universal concepts, such as the power of the king and the destruction or absorption of foreigners. Indeed, some scholars have argued that the various "panoramic vistas" of the Battle of Qadesh on the temples of Ramesses II were not so much historical records as elaborate substitutes for the traditional scene of the king smiting foreigners, depicted ad nauseam on temple pylons. The ideology that the New Kingdom battle reliefs express was no doubt fossilized to some extent, but it continued to be useful in the context of propaganda, and the common placement of battle reliefs in full view on the exterior walls of temples (and on the inside, as at Abu Simbel) seems to make it clear that this was at least one of their aims.

The Small Temple

The smaller rock-cut temple at Abu Simbel is about 100 yards (90 meters) north of the Great Temple. Like the earlier eighteenth-dynasty temple of

so that it greatly increased knowledge both of ordinary daily life and of previously neglected periods such as prehistory and the Middle Ages. Finally, it affected the trend of Egyptian archaeology by introducing a new generation of archaeologists to previously neglected areas of study in the Nile Valley.

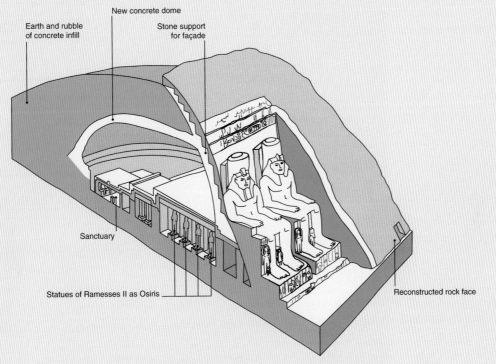

A three-dimensional drawing of the reconstructed Great Temple (after Annick Petersen, 1994).

Queen Tiy at Sedeinga, farther south in Nubia, this monument is unusual in being dedicated to a royal wife—Queen Nefertari—as well as to the goddess Hathor of Abshek (Abshek being the ancient Egyptian name for the site of Abu Simbel). Its façade features four colossal standing figures of Ramesses and only two of Nefertari, despite the fact that this is supposed to be her temple. As in the Great Temple, the king's statues (but not the queen's) are each given names, this time in an inscription running along the top of the façade. Four of the royal children are represented in the form of smaller statues beside the legs of their parents.

The whole structure extends for about 80 feet (25 meters) from front to back wall, almost exactly half the length of the Great Temple. A short passage leads from the façade to a hall containing six columns, each with a distinctive capital in the form of a sistrum, a kind of rattling instrument played mainly by women. The hall is followed by a vestibule, and finally the sanctuary. The painted reliefs, like those in the Great Temple, mainly feature the

This statue of Ramesses II was moved to its present location during the Nubian rescue campaign.

colors red, yellow, and black, but the content of the scenes is less aggressive; the eastern wall of the pillared hall is the only one to include depictions of the ritual slaughter of foreigners. Ramesses appears frequently in the reliefs throughout the interior, although there are a number of scenes showing Nefertari alone, usually presenting offerings to deities. In one scene, on the east wall of the vestibule, the queen is shown being crowned by the goddesses Isis and Hathor.

On the rear wall of the sanctuary is a statue of the goddess Hathor represented as a cow emerging from the rock-face, with a figure of Ramesses II protected beneath her. The surrounding reliefs show both king and queen in the presence of various deities. The most interesting of these, with regard to Nefertari's importance, shows her alongside Ramesses, burning incense and pouring libations not only to the deified form of the king but also to a deified figure of herself.

The Moving of the Abu Simbel Temples

From a modern visitor's point of view, perhaps the most spectacular aspect of the temples is the fact that they still appear largely as they did when Belzoni first cleared them, despite the fact that their original location is now 700 feet (210 meters) away, submerged under the waters of Lake Nasser. Lower Nubia was first subjected to artificial flooding when the earliest and smallest of the Aswan dams was constructed by the British (and heightened in three phases) between 1902 and 1933, triggering a campaign to survey as much of the archaeology of Nubia before it was submerged. When work began on the new Aswan High Dam in 1960, the creation of Lake Nasser, one of the largest reservoirs in the world, was under way. A UNESCO-coordinated operation was launched on 8 March 1960, not only to record the Nubian monuments threatened by this much more extensive flooding but also to dismantle and move certain monuments to higher ground before the completion of the dam in 1971. The Abu Simbel temples were among the largest and most complex of the stone-built monuments threatened by the new lake.

In an operation costing around $40 million, the temples were carved up into separate blocks, the Great Temple making up 807 blocks and the Small Temple comprising 235. These blocks were then reassembled in a concrete matrix at a location 210 feet (64 meters) higher and 700 feet (213 meters) to the west of the original site. The process of moving them took over four years, from 1964 to 1968. Even the alignment of the relocated Great Temple was maintained so that the sanctuary would still be illuminated twice a year. This project was probably the most spectacular achievement of the entire UNESCO campaign, primarily because the temples were largely cut into the living rock, rather than free-standing like those at Philae and Kalabsha.

Further Reading

Burckhardt's description of the rediscovery of Abu Simbel forms part of his *Travels in Nubia* (London, 1819). Giovanni Belzoni's account of his pioneering archaeological work at the site features in his *Narrative of the Operations and Recent Discoveries . . . in Egypt and Nubia* (London, 1820). More recent general books on the site are William MacQuitty's *Abu Simbel* (London, 1965),

Christiane Desroches-Noblecourt's *Grand temple d'Abou Simbel* (Cairo, 1971), and Christiane Desroches-Noblecourt and Charles Kuentz's *Le petit temple d'Abou Simbel* (2 vols., Cairo, 1968).

Temples and Tombs of Ancient Nubia (London, 1987), edited by Torgny Säve-Söderbergh, is one of several books dealing with the UNESCO-backed Nubian salvage operation in the 1960s.

Further Viewing

The Nubia Museum at Aswan, which opened in November 1997, contains a magnificent selection of Egyptian and Nubian sculptures and artifacts, many of which derive from the temples and towns of Ramesses II in Nubia, such as the colossal statue of the king from his temple at Gerf Hussein.

Five of the smallest Nubian temples were given to various countries as rewards for their efforts in saving the Nubian monuments from Lake Nasser. The Roman temple of Dendur was given to the United States and is now in the Sackler Wing of the Metropolitan Museum, New York; the temple of Dabod (an unusual Meroitic/Ptolemaic combination) was given to Spain and can now be viewed in the City Park, Madrid; the undecorated Roman temple of Tafa is now in the Rijksmuseum van Oudheden, Leiden; the Tuthmosid temple of el-Lesiya is in the Museo Egizio, Turin; and a Ptolemaic granite gateway from Kalabsha is now in the Berlin Museum.

Medinet Habu

c. 1279–1153 B.C.

The Mansion of Millions of Years

of Ramesses III

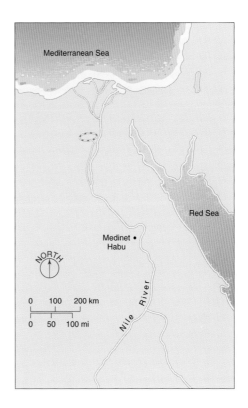

The vast and beautifully preserved temple complex of Medinet Habu, constructed over many years from the early New Kingdom to the Late Period, is situated at the southern end of the Theban west bank, opposite modern Luxor. The earliest section of the complex is a small temple built by the eighteenth-dynasty rulers Hatshepsut and Thutmose III in the fifteenth century B.C., but this was later thoroughly outshone by the mortuary temple of Ramesses III, built in the twelfth century B.C. Unlike the rest of the Theban royal mortuary temples, that of Ramesses III seems to have survived primarily because it was the last great royal monument of the New Kingdom to be constructed on the west bank at Thebes. This meant that, unlike its predecessors, it was not dismantled and robbed to provide building material for later kings' constructions, so it has survived very well to the present day.

Because of its strong fortifications, the temple became a refuge in unsettled times, and the residents of the royal tomb-workers' village at Deir el-Medina moved there during the late twentieth dynasty (c. 1100–1070 B.C.). Eventually, however, the temple defenses were breached and the western gate was demolished. A little less than midway between the eastern gate and the first pylon of the main temple is a group of mortuary "chapel-tombs" of several "god's wives of Amun" of the twenty-fifth and twenty-sixth dynasties. In the Byzantine period, the town of Djeme (the Coptic version of "Tjamet," the site's

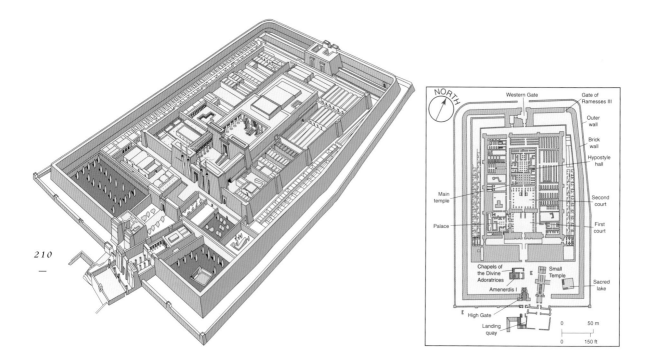

In the plan diagram (right):

NORTH

Western Gate

Gate of
Ramesses III

Outer
wall

Brick
wall

Hypostyle
hall

Main
temple

Second
court

Palace

First
court

Chapels of
the Divine
Adoratrices

Small
Temple

Sacred
lake

Amenerdis I

High Gate

Landing
quay

0   50 m

0   150 ft

Overall plan of the temple complex of Medinet Habu in western Thebes.

name during the pharaonic period) grew up inside the main walled compound of Medinet Habu, and the second court was reused as a church.

The Design of Medinet Habu and the Celebration of the Cult of Ramesses III

Like most of the preceding pharaohs of the New Kingdom, Ramesses III had a tomb excavated and decorated for himself in the Valley of the Kings. Whereas the rulers of the Old and Middle Kingdoms had built pyramid complexes in which the tomb and mortuary temple were all part of the same monument in one location, the New Kingdom pharaohs separated the burial place from the cult temple (the "mansion of millions of years") by a considerable distance. Thus, the royal tombs were dug deep into the Theban cliffs, and the corresponding mortuary temples were constructed in a long row by the edge of the cultivation. Since Medinet Habu was down at the southern end of the row of temples, the distance between it and Ramesses III's tomb was more than a mile as the crow flies. With regard to the cult of the dead king, however, the tomb and temple were still conceived as two halves of a single monument, intimately connected by their joint role in ensuring the survival of the king in the afterlife.

The entire complex of Medinet Habu is enclosed by massive mud-brick walls, originally 35 feet (10.7 meters) thick and 60 feet (18.3 meters) high, with entrances to both west and east. The west gate was destroyed many centuries ago, but the eastern one (sometimes known as the "pavilion gate") has survived. It takes the form of a Syrian fortress, or *migdol*. This establishes a suitably intimidating atmosphere as visitors enter the temple from the direction of the Nile, although the full dramatic effect of the frontage is now slightly spoiled by the protruding Ptolemaic and Roman additions to the adjacent eighteenth-dynasty temple. Like the main temple pylon, the outside walls of the gateway are decorated with large relief scenes of the king smiting his enemies—Nubians and Libyans on the left, and Asiatics and various seminomadic peoples on the right. In rooms above the eastern gate, interior wall reliefs have survived showing Ramesses III relaxing in his private apartments, playing board-games with the women of his harem. In a recess on the south side of the passage leading through the gate there is a relief depiction of the king offering to the god Ptah, whose image was evidently originally inlaid with colored faience and perhaps covered with a veil. Close to the eastern gate, and covered by the modern road approaching the site, are the remains of a landing stage at the end of a canal running westward from the Nile.

The three-storey East Gate of Ramesses III's mortuary temple at Medinet Habu takes the form of an Asiatic *migdol,* or fortress.

The temple itself consists of a sequence of two pylons, two courts, two hypostyle halls, and a suite of treasuries and sanctuaries devoted to the gods Osiris and Ra-Horakhty. Its alignment is roughly southeast to northwest, but conventionally the side facing the Nile is known as the east. As in most Egyptian temples, the overall design of Medinet Habu conveys a sense of penetrating deeper and deeper into the darkness: the pylons and open courts lead into dense columned halls, with the floor gradually rising and the ceilings lowering as the visitor draws closer to the clusters of hidden shrines in the innermost parts of the building.

All around the outside walls of the temple are relief carvings depicting scenes from the king's various military campaigns, notably his wars with the Libyans and the Sea Peoples, who also appear in continued battle scenes inside the first court of the temple. The northern and southern halves of the first pylon are carved with scenes showing the king smiting his enemies, while rows of human-headed "name rings" depict the conquered lands.

The first court of the temple, which served as the "hall of royal appearances," seems to have had its huge, heavy wooden door almost permanently open (the wall behind it is described in inscriptions as "shadow of the door").

A detail of Ramesses III's naval battle with the so-called Sea Peoples, on the northern exterior wall of his mortuary temple. The soldiers in this Sea Peoples' boat include both Sherden (with horned helmets) and probably Tjekker (those wearing the distinctive high headdress sometimes described as a "feathered crown").

212

CHAPTER FIFTEEN

213

Nevertheless, there are interesting archaeological traces suggesting that access to the first court and the rest of the temple was limited to a favored few. We know this because there are also remains of a smaller double-leafed door that lay at the end of the passageway through the center of the pylon and probably served as a regular means of entering and exiting the temple for those who were allowed this privilege. Once the elite passed through this door, they found themselves—like modern visitors to the temple—standing in a large open court with an eight-pillared portico to the left (or south), and to the right a set of seven pillars, each fronted by a huge standing figure of the king. Beyond the southern portico was the king's palace; the court owes its name to the fact that the pharaoh was able to appear ceremonially at a window in the south wall, thus providing a link between his apartments and the temple proper. The window was at some point widened, presumably to give Ramesses a better view of ritual events within the first court. The reliefs around the walls of the first court generally continue the theme of military conquest, and it is clear from the inscriptions that the booty from the king's campaigns (including the severed hands and foreskins of his enemies) was brought here to be piled up in the presence of the great god Amun-Ra. Some of the reliefs below the window show that the king would also have viewed wrestling matches in which Egyptians competed against Libyans, Nubians, or Asiatics. In front of the visitor, at the western end of the first court, is the second pylon, which provides access to the second court.

All four sides of the second court consist of colonnades. The decoration on the walls is devoted to scenes of religious processions, notably those of the gods Min and Sokar. As the reliefs suggest, it was in this court that many of the temple's regular festivals were celebrated. The scenes on the north wall show parts of the enactment of the Feast of the Valley, in which the cult-statues of Amun, Mut, and Khonsu, the three deities of Karnak temple, were brought over the Nile to the reigning king's mortuary temple. They also show the key moments in the Feast of Sokar, which occurred annually over a period of ten days in mid-September. This festival was evidently the most important of the ritual events celebrated at Medinet Habu, since a calendar on the temple's southern exterior wall lists more offerings set aside for it than for any other event. At the climax of the Feast of Sokar, the statue of the god was placed in a bark (a portable boat-shaped shrine), carried out of the temple by the priests, and then taken round and round the temple walls. The festival concluded with the ceremonial erection of the djed-pillar, a ritual celebrating the burial of Osiris, the god of the dead.

Beyond the second court is the hypostyle hall. Despite the generally good state of preservation of the temple as a whole, the hypostyle hall has suffered greatly, the columns being reduced to only a few feet in height. However, in the southwest corner is a treasury building with scenes depicting some of the temple equipment. Other temple valuables were probably kept in a better concealed building immediately in front of the north wall of the sanctuary. The focus of the main axis of the temple is the sanctuary of Amun, behind which lies a false door dedicated to "Amun-Ra united with eternity," a title of Ramesses III in his divine form.

The royal palace, situated on the southeastern side of the temple, was probably much smaller than the king's main residences in Thebes, Memphis, and Piramesse. It served partly as a symbolic home and partly as a setting for Ramesses' occasional visits to his mortuary temple. It was originally deco-

The throne-room in Ramesses III's symbolic or ceremonial palace at Medinet Habu.

rated with glazed tiles, many of which are now in the Cairo Museum, and its bathrooms were lined with limestone to protect the mud brick. From the palace, the king could enter the first court or observe it from the "window of appearances" on its southern side.

The Temple as Settlement and Fortress

Ramesses III's mortuary temple was constructed with four rows of small houses, thirty-three in all, between the inner and outer enclosure walls. The German excavator Uvo Hölscher has supplied little information about the domestic objects found there, but the purely architectural aspects of these houses make interesting comparisons with earlier planned residential blocks at Amarna, Malkata, and Deir el-Ballas. These rows of houses at Medinet Habu are of two different types. The two rows nearest to the temple were each just over 1,100 square feet (100 square meters) in area, and their roofs were held up by impressive octagonal columns; Hölscher therefore suggested that "they were intended not for people of lowly position, such as poor workmen or slaves, who were no doubt employed in great numbers in the temple precinct, but probably only for employees or officials."

The two rows farther from the temple consisted of smaller houses, each only about 759 square feet (70 square meters) in area; these Hölscher described as "vastly different from dwellings known to us before." He suggested that these smaller houses, whose plan is unlike those at Deir el-Medina or the Amarna "workmen's village," may have been barracks-style housing for slaves or soldiers. The inner row of the larger houses was separated from the two outer rows only by a narrow street, but there was evidently no regular traffic between the larger and smaller "classes" of dwelling.

In the reign of Ramesses XI (c.1098–1069 B.C.), at the very end of the New Kingdom, a combination of civil war and the presence of hostile Libyans in the western desert made western Thebes relatively unsafe, so the royal tomb-workers at Deir el-Medina moved into the interior of Medinet Habu. A building still partially standing at the western end of Medinet Habu has been identified as the house of a scribe of the workmen called Butehamon, whose name appears on the stone lintels and columns. The lintel of his father Thutmose's house was found nearby. Thutmose and his son Butehamun were part of a Deir el-Medina family who had been scribes for about a hundred years, since the appointment of Amennakhte son of Ipuy in the reign of Ramesses III (c.1171 B.C.). After the move to Medinet Habu, work at first continued as usual on Ramesses XI's tomb, which was to be the last one built in the Valley of the Kings.

An archive of letters sent by the scribe Thutmose has survived. In one, he describes the general situation of the tombworkers:

> We are living here in Medinet Habu . . . However, the boys of
> the Tomb have gone. They are living in Thebes while I am living

here alone with the scribe of the army Pentahunakhte. Please have the men of the Tomb who are there in Thebes assembled and send them to me to this side [of the river] . . . Put them under the supervision of the scribe Butehamun.

Later, Thutmose was posted down in Nubia, and his letters were then being sent to his son, who had been put in charge of the tomb-workers in his absence. Thutmose died in about year 28 of the reign of Ramesses XI. It is possible that the inhabitants of Medinet Habu at this date might have been some of those mentioned in a list of households on the verso of one of the twelve so-called Tomb Robbery Papyri (BM 10068), which record judicial inquiries at Thebes in years 16 and 17 of the reign of Ramesses IX (c. 1115 B.C.).

After the Ramessid Period, the area between the inner and outer enclosure walls became honeycombed with winding streets and houses that were built on top of the remains of the original planned rows of buildings. The British Egyptologist Barry Kemp has suggested that this somewhat disorganized growth reflects the fact that the role of the residential part of Medinet Habu "was extended beyond that of simply housing the personnel for this one temple." The transformation of the settlement from orderly blocks and rows into a more haphazard arrangement may reflect the appearance of a new set of inhabitants. It may therefore show the two extremes of Egyptian settlement organization, with the plan of the late eighteenth-dynasty city at Amarna (see chapter 11) midway between them.

The Chapels of the God's Wives of Amun

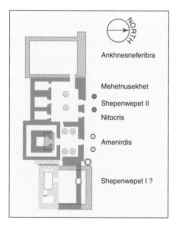

Plan of the tomb-chapels of the god's wives of Amun, in the forecourt of the mortuary temple of Ramesses III.

Near the eastern gate of Medinet Habu is a pair of imposing stone buildings, the remains of a group of mortuary "chapel-tombs" beneath which several of the twenty-fifth- and twenty-sixth-dynasty priestesses known as "god's wives of Amun" were buried. The two surviving buildings housed the funerary cults of the god's wives from Amenirdis I to Netiqret. Only faint traces of two other chapels (the earliest and latest in the sequence) have survived at either end of these structures.

Amenirdis I, the daughter of the Kushite ruler Kashta, adopted as "god's wife" in about 740 B.C., was eventually buried in a tiny crypt under the floor of her chapel, just large enough to have held a stone sarcophagus and a few items of funerary equipment. This chamber was completely plundered in ancient times, and not even the sarcophagus has survived. The second part of the structure belonged to Shepenwepet II (daughter of Piye, adopted in 710 B.C.), Netiqret, and Mehetnusekhet (mother of Netiqret and wife of Psamtek I). The shrine of Mehetnusekhet differs from the others, having a false door at the back and generally resembling the tombs of high officials at this time rather than the chapel-tombs of the god's wives of Amun. Almost

216

nothing is left of the chapel of Shepenwepet I (daughter of Osorkon III, adopted c. 754 B.C.) at the eastern end, but a burial shaft leads down to the tomb chambers of Shepenwepet and the rest of her family. At the western end, it is evident from peculiarities of the walls that there was originally a chapel of Ankhnesneferibra (daughter of Psametek II), the last of the god's wives, but none of its masonry has survived. The sarcophagus of Ankhnesneferibra was found reused at Deir el-Medina and is now in the collection of the British Museum.

The function of the god's wife of Amun was to play the part of the consort of Amun in religious ceremonies, emphasizing the belief that kings were conceived from the union between Amun and the great royal wife. The title "god's hand" was also sometimes used, referring to the act of masturbation by which the Creator Atum produced Shu and Tefnut; Atum's hand was thus regarded as female. In the late twentieth dynasty, Ramesses VI conferred on his daughter Isis a combined title of both god's wife of Amun and divine adoratrice, thus creating what was largely a political post. From then on, this office was bestowed on the king's daughter, who, as a priestess, would have held great religious and political power in the city. She was barred from marriage, remaining a virgin, and so she had to adopt the daughter of the next king as heiress to her office. In this way, the king sought to ensure that he always held power in Thebes, and he also prevented his elder daughters from aiding rival claimants to the throne. The god's wife was in fact the most prominent member of a group of "Amun's concubines," all virgins and all with adopted successors.

In the twenty-fifth and twenty-sixth dynasties, the god's wife and her adopted successor played an important role in the transference of royal power. This office was sometimes combined with that of chief priestess of Amun. The god's wives of Amun are attested only in the Theban region. We know a fair amount about the office of god's wife in general because of the survival of a stele (found at Karnak temple) dealing with the adoption of Netiqret as the new god's wife in the reign of Psamtek I. The occasion of Netiqret's adoption was also celebrated on the walls of the Karnak temple of Mut, with a set of reliefs depicting a number of boats arriving at the main quay at Karnak, where they were greeted by the two existing god's wives, Shepenwepet II and Amenirdis II, as well as by Mentuemhet, the powerful mayor of Thebes.

Each of the twenty-fifth- and twenty-sixth-dynasty god's wives of Amun had at least one chief steward, who appears to have been charged with the control of her estates. Between them, the god's wife and the chief steward probably wielded power equivalent to that of chief priests of Amun at the end of the New Kingdom, such as Piankh and Herihor. Eight statues of a twenty-fifth-dynasty chief steward called Harwa have survived. An inscription on one statue of Harwa in Berlin describes how his career was advanced both by the god's wife and the king: "My lady made me great when I was a small boy, she advanced my position when I was a child. The King sent me on missions as a youth; Horus, lord of the palace, distinguished me."

The last two god's wives of Amun, Netiqret and Ankhnesneferibra, were also the chief priestesses of Amun, thus holding complete supremacy over the Theban region. The Persian conquest brought a temporary end to both the Saite Dynasty (the twenty-sixth-dynasty rulers whose capital was the city of Sais) and the post of god's wife of Amun. Some measure of the wealth and influence of these women has survived in the form of their "temple-tombs" at Medinet Habu.

The Tomb of the Eight Gods and Goddesses

In the northeast corner of the temple enclosure is a building that incorporates both the earliest and the latest phases of monumental construction at Medinet Habu. Beneath its foundations are traces of a temple dating at least as far back as the early eighteenth dynasty, and perhaps even to the Middle Kingdom. The earliest parts of the building itself—the sanctuary and bark-shrine, at the western end of the temple—date to the reigns of Hatshepsut and Thutmose III (mid-eighteenth dynasty); the latest parts, a small portico and forecourt, are of the Roman Period.

The purpose of the building was to celebrate rites connected with the so-called Ogdoad, a group of eight gods and goddesses whose cult was particularly important in the region of Hermopolis in Middle Egypt. The small temple at Medinet Habu was known as "the genuine mound of the West" and was regarded as the final resting place of the Ogdoad. Because the Theban god Amun was thought to manifest himself in the form of various deities within the Ogdoad, there were weekly festivals in which Amun (in the form of his statue) traveled across from Luxor temple to Medinet Habu in order to "see his father in the company of his children, who came into being from his limbs." Since the temple was the tomb of the Ogdoad, it is possible that the regular visits by Amun were a way of ritually linking the east bank at Thebes (the land of the living) with the cemeteries on the west bank (the land of the dead).

Usually modern visitors to Medinet Habu would be able to enter the small temple through a doorway on the southern side, between the sanctuary and bark-shrine, but at the time of writing (2002), the Chicago Oriental Institute is engaged in epigraphic work and conservation in these earliest parts of the temple, and so they are not open to the public. Instead, we have to enter the temple through a gateway to the south of the columned hall that was added onto the bark-shrine in the twenty-fifth dynasty and later rebuilt by Ptolemy X. It is no longer possible to enter the small temple through its easternmost gate, which has been blocked in modern times in order to leave only one tourist entrance to Medinet Habu as a whole. A visitor in the third century A.D., however, would have passed through the eastern gateway into a large forecourt, at the west end of which was an unfinished stone portico built by the Roman emperor Antoninus Pius in the mid-second century. This was dominated by the towering stone Ptolemaic pylon to which it was attached. The pylon, with a huge painted winged disk on its cavetto cornice (a distictive form of concave molding projecting from the top of the pylon), is one of the most impressive surviving parts of the temple.

The third-century visitor who passed through the pylon gradually walked back through the history of Egypt, as is often the case in Egyptian temples. Beyond the pylon, he found himself standing in front of a six-columned portico built by an unknown twenty-sixth-dynasty ruler whose name was excised and replaced by that of Nectanebo I, one of the last few native rulers of Egypt before the Persian conquest. Beyond the twenty-sixth-dynasty por-

Reassembled dyad of Thutmosis III and Amun, granodiorite, 3 meters in height.

219
—

The mortuary temple of Ramesses III is the southernmost of a long row of royal mortuary temples that extends along the edge of the desert for a distance of 2.5 miles (4 kilometers). Up at the far northern end, near the village of Gurna, is the temple of Sety I, the prototype for Ramessid mortuary temples such as the Ramesseum and Medinet Habu. Its two courtyards, each entered by a large pylon, led westward to a portico, hypostyle hall, and sanctuaries—an architectural blueprint repeated throughout the nineteenth and twentieth dynasties.

Most of the mortuary temples, here as elsewhere in Egypt, were built by cannibalizing earlier structures in the vicinity, no doubt primarily to save effort and cost, but perhaps also to benefit from their associations with earlier pharaohs and their cults. The temple of Merenptah, for instance, reused many stone blocks taken from its neighbor, the mortuary temple of Amenhotep III, built nearly 200 years earlier. The latter temple was thus robbed down to its foundations, but its site is still unmistakably marked by two colossal statues of the deified Amenhotep that once flanked its eastern entrance. These two huge seated statues, now known as the Colossi of Memnon, are matched in size only by the statues of Ramesses II at Abu Simbel and the Ramesseum. It is probably no coincidence that all these colossi represent not merely the king or one of the Egyptian pantheon (such as Amun or Horus), but the deified king, who may have been regarded as a kind of super-deity combining the powers of both kingship and divinity and therefore portrayed on as large a scale as possible. At the time of writing (2002), the temple of Amenhotep III is the subject of extensive excavations led by the German archaeologist Rainer Stadelmann.

The second court of the mortuary temple of Ramesses II (the Ramesseum).

The Ramesseum, Ramesses II's mortuary temple, is situated about a mile (1.6 kilometers) north of Medinet Habu. Many aspects of Ramesses III's reign seem to have consciously imitated his illustrious predecessor, and this is especially true of the mortuary temples. Although the Ramesseum is not as well preserved as Medinet Habu, enough of the walls, columns, and statuary survives to show that it served as the closest model for Ramesses III's temple. Like Medinet Habu, the complex also includes the remains of a royal palace and numerous mud-brick granaries and storerooms. Both pylons of the Ramesseum are decorated with scenes from the Battle of Qadesh, which Ramesses III was to imitate with his scenes of the battles with Libyans and Sea Peoples. Beneath the floor of the Ramesseum, a shaft-tomb of a priest of the late Middle Kingdom (c.1700 B.C.) was excavated by James Quibell in the nineteenth century; its burial chamber contained a box of Middle Kingdom papyri and a range of religious and magical artifacts.

tico was a pylon built by the Kushite twenty-fifth-dynasty rulers, whose names were excised from their cartouches in the Ptolemaic period. Walking westward through this small pylon, the visitor passed through the middle of two rows of eight columns before reaching the frontage of the eighteenth-dynasty core of the temple. The reliefs and inscriptions decorating this façade are a fascinating mixture of styles deriving from many different phases of the temple. Beyond the façade are the bark-shrine and the various chambers of the sanctuary.

When Uvo Hölscher cleared the small temple, he found that the paving blocks in the entrance chamber of the sanctuary had been torn up, and among the debris were three fragments of a colossal gray granodiorite statue of Thutmose III seated beside the god Amun. Many more fragments of this statue were found by the epigraphic survey in the floor debris prior to restoration of the flooring in 1999. Hölscher recognized evidence that the front wall of the sanctuary was left unfinished and was only added by Thutmose III after the statue was in place because the statue was considerably larger than the doorway. The Amun figure was later mutilated during Akhenaten's reign and new evidence shows that the Amun element was restored in the post-Amarna period. The statue was broken into pieces in the medieval period when Medinet Habu was the center of the Christian community in western Thebes. The pieces were buried in a large robber's pit in the middle of the sanctuary. The statue has recently been restored by the Epigraphic Survey of the Oriental Institute, University of Chicago.

By sheer chance, the small temple has also preserved another relic of the reign of Thutmose III. Out in the Roman forecourt, Hölscher found a magnificent granite false door that originally stood in the mortuary temple of Thutmose III, a short distance north of Medinet Habu. It had been reused as a threshold in the forecourt, and being laid face down it was much better preserved than it might have been if it had been left exposed to the elements. This monument has been reerected close to the spot where it was found.

Further Reading

The most comprehensive description of the monuments at Medinet Habu was published by the epigraphers of the Chicago Oriental Institute in *Medinet Habu* (8 vols., Chicago, 1930–1970). The early excavations of Harold H. Nelson and Uvo Hölscher were published as *Medinet Habu, 1924–1928* (Chicago, 1929). The later excavations were published by Hölscher in *The Excavation of Medinet Habu* (5 vols., Chicago, 1934–1954). An excellent shorter account of the site is William Murnane's *United with Eternity: A Concise Guide to the Monuments of Medinet Habu* (Chicago and Cairo, 1980).

The architecture and reliefs of the mortuary temple of Ramesses II were published by James Quibell in *The Ramesseum* (London, 1898), and by

Wolfgang Helck in *Die Ritualdarstellungen des Ramesseums* (Wiesbaden, 1972). B. J. J. Haring discusses the general phenomenon of New Kingdom mortuary temples in *Divine Households: Administrative and Economic Aspects of the New Kingdom Royal Mortuary Temples in Western Thebes* (Leiden, 1997).

Further Viewing

Wall tiles from the palace at Medinet Habu are displayed in the Egyptian Museum, Cairo, and the stone sarcophagus of the last god's wife of Amun, Ankhnesneferibra, is part of the collection of the British Museum. The Swiss excavators of the mortuary temple of Merenptah opened a museum at the site in 2002.

Tanis

c. 1069–747 B.C.

Capital of the Libyan pharaohs

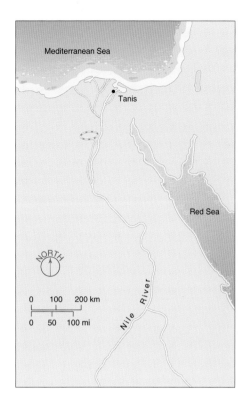

In Mesopotamia and the Indus, many of the excavated sites are towns and cities, but in Egypt, the majority of sites are tombs and temples. Egyptian cemeteries are largely situated in the desert, and the temples are mainly built of stone; both these factors have ensured the preservation of religious and funerary monuments in greater numbers than settlement-sites, since the latter are mostly constructed of mud brick and nearly all situated in the densely populated Nile Valley. Moreover, archaeologists working in Egypt historically have tended to focus on stone temples and decorated tombs and to neglect the sites where the ancient Egyptians were actually living. Thus, until recently our knowledge of Egyptian daily life was based either on tomb-scenes or on the evidence from a tiny group of excavated settlements, primarily dating to the Middle or New Kingdom (Lahun, Amarna, and Deir el-Medina are the best known). Fortunately, the balance is now slowly shifting: over the last three decades of the twentieth century, excavation began on a number of significant town sites, including the Third Intermediate Period city of Tanis in the eastern Nile Delta.

The modern Delta region of Egypt is the main center of the Egyptian population, but comparatively few archaeological sites have survived well in this northernmost part of the country, and even fewer have actually been excavated to any great extent. In fact, these demographic and archaeological

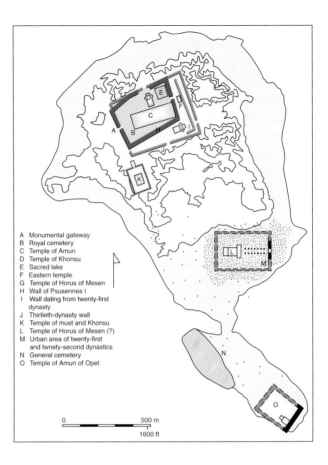

A Monumental gateway
B Royal cemetery
C Temple of Amun
D Temple of Khonsu
E Sacred lake
F Eastern temple
G Temple of Horus of Mesen
H Wall of Psusennes I
I Wall dating from twenty-first
   dynasty
J Thirtieth-dynasty wall
K Temple of must and Khonsu
L Temple of Horus of Mesen (?)
M Urban area of twenty-first
   and twnety-second dynastics
N General cemetery
O Temple of Amun of Opet

scenarios are closely linked because of the disastrous damage that intensify-
ing agriculture has wreaked on the ancient settlements of the Delta. Many
tell sites that are known to have been well preserved as recently as the nineteenth and early twentieth centuries were rapidly destroyed by farmers who
removed the archaeological deposits for use as fertilizer. Miraculously, the
site of Tanis (modern San el-Hagar) survived this agricultural pillaging, primarily because its location, surrounded by the Manzala salt lake, is more isolated than most major sites. Ironically, it was the gradual salinization of the
waters surrounding Tanis that caused its decline in the Byzantine period,
when it was replaced by other cities enjoying more favorable ecological conditions to the north and east.

The principal excavations at Tanis were carried out in 1860–1880 by
Auguste Mariette, in 1883–1886 by Flinders Petrie, and in 1921–1951 by
Pierre Montet. The site is still being studied by French archaeologists at the
beginning of the twenty-first century. Today its huge mound, measuring 2
miles (3.2 kilometers) from north to south and about 1 mile (1.6 kilometers)
from east to west, is the only site in the Delta, apart from Alexandria, that
is visited with any frequency by tourists.

The landscape consists of heavily eroded hills between which seasonal watercourses run. Although the mound of Tanis is largely manmade, at its core is a natural deposit consisting of fossilized Pleistocene sand dunes, known in Arabic as a *gezira* (literally, "island"). Such islands, or "turtle-backs," would have been the only parts of the ancient Delta landscape to remain dry during the annual Nile inundation, so they were obvious places to establish settlements. In the 1980s, the French expedition working at Tanis undertook geophysical survey in an attempt to establish the original height of the gezira across the mound as a whole. The results were inconclusive, primarily because of the presence of groundwater and the large amount of salt in the soil.

The earliest recorded building at Tanis dates to the reign of the twenty-first-dynasty ruler Psusennes I (1039–991 B.C.), who was responsible for constructing the huge mud-brick enclosure wall (1450 by 1230 feet, 435 by 370 meters) surrounding the temple of Amun. Later rulers of the twenty-first and early twenty-second dynasties added to the temple complex; Nectanebo I of the thirtieth dynasty also built there, removing stone from the temple buildings of Sheshonq V and Psamtek I for use in the construction of the Sacred Lake. On the southeastern side of the site, beyond the temple enclosure, is a smaller temple dedicated to Mut and Khonsu, where the Asiatic goddess Astarte was also worshipped; this building was reconstructed during the reign of Ptolemy IV (221–205 B.C.).

By the first century A.D., Tanis had dwindled to little more than a village, probably because its harbor silted up, severely reducing its commercial opportunities. Although it retained some importance as the center of a minor Byzantine bishopric, the settlement appears to have been entirely abandoned by the Islamic period.

Early Fieldwork at Tanis

In 1800, the site was first mapped by the French topographer Jacotin, and a year later the British diplomat Sir William Hamilton excavated a deep pit in the middle of a large mud-brick enclosure. This part of the site would later be identified as a temple of the god Amun, and a sphinx that Hamilton found was the first of many statues to be unearthed at the site. In 1857, the French archaeologist Auguste Mariette persuaded the Egyptian Viceroy Said Pasha to allow him to set up an Antiquities Service to protect the monuments of Egypt. In 1860, Mariette began large-scale excavations at Tanis, creating huge spoil heaps as he worked his way along the axis of the Temple of Amun.

Because Mariette found a great deal of statuary of Ramesses II and his immediate successors, he assumed that Tanis was the site of the great capital of Piramesse, which was known to have been established by Ramesses as a new capital in the eastern Delta. Some of the sculptures were carved with inscriptions referring to the god Seth "Lord of Avaris," and so he also deduced that this was the site of Avaris, the capital established by the Asiatic Hyksos kings about four centuries earlier. The latter assumption appeared to be supported by Mariette's discovery of the so-called Four-Hundred-Year Stele, which commemorates the revival of the cult of Seth four centuries after its first introduction. Mariette also found four outlandish sphinxes that were formerly assumed to depict Hyksos rulers; they are now recognized as sphinxes of the twelfth-dynasty ruler Amenemhat III, probably emphasizing his identification with the sun god. It is now known that the many blocks and fragments of reliefs and statuary at Tanis dating to the Middle Kingdom, the Hyksos Period, and the reign of Ramesses II were actually transported there during the Third Intermediate Period from the real sites of Piramesse and Avaris, ultimately to confuse a whole sequence of excavators from Mariette to Montet.

In the early 1880s, many archaeological expeditions were motivated by the desire to find physical authentication for episodes in the Bible. Indeed, the Society for the Promotion of Excavation in the Delta of the Nile (the early name for the Egypt Exploration Fund) was dedicated to the search for "the documents of a lost period of biblical history" in the Delta region. Flinders Petrie was therefore appointed by the Egypt Exploration Fund to excavate the Delta sites of Tanis, Naukratis, Nabesha, and Defenna. Like the French excavators, he concentrated on the area of the Temple of Amun at Taris, and his plan of the main enclosure and the many decorated stone blocks scattered over the surface was used by subsequent excavators until a new survey was undertaken in the 1990s. Most of Petrie's finds, including a fascinating set of partly burned papyri, date to the Ptolemaic and Roman phases of the site.

Pierre Montet's Excavations: The Royal Tombs

The French archaeologist Pierre Montet began work at Tanis in 1928. Despite the fact that Alan Gardiner had published an article in 1918 in which he argued convincingly that Tanis was not the site of Piramesse, Montet, like Mariette, remained convinced that it was to be identified with both Avaris and Piramesse. Indeed, it was primarily because of the supposed links with the Hyksos capital Avaris that he became interested in the site, having spent many years working at the Levantine port of Byblos, a strongly Egyptian-influenced town in Palestine; he was therefore eager to explore what appeared to be a strongly Asiatic-influenced site within Egypt. Montet held to this belief until the completion of his work at the site three decades later, even though the finds he made would ultimately form part of a broader framework of evidence proving that Tanis was simply a Third Intermediate Period capital, that Piramesse was situated at Qantir, 13 miles (21 kilometers) to the south, and that the city of Avaris was at Tell el-Dab'a, adjacent to Qantir on the southwest.

Despite his erroneous view of Tanis, Montet's actual finds turned out to be some of the most exciting made at any site in Egypt. He began by exploring the northern part of the mound, where he hoped to find traces of Asiatic influence. He discovered a new temple southwest of the Temple of Amun, which he described as the Temple of Anta (an Asiatic goddess) on the basis of a statue mentioning this deity; however, it is now clear that the temple is dedicated to various aspects of the Egyptian goddess Mut, including Anta. Transferring his attention back to the main temple enclosure, Montet eventually made a series of finds that would no doubt have rivaled Howard Carter's discovery of Tutankhamun's tomb, had it not taken place in 1939 and been overshadowed by the outbreak of World War II. Montet's main discoveries took place just as Germany was invading Czechoslovakia.

Montet initially concentrated on a great heap of granite blocks at the western end of the enclosure, which he was able to reconstruct into a partially decorated monumental gateway of Sheshonq III. Inside the enclosure, he made a number of interesting discoveries, including a limestone well, granite columns inscribed with the name of King Apries, and a magnificent statue of Ramesses II as a child in front of a large falcon statue. It was evidently the last find that led Montet to begin excavating systematically westward across the enclosure. In February 1939, he found a set of stone-lined subterranean chambers. The first four of these, lined with stone slabs decorated with painted funerary scenes, were identified by inscriptions as the plundered tomb of Osorkon II. This tomb was certainly an interesting discovery, but the real excitement came on 18 March, when Montet entered a chamber bearing the name of Psusennes I. He knew almost at once that this tomb, unlike that of Osorkon II, was intact: "There was a gap, and through it I could see the gleam of gold within."

NORTH

0   10 m

0   30 ft

A Tomb of Osorkon II
B Tomb of unidentified person
C Tomb of Psusennes I
D Chamber prepared for Amenemope
E Tomb of Shoshenq III
F Chamber dismantled in antiquity
G Chamber dismantled in antiquity

228

Montet had found several of the royal tombs of the twenty-first and twenty-second dynasties. For some reason, probably in part because of a desire for greater security, the practice of burying the pharaohs in the secluded Valley of the Kings at Thebes had been replaced by the safer—though less grandiose—expedient of creating burials within the main temple enclosure at the new capital, Tanis, where it would be more difficult for tomb-robbers to gain access. Montet and his team found six tombs altogether. All of them are subterranean and constructed of a combination of mud brick and reused stone blocks, many of the latter inscribed. The occupants of two of the tombs are unknown, but the remaining four belonged to Psusennes I, Amenemope, Osorkon II, and Sheshonq III. Moreover, three further royal burials had been placed in these tombs: the tomb of Psusennes I contained the hawk-headed silver coffin of Sheshonq II and the coffin and sarcophagus of another ruler, Amenemope, while the tomb of Osorkon II held the sarcophagus of Takelot II. The goldwork from the Tanis necropolis is the most important surviving source of knowledge concerning royal funerary goods of the Third Intermediate Period.

In 1985, a reexamination of the necropolis revealed that there was once another tomb at the site (perhaps belonging to Amenemope or Siamun), which seems to have been dismantled by Osorkon II in order to reuse the blocks for his own tomb. Indeed Philippe Brissaud's reexamination of the site suggested that the necropolis was extensively remodeled by the twenty-second-dynasty ruler Shoshenq III in the ninth century B.C. He built his own tomb at the roof level of the existing tombs and also constructed a massive mud-brick building surrounding the whole necropolis. It is likely that the tombs of the "missing" Third Intermediate Period pharaohs were demolished in the course of this reorganization. It also appears that the twenty-first-dynasty royal tombs at Tanis, such as that of Psusennes I, were built so that royal women could be interred in the same tombs as their husbands (in the case of Psusennes, his wife Mutnodjmet); in contrast, the twenty-second-dynasty tombs appear to have been designed to accommodate only the rulers themselves.

Many so-called primitive burials were found under the Temple of Amun. These often consisted of bodies laid directly in the sand, frequently with no real grave or equipment, although occasionally they are accompanied by some grave-goods and placed in baked clay coffins with anthropomorphic covers. When Montet found these, he interpreted them as human sacrifices and claimed that they were evidence of Semitic influence on the city, but it is now thought that they were simply an attempt by the earliest inhabitants of Tanis to protect their dead from the humidity in the Delta plains by placing the bodies high up on the sandy gezira. These burials date to the late Ramessid Period, and they show that the Third Intermediate Period Temple of Amun was built directly on top of the local Ramessid cemetery.

Golden funerary mask of King Psusennes, from his twenty-first dynasty tomb at Tanis. Gold inlaid with lapis lazuli (beard) and black and white glass (eyes and brows)—one of four masks found at Tanis.

Did the Rulers of Tanis Come from Libya?

A number of aspects of the Third Intermediate Period remains at Tanis and elsewhere in the Delta are very different from the standard funerary practices of Egyptians in the New Kingdom. These distinctive traits of the Tanite rulers and their burials are thought to indicate that the new rulers were not Egyptians but Libyans, who had risen to positions of great power in the Egyptian administration in the years following the end of the twentieth dynasty. This suggestion raises two principal questions: How did the Libyans gain such great influence in Egypt? And why have these Third Intermediate Period rulers been identified as Libyan?

To answer the first question, we need to look at several factors in the lead-up to the twenty-first dynasty: first, the evidence for Egyptian wars with Libyans in the late New Kingdom; second, the capture of Libyans as prisoners of war and their subsequent employment as mercenaries and resettlement in Egypt; and third, the historical data suggesting that Libyan peoples were increasingly posing a security threat to Egypt and beginning to settle within its borders (particularly in the western Delta). The Wilbour Papyrus, dating to the reign of Ramesses V, mentions a community of Tjuku Libyans at Herakleopolis; Papyrus Louvre 3169, from the time of Ramesses XI, describes the Meshwesh Libyans as living in the Delta somewhere near Per-hebyt (modern Behbeit el-Hagar). While it is fairly easy to find evidence for the arrival of large numbers of Libyans in Egypt, it is much more difficult to understand how or why they rose to positions of influence, and studies of their rise to power tend to be hampered by a tendency for immigrants to adopt Egyptian names within a generation or two.

The identification of the Libyan origins and influences of many of the rulers and local princes of the Third Intermediate Period rests on the meticulous study of differences between the elite culture of the late New Kingdom and that of the twenty-first to twenty-third dynasties, much of which has been undertaken by the British Egyptologist Anthony Leahy. First of all, there seems to have been a deliberate political "Balkanization" of the administration—in other words, a fragmentation of the kingship, not only splitting it between north and south but also creating smaller "kingships" in a number of different regions, and thus only nominally preserving the quintessential Egyptian idea of a "king of Upper and Lower Egypt." Many scholars in the past tended to assume that this was simply a chaotic situation resulting from the administration's inability to maintain a traditional pharaonic system of government. Leahy, however, has suggested that this political situation was a process of deliberate decentralization, evidently attempting to impose on Egypt a "federal" system of government that would perhaps have come naturally to Libyan "chiefs."

There appear to have been linguistic changes brought about by the inexperience of Libyan scribes, perhaps indicated by greater use of Late Egyptian forms in northern texts. There were also changes in the way that the language was written down. Two different, more cursive forms of hieratic appeared in the reigns of the Tanite kings: "abnormal hieratic" in the south, and demotic in the north. This process of linguistic change emphasizes the clear division between the more Egyptian-dominated Theban culture of the south and the Libyan-dominated system operating at cities such as Tanis in the north. It is also notable that stone donation stelae carved in hieratic script became very common in the north.

At Tanis itself, there were obvious changes in the style of royal funerary architecture, such as the introduction of much smaller burial chambers and the use of family vaults rather than large tombs for individuals. These tombs were apparently constructed hastily, often reusing material from elsewehere. All this suggests a distinctly un-Egyptian lack of interest in creating funerary monuments well ahead of one's death. In addition, the "judgment of the heart" scene characteristic of nonroyal burials and *Book of the Dead* papyri throughout the New Kingdom appears in a royal context for the first time in the tombs of Osorkon II and Shoshenq III at Tanis. The kings buried at Tanis had evidently begun to be viewed less as gods and more as human rulers, judging from the unusual air of familiarity in a lament inscribed at the entrance to the tomb of Osorkon II by his general Pasherieniset.

Tanis as a Northern Version of Thebes: Brissaud's Discoveries

The strategy underlying the seasons of survey and excavation at Tanis in the late twentieth and early twenty-first centuries has been guided mainly by the

In a letter to his wife dated 27 February 1939, Montet described his find of the first of the intact royal tombs:

> At Ibrahim's, in front of the house from last year, there is a handsome pavement, quite deep. I had as much cleared away as possible. One of the flagstones was jutting out—I had it removed. From the hole we gathered remains of ushabtis belonging to the Sesac [Sheshonq] of the monumental gateway, a buckle of Isis of gold cloisonné, which is a superb piece, and also a small coffer. We removed the earth and saw a larger slab, like a lintel stone, in front of two small flat stones, like the doors of a wardrobe. I took a quick look and tested it with Ibrahim's cane. It sounded empty, like an underground chamber that is not entirely filled . . . I sent for the two brothers [Fougerousse and Goyon]. I write this note and I shall then go down to the site, as it seems to be an important moment as we are wondering if it isn't Sesac's tomb! —3 o'clock. No, it's Osorkon's. At exactly 2 o'clock, I had the earth and stones blocking the entrance removed, and went down into a square chamber with walls covered with figures and hieroglyphics; this led into another chamber with a large sarcophagus emerging from the earth which filled three-quarters of two rooms. The cartouche is that of Osorkon . . . Goyon, then Fouge[rousse] came in, and then the overseer. Everyone is overjoyed. I had Hassanein's team come with all the carts so that we could clear this remarkable tomb as quickly as possible— its discovery rewards all our year's efforts.

hypothesis that the rulers of the Third Intermediate Period deliberately set out to create a northern counterpart of the religious geography of Thebes. In other words, the Temple of Amun at Tanis was intended to replicate the main Theban religious complex at Karnak. Like Karnak, the sacred precinct at Tanis consisted of a major temple dedicated to Amun and two smaller temples dedicated to the other two members of the Theban triad, Amun's "wife," Mut, and his "son," Khonsu. However, there was no counterpart here of the western Theban cliffs into which the New Kingdom pharaohs dug their tombs, and so the Third Intermediate Period rulers simply incorporated their new royal cemetery into the plan of the temple itself.

To ensure that these monuments would rival those in the south, Psusennes and his successors brought statuary, reliefs, and dressed stone blocks from the ancient cities of Piramesse and Avaris to provide instant sculpture and masonry for the new structures. Much of the recent work at Tanis has consisted of disentangling great piles of sculpted stone. These relief blocks and sculptures have now been reassembled and reerected, providing a much better idea of the original appearance of the site, such as the monumental gateway of Shoshenq III at the western entrance to the Temple of Amun. Comparatively little has survived of the main temple's three pylons, but the excavators were able to deduce their locations from the presence of various obelisks that originally stood in front of them.

In the central part of the mound (to the south of the temples of Amun, Mut, and Khonsu), the 1980s excavations revealed layers of settlement debris and walls contemporary with the Third Intermediate Period temples and royal cemetery. It is likely, therefore, that future work at the site will begin to reveal details of the actual city and people of Tanis, rather than the religious and funerary monuments of their rulers.

In the southern part of Tanis, at the end of the mound opposite to that occupied by the Amun precinct, there were many stone blocks scattered across the surface. Brissaud's team undertook geophysical surveys during the mid-1980s, and the discovery of two electromagnetic anomalies suggested that this southernmost part of the mound might also have been the site of a large monumental structure. In 1988 the area was excavated, revealing a thick temple enclosure wall within which were found many blocks with inscriptions mentioning "Amun of Ipet." This "temple of Amun of Ipet" appears to have been the counterpart of Luxor temple at Thebes, which, like this structure, lay some distance to the south of the larger complex and was known as the *ipet resyt* ("southern private chambers'; see chapter 12). This discovery is further confirmation of a grand scheme to create a complete "Thebes of the north" rivaling the original.

Further Reading

The reports on the early excavations at the site include Flinders Petrie's *Tanis* (2 vols., London, 1885–1887), Pierre Montet's *La nécropole royale de Tanis* (3 vols., Paris, 1947–1960), and Georges Goyon's *La découverte des trésors de Tanis* (Paris, 1987). The work during the 1980s and 1990s has been summarized by its director, Philippe Brissaud, in his chapter in *Royal Cities of the Biblical World,* edited by J. Goodnick Westenholz (Jerusalem, 1996).

Kenneth Kitchen's *The Third Intermediate Period in Egypt (1100–650 B.C.)* (3rd ed., Warminster, 1995) is still the best and most detailed historical summary of the historical context of the Third Intermediate Period kings buried at Tanis. An exhibition of items from Tanis (particularly the coffins, jewelry, and offerings from the royal tombs), which toured various European and American museums in the late 1980s, was accompanied by a detailed and well-illustrated French catalog by J. Yoyotte et al., *Tanis, l'or des pharaons* (Paris, 1987), and a shorter version in English, *Gold of the Pharaohs* (Edinburgh, 1988). Henri Stierlin's popular account of Egyptian jewelry, *The Gold of the Pharaohs* (Paris, 1993), includes a description of Montet's discovery, illustrated with excellent photographs of much of the royal funerary equipment from Tanis.

Further Viewing

The funerary equipment from the Tanis royal tombs is currently on display in the Egyptian Museum, Cairo. The same museum has jewelry of roughly similar date from the tomb of Queen Kama(ma), the mother of Osorkon III, at Tell el-Muqdam (Leontopolis).

Edfu

c. 246–51 B.C.

The temple of the hawk god

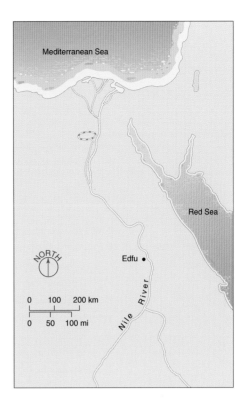

It is one of the ironies of ancient Egypt that the best surviving temples—those that actually give modern visitors the strongest sense of the nature of Egyptian religion—mostly date to the Ptolemaic and Roman periods, when Egyptian art and architecture had become to some extent Hellenicized and Romanized. Nevertheless, the painted reliefs of such buildings as the Temple of Horus at Edfu and the Temple of Isis at Philae lie well within the tradition of Egyptian religious art in that they are concerned principally with the depiction of pharaohs and priests undertaking rituals in the presence of anthropomorphic, often animal-headed deities. Although certain aspects of the artistic style altered during the Ptolemaic Period—including a more voluptuous rendering of the human body and a more complex variety of religious symbols and hieroglyphic signs—most of the reliefs were still designed to convey a sense of the living, day-to-day ritual of the temple.

The principal surviving temples of the Ptolemaic and Roman periods—the last great burst of energy for Egyptian religious architecture—neatly punctuate the banks of the Nile for a distance of more than 160 miles (256 kilometers) from the northernmost, Dendera, near the modern governorate of Qena, to the southernmost, Kalabsha just south of the High Dam at Aswan. Almost exactly halfway between Luxor and Aswan is the best-preserved and most impressive of all these post-pharaonic structures: the Temple of Horus at Edfu.

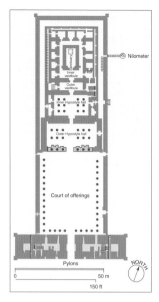

Overall plan of Edfu temple.

Stone implements found in the desert surrounding modern Edfu provide evidence of a Palaeolithic occupation in the Nile Valley about 17,000 years ago, known as the Edfuan (or Idfuan) culture, but the earliest evidence for historic activity at the site is a rock-carving comprising the name of the first-dynasty king Djet (c. 2950 B.C.), discovered in the desert east of the Ptolemaic temple. In the mounds to the west of the temple, a necropolis of the Early Dynastic Period has been excavated. The site as a whole includes settlement and funerary remains covering the entire pharaonic period, but a substantial proportion of these buildings remain unexcavated.

The Temple of Horus the Behdetite

The Ptolemaic temple of Horus the Behdetite was founded on the site of a much earlier pharaonic temple (the term "Behdetite" refers to the cult of Horus that originated in the Delta town of Behdet). Its construction dates to the period between the reigns of Ptolemy III and Ptolemy XII (237–57 B.C.). The reliefs and inscriptions on the walls include the myth of the contendings of Horus and Seth (probably performed annually as a religious drama) and an important account of the ritual foundation of the temple.

The most important concepts in Egyptian religion were secrecy and revelation, and both the myths and the temple architecture were designed to strengthen these two ideas. There were also rituals, festivals, and dramas in which the divine reality was repeatedly acted out, or actualized to reforge the links between myth and reality. One inscription in the Edfu temple vividly

View of the first court of the Temple of Horus at Edfu, taken from the roof of the pronaos.

demonstrates this combination of mystery and epiphany, describing how the chief priest (standing in for the king) goes to the *naos* and opens it to reveal the god's statue. He then says: "I have seen the god, the power sees me. The god rejoices at seeing me. I have gazed upon the statue of the Divine Winged Beetle, the sacred image of the Falcon of Gold."

What Was the *mammisi*?

About 55 yards (50 meters) south of the pylon at Edfu there were once two more temple buildings. Of the eastern one, the "temple of the sacred falcon," only the altar and a few flooring blocks have survived, but the other building—a long rectangular structure surrounded by a colonnade with intercolumnar screen walls, set at right angles to the main temple axis—is preserved almost in its entirety. The reliefs and texts on the walls of this building suggest that the birth of the god Harsomtus (another variant of Horus) was celebrated there.

Known to Egyptologists as a *mammisi*—a Coptic term meaning "birth house," which was invented by the nineteenth-century Egyptologist Jean François Champollion—this is an example of a kind of small temple that was attached to certain temple complexes, such as those at Edfu, Dendera, and Philae, from the Late Period to the Roman Period (712 B.C.–395 A.D.). In the Ptolemaic *mammisi*, the rituals of the marriage of the goddess (Isis or Hathor) and the birth of the child-god were celebrated. The origins of the

The pyon at Edfu. Ptolemaic period.

mammisi can perhaps be seen in the form of eighteenth-dynasty painted reliefs describing the divine birth of the king, found in the mortuary temple of Hatshepsut at Deir el-Bahari (see chapter 10) and in the temple of Amenhotep III at Luxor.

In the temple complex at Dendera, there are two *mammisis* situated in front of the main temple. One of these dates to the Roman Period, but the other is the earliest known *mammisi*, constructed in the reign of Nectanebo I (380–362 B.C.). "Mystery plays" appear to have been enacted in the latter, celebrating the births of the god Ihy and of the pharaoh. The dramas and rituals enacted in *mammisi* were no doubt intended to ensure agricultural success and the continuation of the royal line.

The Triumph of Horus: A Religious Drama

Whereas Egyptian temples in the pharaonic period usually consist of successions of pylons, open courts, and pillared halls surrounded by outer enclosure walls constructed from mud brick, the vast temples built in the Ptolemaic and Roman periods tend to be surrounded by a stone enclosure wall stretching from the edges of the main pylon back to the rear wall of the temple, where the sanctuary and treasuries were located. This outer wall created the so-called ambulatory, a long corridor surrounding the rectangular complex along three of its sides. In the Temple of Horus at Edfu, scenes and texts describing the myth of the Triumph of Horus decorate the inner (east) face of the west enclosure wall. Visitors to the temple can find these scenes by walking through the main pylon at the southern end of the temple, turning left immediately, and then walking along the colonnade around the edge of the court until they reach a small doorway in the northwestern corner of the Court of Offerings. They should next walk through the narrowest part of the ambulatory, along the western side of the thick stone wall surrounding the Outer Hypostyle Hall (or Pronaos), which is the widest part of the temple proper. When the temple proper narrows down to the Inner Hypostyle Hall and the rooms surrounding the sanctuary, the ambulatory correspondingly widens. Along the lower part of this stretch of the enclosure wall are laid out the eleven vignettes (each combining carved scenes and hieroglyphic inscriptions) making up the narrative of the mythical contendings of Horus and the evil god Seth, here represented by a hippopotamus. These eleven sections of relief are intended to be read from north to south, so it is necessary to go almost into the northwestern corner of the ambulatory to find the earliest part of the drama.

It was initially assumed that these inscriptions and relief scenes were simply depictions of mythical tableaux or rituals, but careful analysis of the text by the British Egyptologist H. W. Fairman revealed that the layout and contents take the form of a mixture of speeches and "stage directions," suggesting that this is the only surviving complete Egyptian play. Although the inscriptions themselves date only to the third century B.C., about two centuries later than the Greek tragedies of Aeschylus, it seems almost certain that the drama of Horus and Seth was already being enacted in Edfu at the time of the main New Kingdom phase of the temple (part of the pylon of which has survived) in the nineteenth dynasty (c.1200 B.C.). The Triumph of Horus therefore probably predates the earliest surviving Greek plays by at least a thousand years.

The first section of the Edfu drama combines two scenes: on the right-hand side, a group of deities (Thoth, Horus the Behdetite, and Isis), and on the left-hand side a papyrus boat containing the standing figures of Horus and Isis, with the king standing in front of them on the bank of the lake. Horus holds a long rope and a harpoon, and both he and the king (also hold-

The so-called ambulatory, a long corridor surrounding the rear portions of the Temple of Horus, was decorated with a series of dramatic texts and scenes relating the myth of the Triumph of Horus.

237
—

ing a harpoon) are stabbing a tiny hippopotamus below the surface of the water. The absurdly small scale of the hippopotamus is presumably a compromise between the need to depict the defeat of Seth and a reluctance to allow this symbol of evil to figure too prominently in the temple of his adversary. The scene of the harpooning of the Seth hippopotamus can be traced back at least as far as the first Dynasty (c.3000 B.C.), when it is unequivocally depicted on a seal impression found in the tomb of King Den at Abydos, suggesting the existence of some form of the ritual on which the drama is based as early as the beginning of the third millennium. The content of the play was not simply a retelling of the myth of Horus and Seth but, like so much of ancient Egyptian art and literature, an opportunity to reaffirm and celebrate the kingship and royal victory.

To the left of these two relief scenes is a large section of text consisting of nine vertical columns of hieroglyphs; this is the first long section of dialogue and stage directions, although the hieroglyphs above and around the various figures also provide small sections of speech and identify the protagonists. Fairman has identified this first vignette as a kind of prologue. The next five relief scenes and accompanying inscriptions (the five "scenes" of "Act I") relate the process by which Seth is stabbed with ten harpoons. Act II is taken up by mass rejoicing over Horus's victory and the crowning of Horus as king, and Act III consists of two ceremonies in which the Seth hippopotamus is ritually dismembered. The drama concludes with a celebration of the overthrow of the enemies of Horus, Osiris, and the king.

If the Triumph of Horus was indeed a play, when and where might it have been performed? We know the answer to the first part of the question, since the temple inscriptions indicate that it took place annually on the twenty-first to twenty-fifth days of the second month of the peret season (January 9–13 in the modern calendar), forming part of the Festival of Victory, which commemorated the struggles between Horus and Seth, culminating in the dismemberment of Seth and the triumphant coronation of Horus. As far as the location of the drama is concerned, there are a number of possible answers to the question. The inscriptions suggest that the play was intended to take place in or around the Sacred Lake (see chapter 12). If the lake was located in the same position as the one at Dendera, it would be buried underneath the modern town, a few yards east of the northeastern corner of the temple. It would probably have been a rectangular stone-lined pool covering an area of about 2,500 square feet (750 square meters), with a pavement and low balustrade running around its perimeter. The action of the play might therefore have taken place in papyrus skiffs on the surface of the lake, with the painted east walls of the temple providing an impressive backcloth and a nearby kiosk perhaps serving as dressing room. Against this suggestion, it might be argued that the lake setting, being on the opposite side of the temple from the ancient city, would have prevented the kind of mass audience participation that seems to have been intended. The low level of the

The temple complex at Dendera incorporates one of the best surviving examples of a Greco-Roman "sacred lake," which served several different purposes, including the provision of pure water for religious rituals.

lake, which was probably fed only by the Nile water table, might also have prevented spectators from seeing the play unless they stood at the very edge.

An alternative suggestion is that the play was performed in front of the southern entrance to the temple, but this would probably have been impossible because the *mammisi* and the "temple of the sacred falcon" occupied this area at Edfu. We are therefore left with the open court directly in front of the pylon as the prime contender for the "stage." Although the court would have been surrounded by the thick mud-brick enclosure wall that separates all Egyptian temples from the outside world, it might nevertheless have been clearly visible from the city, the rooftops of which would have overlooked the temple by several feet, since the temple was in a hollow relative to the Ptolemaic city of Edfu, built directly on top of numerous layers of previous occupation. Possibly the two halves of the pylon served as the backdrop, with the two colossal relief figures of Ptolemy XIII slaughtering foreigners in front of Horus the Behdetite no doubt reinforcing the "message" of the play.

The Annual Journey of Hathor from Dendera to Edfu

The most interesting of the many festivals celebrated in the Temple of Horus was the "Sacred Marriage," the ceremonial transportation of a statue of the goddess Hathor by barge from her temple at Dendera to be reunited with her consort Horus at Edfu. We know a great deal about this and other festivals (such as the Coronation of the Sacred Falcon and the Festival of Victory) because, like the *Triumph of Horus,* they are described in texts and reliefs on the walls of the temple (part of the so-called temple grammar, which also describes foundation rituals).

The texts indicate that the celebration of the Sacred Marriage at Edfu itself lasted for fifteen days, from the new moon to the full moon in the third month of *shemu* (the summer season), but the whole process actually began fourteen days earlier in the temple of Hathor at Dendera. There, the cult image of the goddess was carried onto a processional barge that was then towed south to Edfu, stopping at Thebes, Komir, and Hierakonpolis so that Hathor could visit various other deities en route. Once the barge had arrived at a quay a short distance north of Edfu, on the day of the new moon, the image of Hathor was met by an image of Horus of Behdet, and the two deities were then taken to a nearby shrine before continuing their river journey to Edfu temple itself. They entered the temple enclosure wall through a gateway on the eastern side, and Horus and Hathor then spent the first night of their renewed marriage in the sanctuary. The subsequent fourteen-day festival then focused not so much on the marriage as on the cult of Horus of Behdet, including the offering of sacrifices and hymn-singing at an unknown location in the desert to the west or southwest of the temple, known as the "burial ground of Behdet." The ritual acts of the festival would have been accompanied by a period of general feasting and celebration among the local population.

On the day of the full moon, Hathor's cult image was transferred back onto her barge amid numerous ceremonies, and she was taken back to Dendera. The principal aim of this festival seems to have been to celebrate fertility and the harvest, although the annual timing of the celebration around July or August is inexplicably much later than the actual season of harvesting and threshing cereal at the beginning of the summer season around April.

Ptolemaic Priests, Liturgies, and Temple Libraries

What do we know of the priests and other officials whose lives were dedicated to the cult of Horus of Behdet at Edfu? Once again, the inscriptions on the temple walls provide crucial information. The doorways through which the priests entered the temple are inscribed with codes of behavior: "Do not enter unclean," "Be serious in your work," "Do not tell lies in the temple," and "Do not steal from the offerings." There were workers of various types attached to the temple, ranging from the most important officials—the *hemu-netjer* (literally, "servants of the god"), who were drawn only from priestly families and had to be able to read the sacred papyri—down to the groups of laymen who undertook such menial tasks as supplying food for the altars and using brushes to erase the footprints of the priests as they left the temple. There were also priests who specialized in such aspects of the cult as the carrying of ritual boats or images and the slaughter of animals.

Essential priests at every Ptolemaic and Roman temple were the scribal officials attached to the so-called *per-ankh* ("house of life"). Buildings corresponding to the *per-ankh,* where Egyptian scribes generally worked and learned their trade, have been identified at such cities as Memphis and el-Amarna, but libraries and official archives within temples have generally proved more difficult to locate. A number of Egyptian temples, such as those at Esna and Philae, have lists of titles of liturgical texts written on certain walls, but the only definitely identified temple library is a niche-like room in the southern wall of the outer hypostyle hall of Edfu temple. An inscription over the entrance to this room describes it as the "library of Horus," although it is possible that it simply contained the few rolls necessary for the daily rituals.

The term *per-medjat* ("house of papyrus rolls") denotes the repositories of papyri associated with government buildings and temple complexes. The location, or indeed the very existence, of a library in the Ramesseum (c. 1250 B.C.) at Thebes has proved a contentious question; most modern Egyptologists fail to identify any room that equates with the "sacred library" mentioned by the Greek historian Diodorus (c. 300 B.C.), although archives of the late New Kingdom administration were found in the immediate vicinity of the mortuary temple of Ramesses III at Medinet Habu (c. 1170 B.C.).

The "library" at Edfu, the doorway of which is shown here, was actually a large shelved cupboard holding a selection of papyrus rolls bearing the liturgies for various temple rituals.

241

The Abandonment of the Last Temples

The Ptolemaic and Roman temples, of which Edfu, Kom Ombo, Dendera, Esna, and Philae are the best surviving examples, lay so much at the heart of Egyptian culture and society that they survived for many centuries, not merely as inert monuments but as vibrant and potent centers of local power and prestige. Most of them, however, were completed before the end of the second century A.D., and little new religious architecture was then attempted until the appearance of the first distinctive Christian buildings in Egypt, such as the cathedral at Hermopolis and the monastery at Deir el-Abyad, both constructed in the early fifth century.

With the coming of Christianity, the highly visible symbols of idolatrous pagan cults were inevitably abandoned. In some instances, temples were converted into churches, as in the case of the Late Period *mammisi* at Dendera, but many others, particularly in the north of Egypt, were demolished and their stone masonry reused in later buildings. Those in Upper Egypt tended to fare rather better, and the cult of Isis was still being celebrated in Philae temple around 535 A.D., some 200 years after the official recognition of Christianity by Constantine the Great.

Opinions differ as to whether the reliefs in surviving temples were defaced primarily by Christians or Muslims, but by modern times many of the strange animal-headed deities or kings had had their facial features or even their whole bodies deliberately destroyed. Fortunately, by this time the gathering sands had often covered all but the upper areas of decoration, thus preserving many images and texts for posterity.

Dieter Arnold's *Temples of the Last Pharaohs* (Oxford, 2000) provides well-informed and up-to-date discussion of the major Ptolemaic and Roman temples in Egypt. The basic works on the architectural and epigraphic aspects of the temple of Horus at Edfu are published in French and German, including Maxence de Rochemonteix and Émile Chassinat's *Le temple d'Edfou* (Paris and Cairo, 1892; Cairo, 1918–1998), Kazimierz Michalowski's *Tell Edfou* (Cairo, 1937–1950), and Dieter Kurth's *Inschriften aus dem Tempel des Horus von Edfu* (Zurich, 1994). Sylvia Cauville has written a very detailed account of the theological background to the Edfu temple complex in *La théologie d'Osiris Edfou* (Cairo, 1983). Penny Wilson's *A Ptolemaic Lexicon: A Lexicographical Study of the Texts in the Temple of Edfu* (Leuven, 1997) is a study of the inscriptions on the walls of the temple, which seeks to analyze the religious vocabulary typically employed in the Ptolemaic and Roman periods. There are two discussions of the rituals practiced in the temple: H. W. Fairman's "Worship and Festivals in an Egyptian Temple" in *Bulletin of the John Rylands Library, Manchester* 37 (1954), pp.165–203; and Barbara Watterson's *The House of Horus* (London, 1998). In *Ptolemaic Philae* (Leuven, 1989), Eleni Vassilika analyzes the iconography of the reliefs on the walls of Ptolemaic and Roman temples.

Fairman's *The Triumph of Horus: An Ancient Egyptian Sacred Drama* (London, 1974) is still the best English translation of the drama inscribed on the ambulatory wall of the temple, and it includes an interesting description of the practicalities of staging the first modern version of the play at Padgate College, Warrington, England, in 1971.

The *mammisi* at Edfu is described by Émile Chassinat in *Le mammisi d'Edfou* (Cairo, 1939); those at Dendera and Philae are described by François Daumas in *Les mammisis de Dendara* (Cairo, 1959), and by Josef Junker and Erich Winter in *Das Geburtshaus des Tempels der Isis in Philä* (Vienna, 1965). François Daumas's *Les mammisis des temples égyptiens* (Paris, 1958) is a more general discussion of this type of religious building.

There are several other Ptolemaic and Roman temples that can be visited, apart from the Temple of Horus at Edfu. The Temple of Hathor at Dendera has a well-preserved sacred lake as well as two *mammisis,* one dating to the thirtieth dynasty and the other to the Roman Period. The temple at Kom Ombo is notable in that it is actually a "double temple," with parallel axes leading to sanctuaries dedicated to local aspects of Horus and the crocodile god Sobek. The temple of the ram god Khnum at Esna is located in a deep pit and only the first hypostyle hall has been excavated, the rest of the structure being buried underneath the surrounding modern houses. The temple of Isis at Philae is perhaps the most beautiful because of its architecture and setting.

Alexandria

c. 332–30 B.C.

A Greek city in Africa

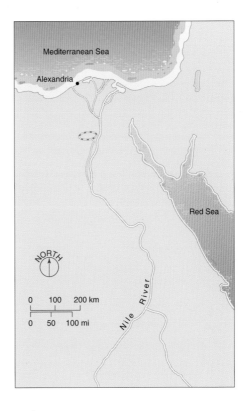

Visitors to modern Alexandria have to use a great deal of of imagination to gain any sense of the ancient town and its elaborate monuments. Amid the concrete office blocks and European-style waterfront are a few surviving Islamic buildings, but the Hellenistic and Roman palaces and temples have left little visible impression on the present-day cityscape. The street plan of the modern city, the second most populous in Egypt after Cairo, is essentially European (and specifically British), reflecting the fact that many of Egypt's European colonial inhabitants chose to make their homes here in the nineteenth and twentieth centuries. Yet although Alexandria has changed radically since Ptolemaic times, the modern Western bias of its architecture and population is nevertheless faithful to its original character as the first city in Egypt to be designed along Greek lines. The city plan was laid out in the overall shape of a traditional Greek cloak, or *chlamys*, covering an area of about 3 square miles (7.7 square kilometers). It was divided into quarters by two principal roads: the Canopic Way, running from the Gate of the Moon in the west to the Gate of the Sun in the east; and the Street of the Soma, running from Lake Maryut in the south to the Mediterranean in the north.

Modern visitors can attempt to make the imaginative leap back from contemporary to ancient Alexandria by walking along Sharia Nabi Daniel, which roughly follows the route of the Street of the Soma, until it intersects with Sharia Hurriya, which is roughly equivalent to the Canopic Way. At the

Map of ancient Alexandria, showing probable locations of such famous landmarks as the Pharos lighthouse and the Serapeum.

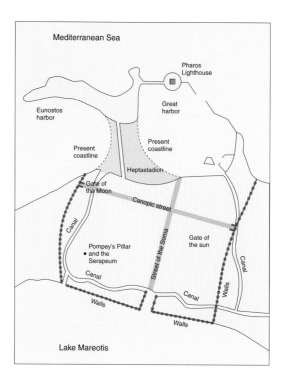

Mediterranean Sea

Pharos Lighthouse

Great harbor

Eunostos harbor

Present coastline

Present coastline

Heptastadion

Gate of the Moon

Canopic street

Canal

Gate of the sun

Pompey's Pillar and the Serapeum

Street of the Soma

Canal

Canal

Canal

Walls

Walls

Walls

Lake Mareotis

northern end of Sharia Nabi Daniel is the Hotel Cecil, an elegant establishment overlooking the Mediterranean, where many famous visitors to Alexandria (such as Lawrence Durrell and Somerset Maugham) stayed; at the southern end of the street is the busy modern bus station. Immediately to the south of the junction of Sharia Nabi Daniel and Sharia Hurriya, beneath the shops and hotels, is thought to be the location of the ancient city's center, where Alexandria's famous museum and library were built. The adjacent Mosque of Nabi Daniel was built on top of a tenth- to twelfth-century Islamic cemetery, which in turn lies on top of the Soma, a temple supposedly surmounting the burial site of Alexander and the Ptolemies, none of whose bodies have yet been found.

With its gridded street plan and freshwater channels running under each street, ancient Alexandria was essentially a Hellenistic rather than an Egyptian city, and it came to symbolize the increasing links between Egypt and the Mediterranean world. Its identity was so strong that it was often called Alexandrea ad Aegyptum, Alexandria "beside" Egypt rather than within it, as if it were a separate country in its own right. By the mid-first century B.C., the Greek historian Diodorus Siculus described it as "the first city of the civilized world, certainly far ahead of all the rest in elegance and extent and riches and luxury"; and in the late first century A.D., the Roman orator Dio of Prusa went so far as to describe Egypt as a mere appendage to Alexandria.

The ancient city was situated on a narrow peninsula at the western end of the Mediterranean coast of Egypt. It was founded by Alexander the Great in 331 B.C. in the vicinity of an earlier Egyptian settlement called Rhakotis, archaeological traces of which have so far been found only in the form of the pre-Ptolemaic seawalls to the north and west of the island of Pharos. The name "Rhakotis" was later applied to a hill in the Ptolemaic and Roman city, presumably corresponding to the original location of the pre-Ptolemaic settlement; it is now largely covered by an Islamic cemetery, precluding any excavation.

The Foundation and Design of Alexandria

Alexander the Great was returning from his momentous visit to the oracle of Amun at Siwa Oasis when he is said to have founded Alexandria (on 7 April 331 B.C., according to ancient biographical texts). Plutarch recounts the tale of the newly crowned and deified Macedonian king being visited in a dream by a prophet who suggests establishing a new city at Rhakotis, mentioning a reference in Homer to the island of Pharos; Plutarch then describes the somewhat unorthodox technique employed to map out the city plan:

> Since there was no chalk available, they used barley meal to describe a rounded area on the dark soil, to whose inner arc straight lines succeeded, starting from what might be called the skirts of the area and narrowing to the breadth uniformly, so as to produce the figure of a military cloak. The king was delighted with the plan when suddenly a vast multitude of birds of every kind and size flew from the river and the lagoon on to the site like clouds; nothing was left of the barley meal and even Alexander was much troubled by the omen. But his seers advised him that there was nothing to fear . . . he therefore instructed his overseers to press on with the work. (translation by Alan Bowman, 1986)

Alexander is said to have entrusted the design of the city to the architect Deinokrates of Rhodes and the viceroy Kleomenes, but it was actually the general Ptolemy son of Lagos, the first Ptolemaic ruler of Egypt, who carried out the earliest program of construction at the site, establishing a thriving cosmopolitan city that was to supplant Memphis as the capital of Egypt by 320 B.C. Alexandria's great prosperity probably derived from two essential factors: first, it took over from the Levantine port of Tyre the role of principal commercial link between Europe and Asia; and second, its population expanded very rapidly, reaching about half a million by the first century B.C., including substantial numbers of Greeks and Jews (indeed, it became the largest Jewish center or population in the world).

The archaeological exploration of the city has been complicated by the fact that antiquities from all over Egypt were gathered together in Alexandria,

The Begram beaker.

either to embellish new temples or in preparation for their transportation to other parts of the Roman Empire. Both Cleopatra's Needle (now on the Embankment in London) and the Central Park obelisk in New York once stood in the Caesareum at Alexandria, having been brought there from Thutmose II's temple to Ra-Atum at Heliopolis.

In 1866, the first major excavations, under the direction of Mahmud Bey, took place in the modern city center, and parts of the road leading from the river port to the sea harbor were examined in 1874. A valuable piece of evidence has survived from this phase of excavation in the form of a plan of the city published by Mahmud el-Falaki in 1872.

Probably the best-known ancient buildings at Alexandria were the Museum, the Library, and the Pharos. The Museum and the Library were burned down, along with an irreplaceable collection of papyri, in the third century A.D, and the Pharos was probably destroyed by earthquakes. The major monuments of the Ptolemaic and Roman periods were the Serapeum (a temple dedicated to the god Serapis, which may have housed part of the library collection), the Caesareum, a Roman stadium, and Kom el-Shugafa (a labyrinth of rock-cut tombs dating to the first two centuries A.D.). Apart from the fortress of Qaitbay on the Pharos peninsula, there are few surviving Islamic monuments at Alexandria.

Where Were Alexander the Great and the Ptolemies Buried?

In May of 323 B.C., Alexander the Great died of a fever (perhaps malaria) in Babylon. Despite the attempts of his half-brother, Philip Arrhidaeus, and his son, Alexander IV, to maintain the unity of Alexander's empire, it eventually dissolved into several different kingdoms ruled by his generals and their descendants. As with so much of Alexander the Great's career, there are conflicting accounts about what became of his corpse. For the first two years after his death, the body seems to have stayed in Babylon, where Philip Arrhidaeus prepared both the corpse and the vehicle in which it was to be transported to its final resting place. Although some accounts claim that the final burial place was Siwa Oasis, where Alexander had visited the oracle of Amun after conquering Egypt, most authorities seem to agree that his immediate successors would never have consented to such an obscure cemetery. The account given by Pausanias suggests that the initial intention was to take the body back to Aegae, the traditional Macedonian royal cemetery, but that Ptolemy son of Lagos, the general acting on behalf of Kleomenes, viceroy of Egypt, intercepted the funeral cortège in Syria and took the body back to Memphis, and then to Alexandria.

Ptolemy—who eventually overthrew Kleomenes to become the first ruler of the Ptolemaic period in 305 B.C.—is said to have placed Alexander's body in a golden coffin inside an elaborate shrine at Alexandria, which was later to be the burial site for the Ptolemaic dynasty's rulers as well. This mausoleum is usually known as either the *soma* ("body") or the *sema* ("tomb"). In 30 B.C., the Roman emperor Augustus reputedly viewed the body in the *soma* after his victory over Mark Antony and Cleopatra VII; the Roman historian Dio Cassius claims that he touched the corpse, accidentally knocking off part of the nose. The same author also suggests that Augustus turned down an opportunity to visit the graves of the Ptolemies, which are assumed to have been somewhere in the vicinity. The last attested visit to the tomb by a Roman emperor was that of Caracalla, in A.D. 215.

The Ptolemaic City, Necropolis, and Pharos

Because the vast majority of the archaeological finds date to the Roman period, our knowledge of the Ptolemaic period (332—30 B.C.) at Alexandria derives largely from written descriptions provided by ancient historians and geographers. The more central part of the city is said to have been divided into three sections along ethnic lines, with the Jewish population primarily settled in the eastern part, the Greeks (immigrants from Thrace, Macedonia, the Aegean, mainland Greece, Asia Minor, and the Levant) in the so-called Brucheion or Royal Quarter in the center, including the Heptastadion and Pharos, and the Egyptian inhabitants mainly in the west in a region known as Rhakotis, presumably because it lay in the area occupied by the original pre-Ptolemaic settlement. Beyond Rhakotis, farther west, was the suburb of Necropolis, which was said to have included impressive gardens.

The Ptolemaic cemetery at Anfushi, close to the western shore of the East Harbor, dates primarily to the third and second centuries B.C. It consists of a number of subterranean structures, each made up of a sunken court leading to suites of funerary rooms in which one or more individuals were interred. Some of the walls were plastered and painted to imitate exotic stones such as marble or travertine. The walls of the stairway leading into one court still bear fragments of scenes depicting the judgment of the dead, including the presentation of the deceased to Osiris, Isis, Horus, and Anubis. The entrance to one of the burial chambers is flanked by sphinxes, and a winged sun-disk is carved on the cornice above.

The Pharos

The building of the famous Alexandrian lighthouse, one of the Seven Wonders of the World, was financed by Sostratos of Knidos, who was perhaps also the designer. It was constructed in the early Ptolemaic period, probably between the reigns of Ptolemy I and Ptolemy II, at the eastern end of the islet of Pharos about a mile (1.6 kilometers) into the sea, where the shallow waters and rocks endangered shipping entering the port. This island is mentioned in Homer's *Odyssey*—"there is an island called Pharos in the rolling seas by the mouth of the Nile"—and Sostratos's building is said to

The Pharos lighthouse at Alexandria. According to E. M. Forster, "It beaconed to the imagination, not only to ships at sea, and long after its light was extinguished, memories of it glowed in the minds of men."

have been the earliest lighthouse in the world. Until the 1990s, it was known only from ancient texts and depictions, according to which it was nearly 400 feet (122 meters) high and consisted of three stories, the lowest of which was square, the middle octagonal, and the top cylindrical. During the day, it is claimed, skillful heliographic use of mirrors allowed the sun's light to be relected far across the Mediterranean, while at night, a fire burning at the top of the edifice was said to have been artificially magnified. Some accounts even suggest that some kind of mirror or telescope was used by the Alexandrians to espy ships while they were still at a great distance from port.

Perhaps the most famous surviving depiction of the lighthouse is the so-called Pharos beaker, a vessel of colorless glass showing the building as a single featureless tower (with no indication of the three different stories) attached to a fortress wall and surmounted by a colossal statue perhaps representing Zeus Soter holding an oar or rudder. A coin dating to the reign of Antoninus Pius protrays the lighthouse as a square tower topped by a circular lantern and a statue of Isis flanked by Triton figures.

The island of Pharos was evidently connected with the mainland by a long causeway known as the Heptastadion because it was seven stadia, or three-quarters of a mile (1.2 kilometers) in length. The causeway originally had two gaps crossed by drawbridges, but it has now become entirely sanded up into a natural isthmus separating the eastern and western harbors, which are known as the Great Harbor and the Eunostos Harbor, respectively. At least two severe earthquakes appear to have contributed to the demise of the lighthouse. It was long believed that the only surviving remains were stray blocks incorporated into the masonry of the Qaitbay fortress, a stalwart building erected on roughly the same spot in 1480 A.D.

The first indication that numerous Ptolemaic and Roman remains—including blocks from the lighthouse itself—might have survived under the sea was provided in 1961 by Kamal Abu el-Sadat's discovery of the upper part of a 40-foot-high (12-meter) colossal statue of the goddess Isis, now in the Maritime Museum at Alexandria. In 1975, the British diver Honor Frost made a series of sketches of the other visible archaeological remains on the seabed. In 1994 and 1995, therefore, a team of French archaeologists led by Jean-Yves Empereur explored a region of the Eastern or "Great" Harbor covering about 6 acres (2.5 hectares) to the east of Qaitbay and discovered large blocks of masonry that seem likely to have formed part of the lighthouse. Empereur's team have also lifted and restored many items of sculpture and architectural fragments dating to the Ptolemaic and Roman heyday of Alexandria, including pharaonic-period blocks and sculptures brought from elsewhere (probably mainly from Heliopolis).

Although the West or "Eunostos" Harbor now provides deep-water anchorage for modern shipping, it is obvious that it was the East Harbor that was the city's main seaport during the Ptolemaic and Roman periods. Another French project during the 1990s, directed by Franck Goddio (an underwater archaeologist who began his career as a mathematician and statistician), has concentrated on the southern and eastern shores of the Eastern Harbor. This work has revealed many hundreds of sculptures and architectural fragments, including such features as timber pilings and stone pavements, which show that this is not merely a set of archaeological material that was thrown into the sea in ancient times. Instead, it is apparent that much of the "Royal Quarter" of Alexandria has been preserved in situ under the sea, which helps to compensate for the destruction or inaccessibility of the land-based remains. These palace buildings may have been occupied by Cleopatra VII and

Diver examining a Ptolemaic column capital in the harbor at Alexandria.

The Naos of the Decades, part of which is in the collection of the Louvre in Paris, can now be reconstructed almost in its entirety because of new fragments discovered by French marine archaeologists working in the Bay of Abukir, near Alexandria.

her court, but they also continued to be used well into the Roman Period, making it difficult to reconstruct the original late Ptolemaic ambience of the area. Among the sculptures retrieved from the Royal Quarter were many that had originally stood in other northern Egyptian cities such as Heliopolis and Sais.

In 2000, Goddio also began to survey and excavate the remains of the important cities of Canopus, Menouthis, and Herakleion, at depths between 20 and 33 feet (6—10 meters) beneath the Bay of Abukir, the modern name for the mouth of the long-silted-up Canopic branch of the Nile. The religious center of Canopus and its harbor, Herakleion, flourished from at least the Late Period to late Roman times, and city of Menouthis, situated midway between the two, was founded in the second century A.D. However, by the eighth century, all three settlements and their associated temples and monuments were largely submerged under the Mediterranean, perhaps partly as a result of an earthquake recorded at Akaba in A.D. 746. Among the surviving sculptures of Menouthis, Goddio found several large fragments of the so-called Naos of the Decades, a black granite shrine dating to the time of Nectanebo I (c. 380—326 B.C.), several pieces of which had earlier found their way into the collections of the Louvre and the Greco-Roman Museum in Alexandria. This naos is covered in hieroglyphic inscriptions and images of animals and humans documenting the astronomical movements connected with each of the 37 "decades" (ten-day cycles) making up the Egyptian year, which seem to have formed one of the earliest sources for Classical astrology.

The Great Library

The Great Library is the best-known feature of Ptolemaic Alexandria. Its reputedly vast collection of hundreds of thousands of papyrus rolls formed a concrete symbol of the molding of Egypt's new capital into the intellectual center of the Hellenistic world in the last three centuries B.C. Countless important early scholars, scientists, and poets—Callimachus, Euclid, Archimedes, Eratosthenes, Apollonius of Rhodes, Aristarchus of Samos, Theocritus, and others—spent at least part of their careers in Alexandria. The Library was part of a Museum (or Mouseion), a temple dedicated to the Muses, the Greek goddesses of art, music, literature, and science. It was founded by Ptolemy I, who had evidently studied under Aristotle in his youth (as Alexander had) and was determined to create an institution that would rival Aristotle's Lyceum in Athens.

Perhaps with the help of the Athenian philosopher Demetrius Phalereus, none of whose written works has survived, Ptolemy created a library at the Museum (c. 290 B.C.). He may also have established a smaller library at the Serapeum, the temple of Serapis, a fusion of Greek and Egyptian deities whose cult was deliberately fostered in the early Ptolemaic Period. The scholars of the Hellenistic age at Alexandria not only produced great literature and preserved earlier poetic masterpieces that might otherwise have been lost, but they also achieved such crucial scientific goals as the calculation of pi, the measurement of the earth's circumference, the principle of displacement of bodies in liquids, and the hypothesis that the earth orbited the sun.

Although the intellectual reputation of the city—Ptolemy I's legacy—lasted into the Byzantine Period, the Library itself, which may have contained 500,000 documents at its height, was doomed to be partially burned down during Julius Caesar's Alexandrian battle against Pompey (48 B.C.). It was in the aftermath of this battle that Pompey was murdered by Egyptian officials and Cleopatra VII was reinstated as queen by Caesar, who left behind a visible reminder of his stay in Egypt in the form of Ptolemy Caesarion, his son by Cleopatra. Mark Antony, the next object of Cleopatra's passion, reestablished the Library with a gift of about 200,0000 manuscripts from Pergamon, but this collection too was eventually destroyed entirely by fire, along with the rest of the original Ptolemaic Royal Quarter, probably in the early 270s. In the fourth century A.D., the historian Ammianus Marcellus stated that virtually all of the Brucheion, where the Museum and Library were situated, had been destroyed. By the time of the Islamic conquest, it is evident that almost nothing survived of the Great Library or the smaller Serapeum library. However, a magnificent new library building, the Bibliotheca Alexandrina designed to play a comparable pivotal role in international research and education, opened in 2002, ushering in a new era of twenty-first-century scholarship at Alexandria.

The Roman City and Necropolis

One of the most striking surviving monuments of the city during the Roman period (30 B.C.—311 A.D.) is a 100-foot-high (30-meter) granite column in Sharia Amoud el-Sawari that has become known as Pompey's Pillar. It was

Pompey's Pillar is surrounded by the remains of the Serapeum, a large religious complex dedicated to the immensely popular deity Serapis, whose hybrid Egypto-Hellenistic cult was virtually invented by the early Ptolemaic rulers of Egypt, combining the attributes of the gods Osiris and Apis.

252

erected at the eastern edge of the Serapeum by a prefect called Pompey in honor of the emperor Diocletian around 297 A.D. A group of sphinxes at the foot of the column are in fact much earlier in date (probably belonging to the reign of Ptolemy VI, 180—145 B.C.) and were actually excavated from the southern part of the Serapeum.

Very little of the Temple of Serapis survives at ground level, but it is possible to visit the subterranean catacombs, in which sacred jackals were interred below the section of the complex devoted to the cult of Anubis. A further set of underground chambers, dating to the Roman Period, appear to be the remains of a smaller and later version of the Ptolemaic Library, judging from the traces of shelving on the walls.

Parts of the Roman-Period central city, now known as Kom el-Dikka, near the Mosque of Nebi Daniel have been excavated, revealing the remains of a small Roman amphitheater with thirteen rows of marble seats, estimated to have held about 800 spectators. Dated to the second century A.D., it originally had a domed roof supported by multicolored marble columns, some of which survive. Graffiti on the seats suggest that the sixth-century audience included supporters of "Blue" and "Green" charioteers in the Alexandrian hippodrome. The same excavators also uncovered a huge mud-brick bathhouse, a gymnasium complex, and a possible schoolroom.

Not far from the Serapeum is the subterranean rock-cut cemetery of Kom el-Shugafa (literally "mound of sherds"), dating mainly to the first half of the second century A.D. Whereas the Ptolemaic cemetery of Anfushi consisted of a small number of elite burials, the Kom el-Shugafa catacombs were created for the numerous members of a kind of "burial society" in which each contributed financially to the provision of funerals at this site, eventually creating a dense labyrinth of tunnels and burial chambers, the majority of which are not accessible to the modern visitor. This communal aspect of the tombs also accounts for the many thousands of pottery sherds that gave the site its name, evidently the remains of shallow vessels brought by grieving relatives for the feasts associated with funerals or commemorative festivals. The only other physical traces of the catacombs that are now visible on the surface are four porphyry sarcophagi and a few fragments of stone architecture.

The modern entrance to the most impressive surviving section of the Kom el-Shugafa cemetery, at the northeastern end of the overall enclosure, was discovered in 1900 when a donkey fell into one of the chambers. The tombs are entered down a spiral staircase, through the center of which the bodies of the deceased were probably lowered on ropes. This stairwell leads down to a short passage with a niche on each side (both with their vaulted tops carved into shell shapes), perhaps intended for older or weaker members of the funeral procession to recover from the exertion of the descent. From this passage, visitors can either turn left into a later burial chamber or go straight ahead into a large central "rotunda" with a domed roof supported by eight columns. A doorway to the left leads from the rotunda to a chamber now known as the triclinium or "banquet hall," a large pillared room with stone benches along three of its sides; it is assumed that there was once a wooden table set in the middle of the benches at which the funerary feast could be consumed. A second doorway on the right-hand side of the rotunda leads to a smaller square room from which about a dozen burial chambers can be entered. A hole in one of the walls also provides access to a later complex that includes a well-preserved painted tomb and the so-called Hall of Caracalla, where many skeletons of men and horses were found. If visitors instead walk straight ahead through the rotunda, they reach a set of steps leading down to the "central tomb." These steps also divide and carry on farther down to a third, even lower level, but this part of the catacombs is now inaccessible because of flooding.

The central tomb consists of two central sections: the vestibule and the main burial chamber. The roof of the vestibule is supported by two pillars and two square piers, while niches on its right and left sides contain statues of a man and a woman, respectively, both wearing traditional Egyptian costume, presumably depicting the two main members of the family originally buried

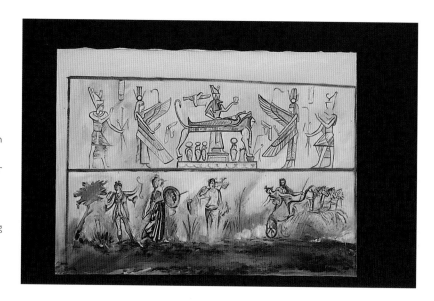

The painted decoration in Tomb 2 at Kom el-Shugafa combined Egyptian funerary scenes (above) with purely Greek myths concerning the underworld (below), demonstrating the combined beliefs in the afterlife held by the mixed Greek and Egyptian population in second century Alexandria. The lower register shows Persephone being carried off by Hades in his chariot on the right, and a row of Greek deities, including Athena and Aphrodite.

here (although they might also have a more universal significance). Farther on, the walls on either side of the entrance to the main burial chamber are painted with bearded serpents wearing the Egyptian double crown (*pschent*) and surmounted by shields bearing Medusa heads, evidently employing both Egyptian and Classical motifs to protect the dead (or perhaps to protect the mourners from the dead). Just inside the burial chamber there are statues on either side, portraying the god Sobek (or perhaps Seth) and the jackal god Anubis, both dressed in Roman armor. Each of the three walls of the chamber comprises a rock-cut niche containing a stone imitation sarcophagus decorated with such motifs as masks and the skulls of oxen. Behind each of the three sarcophagi, the walls of the niches are decorated with painted relief scenes: the central one shows Horus, Anubis, and Thoth protecting the mummy of the deceased, which is laid out on a couch under which three canopic jars are depicted; the two on either side show the king in the presence of the Apis-bull. The vestibule and burial chamber are surrounded by a corridor with numerous niches, including one larger central one at the end, on the main axis of the complex. Each of the niches was designed to hold three corpses, and many still bear writing in red paint announcing the names and ages of the deceased. A passage leading off from the far left-hand corner of the corridor provides access to a long rectangular room provided with many other burial niches.

The Decline of the City

By the Christian period, the city of Alexandria had begun to change, some monuments being transformed into churches and others dismantled. The process of destruction continued in the Islamic period, when many buildings were pillaged for their stone (as in Cairo and other major population centers). The decline was exacerbated by the silting up of the Canopic branch of the Nile by the twelfth century A.D., which cut off the city's major economic link with the Nile Valley. Eventually, Alexandria once more became a port rather than a capital, but it has continued to be a unique Egyptian city in many respects, not only because of the unusually multi-ethnic nature of its population but also because it retains its distinctively Mediterranean character.

The remarkable intellectual heritage of Alexandria is undisputed, but it was different in so many ways from the rest of Egypt at this date that it cannot really be relied on as a source for Greco-Roman Egypt as a whole. Indeed, it could be argued that Alexandria casts far too long a shadow over Ptolemaic and Roman Egypt. Descriptions of Egypt were so often written by Classical scholars based at Alexandria that their accounts had little relevance to Upper Egypt at that date, or even to the Faiyum and some of the Delta cities.

Further Reading

The best-known general monographs on Ptolemaic and Roman Alexandria are E. M. Forster's *Alexandria: A History and Guide* (2d ed., New York, 1961), P. M. Fraser's *Ptolemaic Alexandria* (3 vols., Oxford, 1972), and Evaristo Breccia's *Alexandrea ad Aegyptum* (English translation, Bergamo, 1922). More recently, Alan Bowman has provided a very good summary of the architecture and society of the city in the final chapter of *Egypt after the Pharaohs* (London, 1986, pp. 204—233).

The two sets of French discoveries in the Eastern Harbor are discussed, with excellent color photography, in Jean-Yves Empereur's *Alexandria Rediscovered* (London, 1998) and in Franck Goddio's *Alexandria: The Submerged Royal Quarters* (London, 1998). The Polish excavations at Alexandria since 1959, particularly the discoveries at Kom el-Dikka, are reported by Barbara Tkaczow in *Topography of Ancient Alexandria* (Warsaw, 1993).

Lucio Canfora's *The Vanished Library* (translated by M. Ryle, London, 1989) takes the form of a kind of mystic detective-style quest for the Alexandria Library. In the course of the book's tortuous arguments, Canfora attempts to make spurious and potentially misleading links between the Alexandria Library and the temple libraries of the pharaonic period (particularly that of the Ramesseum).

Further Viewing

Most of the major surviving sculptures and artifacts can be viewed at the Graeco-Roman Museum, Alexandria, including the five marble heads found at the Kom el-Shugafa cmetery, and a terracotta lantern fashioned in the image of the Pharos. Kom el-Shugafa is open to visitors and well worth visiting. It is planned that the Polish-excavated Roman remains at Kom el-Dikka, currently being restored by Polish and Egyptian archaeologists, will eventually be displayed as sections of the overall urban environment. At the site of Abusir (ancient Taposiris Magna), about 30 miles (48 kilometers) west of Alexandria, there is a scale model of the Pharos one-tenth of the size of the original.

The two obelisks that once stood in front of the Caesareum (the massive temple dedicated by Cleopatra to the deified form of Julius Caesar) were in place until the late nineteenth century, but one of them was reerected on the Thames Embankment in London in 1878, while the other has stood in Central Park, New York, since 1881. Fragments of the Naos of the Decades from Menouthis can be seen at the Louvre and also at Alexandria's Graeco-Roman Museum.

CHAPTER

NINETEEN

———

Mons Claudianus

c. 50–400 A.D.

Rome in the desert

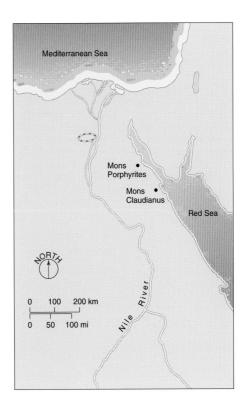

The enormous Roman quarrying complex known in antiquity as Mons Claudianus is situated in the midst of the Red Sea Hills, more than 300 miles (480 kilometers) south of Cairo and 75 miles (120 kilometers) east of the Nile. The region as a whole consists of more than 130 quarry excavations within and between the wadis Abu Marakhat, Umm Hussein, and Umm Diqal. Judging from ostraca and inscriptions found at the Mons Claudianus fortress, the region was worked sporadically and intermittently during the first to fourth centuries A.D., with new quarries being opened whenever fresh supplies of stone were needed for specific construction projects. The peak period of quarrying seems to have been during the reigns of the emperors Trajan and Pius, particularly the years 106–112, when the Basilica Ulpia was under construction in Rome.

During the periods of Roman and Byzantine domination of Egypt, there were high levels of mining and quarrying in the Eastern Desert. Large-scale quarrying operations were established at such sites as Mons Porphyrites (to extract porphyry), Mons Claudianus (tonalite gneiss), and Wadi Barud (quartz diorite). There were numerous gold and emerald mines: the largest Byzantine gold mine was Bir Umm Fawakhir in the Wadi Hammamat, and the main focus for emeralds was the Sikait-Zubara region, roughly midway between Myos Hormos and Berenice. These activities, together with flourishing trade-routes via such Red Sea ports as Myos Hormos (modern Quseir el-Qadim) and Berenice, meant that the desert became a more active region, with the gradual appearance of roads, watch-towers, way-stations, and hydreumata (fortified wells) demonstrating the widespread presence of Roman and Byzantine troops.

The mottled light gray and greenish black stone quarried by the Romans in the Mons Claudianus region, a kind of tonalite gneiss, known as *granito del foro*. Surviving objects made from it are especially common in the cities of Tivoli and Rome, perhaps the best-known examples being the columns in the portico of the Pantheon. It was once thought to have been exported to sites throughout the Mediterranean region, but chemical and petrographic analysis in the 1990s revealed that it was used only for monuments in Rome itself, suggesting that it was restricted for the emperor's use alone. It was used primarily for large columns and basins, as well as for smaller objects such as pedestals and pavement tiles, but there are no known sculptures.

The Mons Claudianus quarry site was rediscovered by Giovanni Brocchi, an Italian traveler and geologist, in April 1823. He provided only a sketchy description of the site, published many years later. It was the visit of two English pioneers in Egyptology, John Burton and John Gardner Wilkinson, only a month after Brocchi's visit, that resulted in the first published descriptions of the quarries and settlement. Wilkinson made the first plan of the site, and, as with many of the plans among his manuscripts (now in the Bodleian Library, Oxford), the basic accuracy of his draftsmanship has been borne out by modern mapping in the 1960s and 1990s.

The Fortress and Surrounding Buildings

The best way to approach the Mons Claudianus settlement is to take the main road east from Qena, through the Eastern Desert toward Safaga, turning north after 120 kilometers. It is eventually possible to walk along the Wadi Farit, turning east down the Wadi Abu Marakhat and then south (after about 200 yards/meters) past a large loading ramp and abandoned columns. After a walk up the slope through various quarries and causeways for a distance of about half a mile (0.8 kilometers) due south, a ridge overlooking the Wadi Umm Husein is eventually reached. From here one has a spectacular view of the main area of settlement in a sheltered bay at the north side of the wadi floor. Surrounded by hills on three sides and open to the wadi at the south, the remains include a large stone-built fortress, a granary, a cistern, a bathhouse complex, a set of stables, a temple, and an adjacent cemetery.

The inscription on one of the many ostraca from the site indicates that its population was at one stage as high as 920; the total figure, including workers involved in transporting stone and supplies, probably exceeded a thousand. Considering the remote location of Mons Claudianus, about 80 miles (128 kilometers) east of the Nile in a desert where the average annual rainfall

is only a quarter-inch (6 millimeters), the logistics of sustaining such a large number of workers must have been challenging, to say the least. Although the accounts given by some ancient authors, such as Josephus and Aelius Aristides, have tended to bolster the misconception that convicts and Jewish prisoners were used as cheap labor in Rome's Egyptian quarries, we know from the ostraca excavated at Mons Claudianus that the work force was in fact made up of soldiers, officials, skilled and unskilled laborers, and even women and children. Far from being an imperial Roman prison colony, Mons Claudianus was a thriving community made up of soldiers and civilian families.

Not surprisingly, the buildings were constructed mainly from the local stone (gneiss and felsite), and mud brick—the favored material for domestic buildings in the Nile Valley—was used only for a single set of dividing walls in the central building of the fort. As at other desert quarrying sites, stone was used instead of brick because there were no local sources of clay; the Roman fortresses in the Eastern Desert employ more or less mud brick according to their distance from the Nile. Occasionally, fired bricks were used at Mons Claudianus, particularly in connection with the underfloor heating of the bathhouses.

What Did the Quarry-Workers Eat?

Undoubtedly the fundamental requirement of the quarry-workers would have been water. Rainfall was as sparse then as now, and the modern water table is about 80 feet (24 meters) below the ground surface, suggesting that

ΓΑΙΟΣΚΟΜΙΝΙΟΣ
ΛΕΥΓΑΣΟΕΥΡΩΝ
ΤΑΜΕΤΑΛΛΑΤΟ
ΥΠΟΡΦΥΡΙΤΟΥΚΑ
ΙΚΝΗΚΙΤΟΥΚΑΙ
ΜΕΛΑΝΟΣΠΟΡ
ΦΥΡΙΤΟΥΚΑΙΠΟΙ
ΚΙΛΟΥΣΛΙΘΟΥΣ
ΕΥΧΗΝΤΕΜΕΝΟ
ΣΠΑΝΙΚΑΙΣΑΡΑ
ΠΙΔΙΘΕΟΙΣΜΕΓ
ΙΣΤΟΙΣΥΠΕΡΤΗΣ
ΣΩΤΗΡΙΑΣΤΩΝ
ΤΕΚΝΩΝΑΥΤΟΥ

ΙᗪΑΤΙΒΕΡΙΟΥ
ΚΑΙΣΑΡΟΣΣΕΒΑ
ΣΤΟΥΕΠΕΙΦ
ΚΘ

This stele erected by the Roman soldier Caius Cominius Leugas near Mons Porphyrites bears a unique text describing his program of geological prospection in the Eastern Desert. The ithyphallic figure represents a syncretic deity combining Pan and the Egyptian fertility god Min.

260

Another major quarrying site of the Roman Period is Mons Porphyrites. Volcanic porphyries (igneous rocks, often purplish, with incorporated feldspar crystals) are widely distributed in the mountains of the Eastern Desert and are especially abundant in the region northwest of Hurghada. Only two ancient quarries are known, both dating from the Roman Period: Gebel Dokhan (Mons Porphyrites) and Wadi Umm Towat. The sources of other porphyries used for vessels in the Predynastic and Early Dynastic periods are unknown.

On the eastern flank of Gebel Dokhan, high on the hillslopes on the west and east sides of Wadi Abu Maamel, are six quarrying areas collectively called Mons Porphyrites by the Romans. From north to south, those on the west side are the northwest, west (or Lycabettus), and southwest (or Rammius) quarries; those on the east side are the northeast, east, and southeast (or Lepsius) quarries. These were all worked from the mid-first to the late fourth centuries A.D.

In 1995, a British expedition to Mons Porphyrites made an astonishing discovery. In the previous year they had found a quarry-workers' village, a set of dry-stone huts clustered near one of the black porphyry quarries (rather than the better-known imperial, or purple, porphyry workings). It was in one of these huts that a slab of porphyry was found lying face down. This turned out to be carved on its face with an intriguing combination of images and text. The curved top of the stele is decorated with the classic Egyptian image of a winged sun-disk with two uraei (cobras) emerging downward from the disc; throughout the pharaonic and Graeco-Roman periods, this was one of the most common images in the upper sections of round-topped stelae. Below the winged disk is a standing figure of a god on the left-hand side, and eighteen lines of Greek inscription on the right. The deity is the ithyphallic god of the desert, Pan-Min, wearing a crown surmounted by tall plumes and holding a flail behind his back.

The inscription not only names the man for whom the stele was created, a Roman called Caius Cominius Leugas, but goes on to say that he "discovered the quarries of porphyry stone and the knekites and black porphyry and . . . found also many-colored stones [and] dedicated a sanctuary to Pan and Sarapis, very great gods, for the well-being of his children." The last three lines of the text provide a date: the twenty-ninth day of the month Epiph in the fourth year of Tiberius. The stele is therefore remarkable not only because it was made for one of the first known geological prospectors, but also because it gives us a precise date (23 July in 18 A.D.) for the Romans' discovery of some of the quarries at Mons Porphyrites.

Colossal column still *in situ* in the Mons Claudianus quarries.

wells would be difficult to excavate. The nearest known well, still used by the Ma'aza Bedouin, is in the Wadi Fatiri, midway between the wadis Umm Diqal and Umm Hussein. To bring food, there must have been a regular supply train running between Mons Claudianus and the present-day Qena region in the Nile Valley.

In addition to the architectural remains at Mons Claudianus, there are also large quantities of refuse in three large middens outside the walls of the fortress, as well as thick layers inside the rooms, many which were entirely filled with such material. The same arid environment that would have prevented the quarry-workers from growing their own crops has significantly enhanced the archaeological value of the site by preserving the remains of their food and feces. Whereas the food remains from the Egyptians' settlements and tombs in the Nile Valley tend to consist mainly of cereals and fish and animal bones, the particularly desiccating conditions at Mons Claudianus have allowed archaeologists to study parts of the Egyptian diet that are usually poorly represented.

Careful study of the organic components of the refuse has begun to reveal a very detailed picture of their diet. The thousands of bones show that the workers ate meat from domesticated animals (presumably imported from the Nile Valley) and also hunted wild mammals and birds (mainly gazelle, ibex, geese, and sand grouse), and that they obtained fish from the Red Sea coast.

Surprisingly perhaps, the two most commonly eaten mammals at Mons Claudianus were not cattle, sheep, or goats but donkeys and pigs. The marks made by knives on the bones of the donkeys show that, as well as being used in teams to transport the huge 20-foot columns of stone from the quarries, they were also consumed. The signs of pig-rearing are part of a steadily increasing body of evidence that this animal was not proscribed, as it is in most modern populations in the Near East, but formed an important element of the diet in many Egyptian communities from Predynastic through Roman times.

Further Reading

A general picture of life in Ptolemaic and Roman Egypt is provided by Alan K. Bowman in *Egypt after the Pharaohs* (London, 1986). David Peacock's short monograph *Rome in the Desert: A Symbol of Power* (Southampton, 1992) gives an excellent account of the activities of the Romans in the Eastern Desert. Survey and excavation reports on Mons Claudianus itself begin with the report by T. Kraus, J. Röder, and J. and W. Müller-Wiener, published in the German journal *Mitteilungen des Deutschen Archäologischen Instituts, Abteilung Kairo*, vol. 22 (1967), pp. 108–205. The site is best described in David Peacock and Valorie Maxfield's *Survey and Excavation at Mons Claudianus, 1987–1993, Volume I, The Topography and Quarries* (Cairo, 1996). Peacock and Maxfield

Encaustic portrait of a young Egyptian woman of the second century A.D. from the Roman-period necropolis at Hawara, in the Faiyum region.

have also edited the most recent archaeological reports on the Mons Porphyrites quarries: *The Roman Imperial Porphyry Quarries: Gebel Dokhan, Egypt. Interim Reports, 1994–1996* (Southampton and Exeter, 1994–1996).

Further Viewing

Tonalite gneiss quarried at Mons Claudianus was used for seven of the eight 40-foot columns in the portico of the Pantheon at Rome, and this stone can also be seen in Trajan's Basilica Ulpia in Rome, Hadrian's Villa at Tivoli near Rome, and Diocletian's Mausoleum in Split, Croatia. The porphyry statues of four Roman emperors (the so-called Tetrarchs) built into the corner of the south façade of St. Mark's Basilica in Venice came from Egypt via Constantinople.

Chronology

This chronology has been compiled on the basis of a number of different criteria, ranging from the interpretation of ancient texts to the radiocarbon dating of excavated materials. The dates from 664 B.C. to 394 A.D. are precise (deriving primarily from Classical sources), but those for prehistory (c. 700,000–3000 B.C.) are approximations based on a combination of stratigraphic information, seriation of artifacts, radiocarbon dates, and thermoluminescence dates.

The dates for the majority of the pharaonic period (c. 3000–664 B.C.) are based mainly on ancient king-lists, dated inscriptions, and astronomical records. In the New Kingdom and Third Intermediate Period, the probably margin of error is about a decade, but this tends to increase as we move further back in time, so that in the Old Kingdom it might be about 50 years, and in the first dynasty it might be as high as 150 years.

When the dates for two or more dynasties overlap (principally in the Second and Third Intermediate Periods), this is because their rule was accepted in different parts of the country. Overlapping dates for reigns within dynasties usually indicate co-regencies (periods when a king and his successor ruled simultaneously). When there are apparent gaps in the chronology, particularly at the ends of dynasties, this is usually because there are one or two very poorly documented rulers whose regnal dates are unknown or difficult to assess.

By the beginning of the Old Kingdom, Egyptian rulers had five names. The oldest of these was the so-called Horus name, and this is the one that we have usually cited for kings of the first through third dynasties (except in the case of Djoser, whose Horus name, Netjerikhet, is given in brackets). From the fourth dynasty on, we have usually given one or both of the so-called cartouche names (the "*nesu-bit*" and "son of Ra" names), and we have also sometimes added the Greek form of the name, especially when this is the name by which they are better known to modern readers (e.g., Cheops for Khufu).

PALAEOLITHIC

Lower Palaeolithic	*c.* 700/500,000–200,000 B.P.
Middle Palaeolithic	*c.* 200,000–35,000 B.P.
Upper Palaeolithic	*c.* 35,000–21,000 B.P.
Late Palaeolithic	*c.* 21,000–10,000 B.P.
Epipalaeolithic	*c.*10,000–7000 B.P.

PREDYNASTIC   *c.* 5300–3000 B.C.

Lower Egypt

Neolithic	*c.* 5300–4000 B.C. (or *c.* 6400–5200 B.P.)
Maadi Cultural Complex	*c.* 4000–3200 B.C.

Upper Egypt

Badarian Period	*c.* 4500–3800 B.C.[1]
Amratian (Naqada I) Period	*c.* 4000–3500 B.C.
Gerzean (Naqada II) Period	*c.* 3500–3200 B.C.

Note: After c. 3200 B.C. the same chronological sequence applies to the whole of Egypt

Naqada III/"Dynasty 0" *c.* 3200–3000 B.C.

EARLY DYNASTIC
PERIOD   3000–2686 B.C.

First Dynasty   3000–2890

Aha
Djer
Djet
Den
Queen Merneith
Anedjib
Semerkhet
Qaʿa

Second Dynasty   2890–2686

Hetepsekhemwy
Raneb
Nynetjer
Weneg
Sened
Peribsen
Khasekhemwy

[1] *The Badarian may have been a culture restricted to the el-Badari region near Asyut in Middle Egypt, rather than being a chronological phase throughout the whole of southern Egypt.*

OLD KINGDOM   2686–2160 B.C.

Third Dynasty   2686–2613

Nebka	2686–2667
Djoser (Netjerikhet)	2667–2648
Sekhemkhet	2648–2640
Khaba	2640–2637
Sanakht?	
Huni	2637–2613

Fourth Dynasty   2613–2494

Sneferu	2613–2589
Khufu (Cheops)	2589–2566
Djedefra (Radjedef)	2566–2558
Khafra (Chephren)	2558–2532
Menkaura (Mycerinus)	2532–2503
Shepseskaf	2503–2498

Fifth Dynasty   2494–2345

Userkaf	2494–2487
Sahura	2487–2475
Neferirkara	2475–2455
Shepseskara	2455–2448
Raneferef	2448–2445
Nyuserra	2445–2421
Menkauhor	2421–2414
Djedkara	2414–2375
Unas	2375–2345

Sixth Dynasty   2345–2181

Tety	2345–2323
Userkara (a usurper)	2323–2321
Pepy I (Meryra)	2321–2287
Merenra	2287–2278
Pepy II (Neferkara)	2278–2184
Nitiqret	2184–2181

Seventh and Eighth Dynasties   2181–2125

Numerous kings, called Neferkara, presumably in imitation of Pepy II.

FIRST INTERMEDIATE
PERIOD   2160–2055 B.C.

Ninth and Tenth Dynasties (Herakleopolitan)   2160–2025

Khety (Meryibra)
Khety (Nebkaura)
Khety (Wahkara)
Merykara

Eleventh Dynasty (Thebes only)	2125–2055
[Mentuhotep I (Tepy-a: 'the ancestor')]	
Intef I (Sehertawy)	2125–2112
Intef II (Wahankh)	2112–2063
Intef III (Nakhtnebtepnefer)	2063–2055

MIDDLE KINGDOM 2055–1650 B.C.

Eleventh Dynasty (all Egypt)	2055–1985
Mentuhotep II (Nebhepetra)	2055–2004
Mentuhotep III (Sankhkara)	2004–1992
Mentuhotep IV (Nebtawyra)	1992–1985

Twelfth Dynasty	1985–1795
Amenemhat I (Sehetepibra)	1985–1965
Senusret I (Kheperkara)	1965–1920
Amenemhat II (Nubkaura)	1922–1878
Senusret II (Khakheperra)	1880–1874
Senusret III (Khakaura)	1874–1855
Amenemhat III (Nimaatra)	1855–1808
Amenemhat IV (Maakherura)	1808–1799
Queen Sobekneferu (Sobekkara)	1799–1795

Thirteenth Dynasty	1795–after 1650
Hor (Awibra)	
Khendjer (Userkara)	
Sobekhotep III (Sekhemrasewadjtawy)	
Neferhotep I (Khasekhemra)	
Sobekhotep IV (Khaneferra) *c.* 1725	

Fourteenth Dynasty	1750–1650

Minor rulers probably contemporary with the thirteenth or fifteenth dynasty

SECOND INTERMEDIATE PERIOD 1650–1550 B.C.

Fifteenth Dynasty (Hyksos)	1650–1550
Salitis/Sheshi	
Khyan (Seuserenra)	*c.* 1600
Apepi (Aauserra)	*c.* 1555
Khamudi	

Sixteenth Dynasty	1650–1550

Minor Hyksos rulers contemporary with the fifteenth dynasty

Seventeenth Dynasty	1650–1550
Intef (Nubkheperra)	
Taa (Senakhtenra/Seqenenra)	*c.* 1560
Kamose (Wadjkheperra)	1555–1550

NEW KINGDOM 1550–1069 B.C.

Eighteenth Dynasty	1550–1295
Ahmose (Nebpehtyra)	1550–1525
Amenhotep I (Djeserkara)	1525–1504
Thutmose I (Aakheperkara)	1504–1492
Thutmose II (Aakheperenra)	1492–1479
Thutmose III (Menkheperra)	1479–1425
Hatshepsut (Maatkara)	1473–1458
Amenhotep II (Aakheperura)	1427–1400
Thutmose IV (Menkheperura)	1400–1390
Amenhotep III (Nebmaatra)	1390–1352
Amenhotep IV/Akhenaten Neferkheperurawaenra	1352–1336
Nefernefruaten (Smenkhkara)	1338–1336
Tutankhamun (Nebkheperura)	1336–1327
Ay (Kheperkheperura)	1327–1323
Horemheb (Djeserkheperura)	1323–1295

RAMESSID PERIOD 1295–1069

Nineteenth Dynasty	1295–1186
Ramesses I (Menpehtyra)	1295–1294
Sety I (Menmaatra)	1294–1279
Ramesses II (Usermaatra Setepenra)	1279–1213
Merenptah (Baenra)	1213–1203
Amenmessu (Menmira)	1203–1200
Sety II (Userkheperura Setepenra)	1200–1194
Saptah (Akehnrasetepenra)	1194–1188
Tausret (Sitrameritamun)	1188–1186

Twentieth Dynasty	1186–1069
Sethnakhte (Userkhaura Meryamun)	1186–1184
Ramesses III (Usermaatra Meryamun)	1184–1153
Ramesses IV (Heqamaatra Setepenamun)	1153–1147
Ramesses V (Usermaatra Sekheperenra)	1147–1143
Ramesses VI (Nebmaatra Meryamun)	1143–1136
Ramesses VII (Usermaatra Setepenra Meryamun)	1136–1129
Ramesses VIII (Usermaatra Akhenamun)	1129–1126
Ramesses IX (Neferkara Setepenra)	1126–1108
Ramesses X (Khepermaatra Setepenra)	1108–1099
Ramesses XI (Menmaatra Setepenptah)	1099–1069

THIRD INTERMEDIATE
PERIOD   1069–664 B.C.

Twenty-first Dynasty	1069–945
Smendes (Hedjkheperra Setepenra)	1069–1043
Amenemnisu (Neferkara)	1043–1039
Psusennes I [Pasebakhaenniut] (Akheperra Setepenamun)	1039–991
Amenemope (Usermaatra Setepenamun)	993–984
Osorkon the elder (Akheperra Setepenra)	984–978
Siamun (Netjerkheperra Setepenamun)	978–959
Psusennes II [Pasebakhaenniut] (Titkheperura Setepenra)	959–945

Twenty-second Dynasty	945–715
Sheshonq I (Hedjkheperra)	945–924
Osorkon I (Sekhemkheperra)	924–889
Takelot I	889–874
Osorkon II (Usermaatra)	874–850
Takelot II (Hedjkheperra)	850–825
Sheshonq III (Usermaatra)	825–773
Pimay (Usermaatra)	773–767
Sheshonq V (Aakheperra)	767–730

Twenty-third Dynasty	818–715
Pedubastis I (Usermaatra)	818–793
Sheshonq IV	c. 780
Osorkon III (Usermaatra)	777–749

Twenty-fourth Dynasty	727–715
Bakenrenef (Bocchoris)	727–715

Twenty-fifth Dynasty	747–656
Piy (Menkheperra)	747–716
Shabaqo (Neferkara)	716–702
Shabitqo (Djedkaura)	702–690
Taharqo (Khunefertemra)	690–664
Tanutamani (Bakara)	664–656

LATE PERIOD   664–332 B.C.

Twenty-sixth Dynasty	664–525
[Nekau I	672–664]
Psamtek I (Wahibra)	664–610
Nekau II (Wehemibra)	610–595
Psamtek II (Neferibra)	595–589
Apries (Haaibra)	589–570
Ahmose II [Amasis] (Khnemibra)	570–526
Psamtek III (Ankhkaenra)	526–525

Twenty-seventh Dynasty (First Persian Period)	525–404
Cambyses	525–522
Darius I	522–486
Xerxes I	486–465
Artaxerxes I	465–424
Darius II	424–405
Artaxerxes II	405–359

Twenty-eighth Dynasty	404–399
Amyrtaios	404–399

Twenty-ninth Dynasty	399–380
Nepherites I [Nefaarud]	399–393
Hakor [Achoris] (Khnemmaatra)	393–380
Nepherites II	c. 380

Thirtieth Dynasty	380–343
Nectanebo I (Kheperkara)	380–362
Teos (Irma Atenra)	362–360
Nectanebo II (Senedjemibra Setepenanhur)	360–343

Second Persian Period	343–33[2]
Artaxerxes III Ochus	343–338
Arses	338–336
Darius III Codoman	336–332

PTOLEMAIC PERIOD   332–30 B.C.

Macedonian Dynasty	332–305
Alexander the Great	332–323
Philip Arrhidaeus	323–317
Alexander IV[2]	317–310

Ptolemaic Dynasty	305–30
Ptolemy I Soter I	305–285
Ptolemy II Philadelphus	285–246
Ptolemy III Euergetes I	246–221
Ptolemy IV Philopator	221–205
Ptolemy V Epiphanes	205–180
Ptolemy VI Philometor	180–145
Ptolemy VII Neos Philopator	145
Ptolemy VIII Euergetes II	170–116
Ptolemy IX Soter II	116–107
Ptolemy X Alexander I	107–88
Ptolemy IX Soter II (restored)	88–80
Ptolemy XI Alexander II	80

[2] *Alexander IV was only the nominal ruler in 310–305 B.C.*

Ptolemy XII Neos Dionysos (Auletes)	80–51
Cleopatra VII Philopator	51–30
Ptolemy XIII	51–47
Ptolemy XIV	47–44
Ptolemy XV Caesarion	44–30

ROMAN PERIOD[3] 30 B.C.– 311 A.D.

Augustus	30 B.C.– 14 A.D.
Tiberius	14–37
Gaius (Caligula)	37–41
Claudius	41–54
Nero	54–68
Galba	68–69
Otho	69
Vespasian	69–79
Titus	79–81
Domitian	81–96
Nerva	96–98
Trajan	98–117
Hadrian	117–138
Antoninus Pius	138–161
Marcus Aurelius	161–180
Lucius Verus	161–169
Commodus	180–192
Septimius Severus	193–211
Caracalla	198–217
Geta	209–212
Macrinus	217–218
Didumenianus	218

Severus Alexander	222–235
Gordian III	238–242
Philip	244–249
Decius	249–251
Gallus and Volusianus	251–253
Valerian	253–260
Gallienus	253–268
Macrianus and Quietus	260–261
Aurelian	270–275
Probus	276–282
Diocletian	284–305
Maximian	286–305
Galerius	293–311
Constantius	293–306
Constantine I	306–337
Maxentius	306–312
Maximinus Daia	307–324
Licinius	308–324
Constantine II	337–340
Constans (co-ruler)	337–350
Constantius II (co-ruler)	337–361
Magnetius (co-ruler)	350–353
Julian the Apostate	361–363
Jovian	363–364
Valentinian I (west)	364–375
Valens (co-ruler, east)	364–378
Gratian (co-ruler, west)	375–383
Theodosius (co-ruler)	379–395
Valentinian II (co-ruler, west)	383–392
Eugenius (co-ruler)	392–394

[3] *The overall dates given here for the Roman Period begin with the official establishment of Egypt as a Roman province (on 31 August, 30 B.C.) and end with the final division of the empire into western and eastern sections in AD 395 (i.e., the beginning of the Byzantine Period, which is usually described as the Coptic or Christian Period in Egypt).*

Acheulean Stone tool industry, characterized by roughly symmetrical bifacial hand-axes and cleavers; linked with the appearance of *Homo erectus* and also with early *Homo sapiens*.

akh One of the five principal elements that the Egyptians considered necessary to make up a complete personality (the other four are the *ka, ba,* name, and shadow); believed to be both the form in which the blessed dead inhabited the underworld, and the result of the successful reunion of the *ba* with its *ka*.

Amarna Letters Set of cuneiform tablets most of which derive from the "Place of the Letters of Pharaoh," a building identified as the official "records office" in the central city at Amarna. All but thirty-two of the 382 documents are items of diplomatic correspondence between Egypt and many rulers of Western Asia.

"anatomically modern" humans The first hominids to (a) resemble modern humans (in anatomical terms) and (b) belong to the subspecies *Homo sapiens sapiens*. The term is rather misleading in that early examples (which have brow ridges and larger teeth) are quite different from genuinely modern humans such as ourselves.

ankh Hieroglyphic sign denoting "life," which takes the form of a cross surmounted by a loop; eventually adopted by the Coptic church as its unique form of cross.

Apis Sacred bull that served as the *ba* (physical manifestation) of the god Ptah, whose cult dates back to the beginning of Egyptian history; the bulls were buried in the Serapeum at Saqqara.

Aten Deity represented in the form of the disk or orb of the sun, the cult of which was particularly promoted during the reign of Akhenaten.

Aterian Palaeolithic industry named after the site of Bir el-Ater in eastern Algeria, characterized by a distinctive type of tanged stone point, implying the use of hafting.

***ba*, *ba*-bird** Aspect of human beings that resembles our concept of "personality," comprising the nonphysical attributes that make each person unique. It was often depicted as a bird with a human head and arms, and was also used to refer to the physical manifestations of certain gods.

bark, bark-shrine The bark was an elaborate type of boat used to transport the cult images of Egyptian gods from one shrine to another. The bark-shrine was a stone structure in which the bark could be temporarily set down as it was being carried in ritual processions from one temple to another during festivals. The Egyptians used the term *wahet* (literally "place of setting down") to refer to the bark-shrine.

benben-stone Sacred stone (perhaps a lump of meteoric iron) at Heliopolis, which symbolized the primeval mound and perhaps also the petrified semen of the sun god Atum-Ra. It was the earliest prototype for the obelisk and possibly even the pyramid.

block statue Type of sculpture representing an individual in a very compressed squatting position, with the knees drawn up to the chin, reducing the human body to a schematic blocklike shape.

Book of the Dead Funerary text known to the Egyptians as the "Spells for Coming Forth by Day," introduced at the end of the Second Intermediate Period. It consisted of about 200 spells (or "chapters"), over half of which were derived directly from the earlier Pyramid Texts and Coffin Texts. The text was usually written on papyrus and placed in the coffin, alongside the body of the deceased.

B.P. Abbreviation for "before present," most commonly used for uncalibrated radiocarbon dates or thermoluminescence dates. "Present" is conventionally taken to be 1950 A.D.

canopic jars A set of four stone or ceramic vessels used for the burial of the viscera (liver, lungs, stomach, and intestines) removed during mummification. Specific elements of the viscera were placed under the protection of four anthropomorphic genii known as the Sons of Horus.

cartonnage Material consisting of layers of linen or papyrus stiffened with plaster and often decorated with paint or gilding, most commonly used for making mummy masks, mummy cases, anthropoid coffins, and other funerary items.

cartouche (*shenu*) Elliptical outline representing a length of knotted rope with which certain elements of the Egyptian royal titulary were surrounded from the fourth dynasty on.

cataracts, Nile The six rocky areas of rapids in the middle Nile Valley between Aswan and Khartoum.

cenotaph Literally meaning "empty tomb," this term is usually applied to buildings constructed to celebrate an individual's funerary cult but containing no human remains.

Coffin Texts Group of more than a thousand spells, selections from which were inscribed on coffins during the Middle Kingdom.

demotic (Greek "popular [script]") Cursive script known to the Egyptians as *sekh shat,* which replaced the hieratic script by the twenty-sixth dynasty. Initially used only in commercial and bureaucratic documents, by the Ptolemaic period it was also being used for religious, scientific, and literary texts.

divine adoratrice (*duat-netjer*) Religious title held by women, originally adopted by the daughter of the chief priest of the god Amun in the reign of Hatshepsut. From the reign of Ramesses VI on, it was held together with the title "god's wife of Amun."

dromos Processional way interconnecting different temples.

encaustic Painting technique employing a heated mixture of wax and pigment, particularly used for the Faiyum mummy-portraits of Roman Egypt.

Epipalaeolithic Chronological term usually applied to the last phase of the Palaeolithic period in North Africa and the Near East. The Egyptian and Lower Nubian Epipalaeolithic is characterized mainly by its innovative lithic technology (microlithic flake tools) and its chronological position between the Nilotic Upper Palaeolithic and Neolithic (c. 10,000–5500 B.C.).

faience Glazed non-clay ceramic material widely used in Egypt for the production of such items as jewelry, *shabtis,* and vessels.

false door Stone or wooden architectural element comprising a rectangular imitation door placed inside Egyptian nonroyal tomb-chapels, in front of which funerary offerings were usually placed.

foundation deposits Buried caches of ritual objects placed at crucial points under important structures such as pyramid complexes and temples. The offering of model tools and materials was believed to maintain the building magically for eternity.

god's wife of Amun (*hemet-netjer nt Imen*) Religious title first attested in the early New Kingdom; later closely associated with the "divine adoratrice." She played the part of the consort of Amun in religious ceremonies at Thebes. From the late twentieth dynasty on, she was barred from marriage and adopted the daughter of the next king as heiress to her office. In the twenty-fifth and twenty-sixth dynasties, the god's wife and her adopted successor played an important role in the transference of royal power.

hieratic (Greek *hieratika,* "sacred") Cursive script used from at least the end of the Early Dynastic period, it enabled scribes to write more rapidly on papyri and ostraca, making it the preferred medium for scribal tuition. An even more cursive form of the script, known as "abnormal hieratic," began to be used for business texts in Upper Egypt during the Third Intermediate Period.

hieroglyphics (Greek "sacred carved [letters]") Script consisting of pictograms, ideograms, and phonograms arranged in horizontal and vertical lines, in use from the late Gerzean Period (c. 3200 B.C.) to the late fourth century A.D.

Horus name The first royal name in the sequence of five names making up the Egyptian royal titulary, usually written inside a *serekh* (see below).

hypostyle hall (Greek "bearing pillars") Large temple court filled with columns and lit by clerestory windows in the roof. The columns were often of varying diameter and height, but those along the axial route of the temple were usually tallest and thickest.

instruction (Egyptian: *sebayt;* wisdom texts, didactic literature) Type of literary text (e.g., *The Instruction of Amenemhat I*) consisting of aphorisms and ethical advice, the earliest surviving example of which is said to have been composed by the fourth-dynasty sage Hardjedef.

ka The creative life-force of any individual, human or divine. Represented by a hieroglyph consisting of a pair of arms, it was considered to be the essential ingredient that differentiated a living person from a dead one.

kiosk Small chapel without a roof, used to contain cult statues of deities during festivals.

Maat Goddess symbolizing justice, truth, and universal harmony, usually depicted either as an ostrich feather or as a seated woman wearing such a feather on her head. Small figurines depicting Maat were frequently offered to deities by Egyptian rulers, indicating the king's role as guarantor of justice and harmony on behalf of the gods.

mammisi ("birth place," "birth house") Coptic term invented by the nineteenth-century archaeologist Champollion to denote a type of building in major temple complexes of the Late Period and Greco-Roman period, in which the rituals of the marriage of the goddess (Isis or Hathor) and the birth of the child-god were celebrated. It was placed at right angles to the main temple axis.

mastaba-tomb (Arabic, "bench") Type of Egyptian tomb, the rectangular superstructure of which resembles the low mud-brick benches outside Egyptian houses. It was used for both royal and non-royal burials in the Early Dynastic Period, but only for non-royal burials from the Old Kingdom on.

Medjay Nubian nomadic people from the eastern deserts of Nubia, often employed as scouts and light infantry from the Second Intermediate Period on. They have been identified with the archaeological remains of the so-called Pan-grave People (see below).

Nilometer Device for measuring the height of the Nile, usually consisting of a series of steps against which the increasing height of the annual inundation, as well as the general level of the river, could be measured.

nome, nome symbols Greek term used to refer to the forty-two traditional provinces of Egypt, which the ancient Egyptians called *sepat.* For most of the dynastic period, there were twenty-two Upper Egyptian and twenty Lower Egyptian nomes. Each nome had its own symbol, sometimes used to designate the nome (e.g., the "Oryx Nome").

nomen (birth name) Royal name introduced by the epithet *sa-Ra* ("son of Ra"), usually the last one in the sequence of the royal titulary, and the only one to be given to the pharaoh as soon as he was born.

offering formula (*hetep-di-nesw* "a gift which the king gives") Prayer asking for offerings to be brought to the deceased, which formed the focus of food offering rituals in nonroyal tombs. The formula is often accompanied by a depiction of the deceased sitting in front of an offering table heaped with food.

Opening of the Mouth ceremony Funerary ritual by which the deceased and his funerary statuary were "brought to life."

ostracon (Gk *ostrakon;* pl. *ostraka;* "potsherd") Sherds of pottery or flakes of limestone bearing texts and drawings, commonly consisting of personal jottings, letters, sketches, or scribal exercises, but also often inscribed with literary texts, usually in the hieratic script.

palace-façade Architectural style comprising a sequence of recessed niches, particularly characteristic of the external walls of Early Dynastic funerary buildings at Abydos and Saqqara.

Pan-grave Culture Material culture of a group of seminomadic Nubian cattle-herders who entered Egypt in the late Middle Kingdom and Second Intermediate Period. Well-attested in the Eastern Desert, their characteristic feature is the shallow circular pit-grave in which they buried their dead.

playa Plain characterized by a hard clay-soil surface and intermittently submerged beneath a shallow lake.

prenomen (throne name) One of the five names in the Egyptian royal titulary, introduced by the title *nesu-bit*, "he of the sedge and the bee," a reference both to the inidvidual mortal king and the eternal kingship (not "king of Upper and Lower Egypt," as it is sometimes erroneously translated).

pylon (Greek: "gate") Massive ceremonial gateway, called *bekhenet* by the Egyptians, which consisted of two tapering towers linked by a bridge of masonry and surmounted by a cornice. It was used in temples from at least the Middle Kingdom to the Roman Period.

Pyramid Texts The earliest Egyptian funerary texts, comprising about 800 spells or "utterances" written in columns on the walls of the corridors and burial chambers of nine pyramids of the late Old Kingdom and First Intermediate Period.

rekhyt-**bird** Egyptian term for the lapwing (*Vanellus vanellus*), a type of plover with a characteristic crested head, often used as a symbol for foreigners or subject peoples.

"reserve head" Type of Memphite fourth-dynasty funerary sculpture, consisting of a limestone human head, usually with excised (or unsculpted) ears and enigmatic lines carved around the neck and down the back of the cranium.

royal titulary Classic sequence of names and titles held by each of the pharaohs, consisting of five names (the so-called "fivefold titulary"), which was not fully established until the Middle Kingdom. It consisted of the Horus name, the Golden Horus name, the Two Ladies name (*nebty*), the birth name (nomen; *sa-Ra*), and the throne-name (prenomen; *nesu-bit*)

sacred lake Artificial pool in the precincts of many Egyptian temples from the Old Kingdom to the Roman Period.

saff-**tomb** Type of rock-cut tomb used in the el-Tarif area of western Thebes by the local rulers of the Theban eleventh dynasty.

satrapy Province in the Achaemenid Empire.

scarab Type of seal found in Egypt, Nubia and Syria-Palestine from the eleventh dynasty until the Ptolemaic Period. Its name derives from the fact that it was carved in the shape of the sacred scarab beetle (*Scarabaeus sacer*).

sed-**festival** (*heb-sed;* royal jubilee) Royal ritual of renewal and regeneration, intended to be celebrated by the king only after a reign of thirty years had elapsed.

Serapeum Term usually applied to buildings associated with the cults of the Apis-bull or the syncretic god Serapis. The Memphite Serapeum at Saqqara, the burial place of the Apis-bull, consists of a series of catacombs to the northwest of the Step Pyramid of Djoser.

serdab (Arabic: "cellar"; Egyptian *per-twt*, "statue-house") Room in mastaba-tombs of the Old Kingdom where statues of the *ka* of the deceased were usually placed.

serekh Rectangular panel (perhaps representing a palace gateway) surmounted by the Horus-falcon, within which the king's "Horus name" was written.

shabti (*ushabti, shawabti*) Funerary figurine, usually mummiform in appearance, which developed during the Middle Kingdom out of the funerary statuettes and models provided in the tombs of the Old Kingdom. The purpose of the statuettes was to perform menial labor for their owners in the afterlife.

shaduf Irrigation tool comprising a long wooden pole with a vessel at one end and a weight at the other, by means of which water could be transferred between rivers and canals.

sistrum (Egyptian *seshesht;* Greek *seistron*) Musical rattling instrument played mainly by women, except when the pharaoh was making offerings to the goddess Hathor.

solar boat (solar bark) Boat in which the sun god and the deceased pharaoh traveled through the netherworld; there were two different types of bark, that of the day (*mandet*) and that of the night (*mesektet*).

speos (Greek: "cave") Type of small rock-cut temple.

sphinx Mythical beast usually portrayed with the body of a lion and the head of a man, often wearing the royal *nemes* headcloth, as in the case of the Great Sphinx at Giza. Statues of sphinxes were also sometimes given the heads of rams ("criosphinxes") or hawks ("hierakosphinxes").

talatat **blocks** Small sandstone relief blocks dating to the Amarna Period; the name probably derives from an Arabic word meaning "three handsbreadths," describing their dimensions (although the word may also have stemmed from Italian *tagliata*, "cut masonry."

throne name See **prenomen**.

triad Group of three gods, usually consisting of a divine family of father, mother, and child, worshipped at particular cult centers.

triad-statue Statue comprising a group of three individuals.

Two Ladies name (*nebty*) One of the royal names in the "fivefold titulary"; the term derives from the fact that this name was under the protection of two goddesses, Nekhbet and Wadjet.

uraeus Serpent-image that protruded just above the forehead in most royal crowns and headdresses. The original meaning of the Greek word *uraeus* may have been "he who rears up."

viceroy of Kush (King's son of Kush) The Egyptian official governing the whole of Nubia (Wawat and Kush) in the New Kingdom.

vizier Term used to refer to the holders of the Egyptian title *tjaty*, whose position is considered to have been roughly comparable with that of the vizier (or chief minister) in the Ottoman Empire. The vizier was usually the next most powerful person after the king.

275
—

Picture Credits

Index